Anastasia Karamalidou

Embedding Human Rights in Prison

English and Dutch Perspectives

palgrave
macmillan

Anastasia Karamalidou
Health & Social Sciences
University of the West of England
Bristol, UK

ISBN 978-1-137-58501-1 ISBN 978-1-137-58502-8 (eBook)
DOI 10.1057/978-1-137-58502-8

Library of Congress Control Number: 2016963569

Cover illustration: cover design by Samantha Johnson

Printed on acid-free paper

This Palgrave Macmillan imprint is published by Springer Nature
The registered company is Macmillan Publishers Ltd.
The registered company address is: The Campus, 4 Crinan Street, London, N1 9XW, United Kingdom

To my parents

Contents

1 Human Rights and Prisons 1

2 English and Dutch Prisons: 'Contrasts in Tolerance' 17

3 English Penal Policy and Prisoners' Human Rights 37

4 Dutch Penal Policy and Prisoners' Human Rights 89

5 Human Rights in English Prisons: Prisoners' Views 115

6 Human Rights in Dutch Prisons: Prisoners' Views 151

7 Embedding Human Rights in Prison 189

Bibliography 199

Index 217

1

Human Rights and Prisons

Introduction: Prisoners' Human Rights in Europe: A Snapshot

In the European context, in the field of human rights and prisons, the Council of Europe (CoE) has made great strides in the advancement of prisoners' human rights in terms of recognition and protection. It has achieved this primarily through the 1950 European Convention for the Protection of Human Rights and Fundamental Freedoms (ECHR) and its enforcement organ, the European Court of Human Rights in Strasbourg (ECtHR). The ECHR is not a prison treaty, but prisoners have invoked its provisions numerous times and with success (van Zyl Smit and Snacken 2009). For example, based on the latest ECtHR historical review of its activity, between 1959 and 2009, Article 6 violations (right to fair trial) featured in 47.47% of the ECtHR judgments and Article 5 violations (right to liberty and security) in 10.72% of the judgments (ECtHR 2010).

Prisoner victories in Strasbourg are many and important. *Golder v UK* (1975) challenged successfully for the first time the hitherto ECtHR view that prisoners' rights were inherently and expressly limited by vir-

A. Karamalidou, *Embedding Human Rights in Prison*,
DOI 10.1057/978-1-137-58502-8_1

tue of their incarceration (van Zyl Smit and Snacken 2009: 10), finding a violation of Articles 6 and 8 (rights to a fair trial, and respect for private and family life). The gist of the ruling was that while it was reasonable to have interferences with inmates' fundamental rights and freedoms, reasonableness alone was not a sufficient criterion; it ought always to be accompanied by the principles of proportionality and legality with regard to the aims that the additional restrictions intended to serve (Kaufmann 1999).

Another instance of the gradual divergence from its once unsympathetic approach to prisoner litigation is found in the Court's interpretation and application of Article 3 (prohibition of torture) to the prison context. In the 1970s and 1980s, the Court was inclined to find breaches of Article 3 mainly in respect of overcrowded living conditions of and inadequate healthcare for political prisoners and when such treatment was deliberate (Snacken and van Zyl Smit 2009: 12). Substandard living conditions brought about by prisoners as a form of protest or experienced as a result of disciplinary punishment or generally on grounds of security did not meet the minimum required threshold to engage Article 3. The same applied to close body searches (Kaufmann 1999: 459–462, 464). This contrasts sharply with later rulings in favour of prisoners where, for example, their overcrowded living conditions were not deliberate (Dougoz v Greece 2001), they had been subjected to daily strip-searching and close body searches on security grounds (Van der Ven v Netherlands 2003), and they had been left naked for seven days in solitary confinement (Helling v Germany 2011). To these findings we can add *Ocalan v Turkey* (2003) and *Vinter and Others v UK* (2013) in which the death penalty and lifelong imprisonment without the possibility of review and release on parole were found in contravention of Article 3. Other circumstances ruled to engage Article 3 involve being sentenced or likely to be sentenced to the death penalty or being placed in conditions such as chain gangs following extradition to the USA (Dumortier et al. 2012).

Moreover, the Court has taken a stance against the concept of joint enterprise in criminal matters, finding it incompatible with Article 6 in *Gotkepe v Belgium* (2005; cited in Dumortier et al. 2012: 117–118). Also, through a series of rulings, life and indeterminate sentenced prisoners have seen their procedural rights under Articles 5 and 6 gradually being strengthened, with the Court delivering damning judgments on (a) the lack of periodic reviews of the prolongation of their detention beyond their tariff and of inadequate provision of rehabilitative courses and access to them so as to prepare for such reviews, (b) on the executive's exercise of sentencing functions in respect of tariff-setting and release procedures, and (c) on the quality of correspondence between the grounds of the original sentence and those employed for its continuation beyond the set tariff and following recall.

Last but not least, with regard to the right to life, the Court has ruled that prison authorities are not to act in a way that is likely to physically endanger prisoners and their relatives or that is foreseeable to have such an effect. At the same time, they are required to have in place measures that safeguard prisoners' lives, including when a prisoner poses a risk to themselves such as in cases of self-harm and suicide (Keenan v UK 2001). Prisoner-on-prisoner homicide that is the outcome of ineffective communication between agencies regarding prisoners' medical records and of inadequate screening procedures for cell-sharing purposes is another relevant example.

Next to the CoE, since the mid-1990s, the European Union (EU) has been also positioning itself as a major player in human rights advocacy, as well as criminal justice matters, leading scholars to talk about the emergence of the EU as a penal actor (Baker 2013) and of a distinct European penology (Girling 2006; Snacken and van Zyl Smit 2013; Daems 2013). Situated within the wider EU project on economic (and also political in more recent years) integration, the 1997 Treaty of Amsterdam provided the main impetus to EU activity in these spheres. It laid out for the first time 'liberty, democracy, human rights, and the rule of law' as the foundations of the EU and firmly established 'freedom, security and justice' as EU competences whose importance and dominant place in EU affairs were consolidated by the 2007 Lisbon Treaty (Alston and Weiler 1999; Baker 2013: 78). This is evidenced in the planned (albeit currently stalled) EU accession to the ECHR[1] as

[1] The EU accession to the ECHR is a legal requirement under the 2007 Lisbon Treaty, which came into force in 2009. For these purposes, an accession treaty between the CoE and the EU was negotiated in 2013, which the Court of Justice in its Opinion 2/13 found, however, incompatible with EU Law.

well as in standard-setting initiatives and the setting up of EU bodies with a human rights and a justice mandate.[2]

Pertinent EU standard-setting initiatives, which are intrinsically relevant to a human rights compliant prisoner treatment, are, for example, the 2000 Charter of Fundamental Rights of the European Union, which became justiciable before the European Court of Justice (ECJ) under the Lisbon Treaty (Baker 2013: 79), and the 2004 European Recommendation on the Rights of Prisoners in the European Union.[3] They contain provisions and call for the implementation by member states of standards found in the ECHR (and its case law), as well as in other hard and soft CoE human rights law, such as the European Convention for the Prevention of Torture and Inhuman or Degrading Treatment or Punishment (ECPT) and the European Prison Rules (EPRs). For example, among the provisions of the Charter we find the rights to an effective remedy, to one's defence and to a fair trial, a re-affirmation of the principles of the presumption of innocence, double jeopardy, legality and proportionality of criminal offences and penalties. It also recognises the inviolability of human dignity, the rights to life and the integrity of the person, and the prohibition formula of torture and the death penalty, all of which are directly relevant to a human rights informed prisoner treatment.

Moreover, promoting (not without controversy as we shall see) the 'free movement of criminal justice' based on the principles of mutual trust and recognition (Baker 2013: 88–89), developments in the area of justice have seen Framework Decisions on the implementation of judicial measures, such as custodial sentences and probation orders across

[2] See, e.g. Eurojust, Europol, and FRA. Eurojust is a judicial co-ordination unit that is tasked with the co-ordination of investigations into and prosecutions of transnational crime between relevant authorities in different member states. It comprises prosecutors, judges and police officers drawn from member states. Europol is the EU's law enforcement agency. It focuses on combatting transnational organised crime and terrorism and provides expert assistance to national law enforcement agencies. FRA is the European Union Agency for Fundamental Rights and is tasked to provide expert advice to EU institutions and nation states on human rights protection.

[3] It is worth noting that the 2004 European Recommendation on the Rights of Prisoners in the European Union proposed the adoption of a Prisons Charter by ECHR and non-ECHR member states. The proposal was rejected by the CoE Committee of Ministers on grounds of avoiding duplication of existing standard-setting instruments and monitoring arrangement (CoE Parliamentary Assembly 2006).

member states. Carrying some positive implications for prisoner rights, the Framework Decisions identify 'social rehabilitation and successful reintegration' as the aims of such punishment. Impregnated with the aforementioned principle of mutuality, they create the expectation that a criminal sanction ordered by one member state can be (and is when the need arises) executed by another despite differences in their criminal justice systems. In such cases, sanctions are treated as 'different but equal' (Chalmers et al. 2010: 764; cited in Baker 2013: 89), a treatment that is facilitated by (aspiring) member states' acceptance and observance of the foundations of the EU in respect of EU and non-EU citizens who reside in them. This common obligation among member states unavoidably necessitates the harmonisation of their respective national criminal justice policies, which can be a positive development if states do honour their obligations derived from their EU membership.

European human rights policy in general and in relation to offenders in particular is best exemplified in the concerted CoE and EU campaigns against the death penalty both at global and regional levels. Effecting the abolition of the death penalty on the European continent in times of both war and peace via Protocols 6 and 13 to the ECHR, European opposition to the death penalty has become an integral feature of EU foreign policy and has been elevated to a distinguishing mark of European sensibilities (Snacken and van Zyl Smit 2013: 16–17). In this respect, back in 2006, Girling argued that the strongly pursued European abolitionist agenda contributed to the formation of a wider European consciousness that treated opposition to the death penalty as an intrinsically European cultural value and thus a characteristic attribute of European identity (pp. 71–73). The argument has been that adoption of this abolitionist qua European moral value has enabled the emergence of a European penal 'community of sentiment' whose espousal of tolerance, inclusivity, parsimony and humanity can be contrasted to approaches fostering intolerance, exclusion and staunchly retributive modes of punishment (Girling 2006: 73–81).

While we should celebrate the above successes in the promotion of human rights values and their application to prisoners, we should also be vocal about a number of parallel negative developments whose undermining force cannot be underestimated. What I principally refer to here are (a) the hijacking of human rights by a strong risk discourse and public punitiveness that has sustained the prison's popularity as punishment in Europe and (b) the reactive nature and painstakingly slow implementation of ECtHR judgments, as well as the latest amendments to the ECtHR procedure.

The Precarious Position of Human Rights

The Hijacking of Human Rights by Risk Discourses

Numerous scholars writing in the fields of (comparative) penology and risk have drawn our attention to the impact of late modernity on the organisation and governance of our lives, and consequently on our attitudes to social and difference(s), crime and its punishment (see, e.g. Beck 1992, 2002; Young 1999; Garland 2001; Boutellier 2004). They have highlighted that our experiences, the meanings attached to them and our outlook are coloured and influenced by inextricably linked international, national and local forces (Beck 2005, 2008; cited in Daems 2013: 32–34). These unprecedentedly divergent forces follow from globalisation, which takes shape in and is shaped by migratory movements and cultural exchanges of ideas and lifestyles, being supported by free market capitalism (neoliberalism) and technological advances (Cavadino and Dignan 2006a).

This confluence of external and internal factors impacting on states' ability to exclusively shape their sovereign affairs and subsequently on their citizenry's lives poses all kinds of challenges that need to be negotiated at political and societal levels, giving rise in the process to all sorts of conundrums and risks (e.g. environmental, financial, political and security ones) (Beck 2002 [2013]: 632–634, 636–637; Garland 2001: 107–113). Against this background, and even more so after 9/11 and subsequent events related to international terrorism, we have witnessed the conflation of crime, social, cultural and religious difference, and immigration and their evolution into potent, ever-present and highly politicised risks that for our safety and security at national and international levels we must strive to control and contain (Beck 2002 [2013]: 636; Broeders 2010; Aas 2011).

To effectively control and contain the presumed harmfulness of these risks, states have increasingly adopted an actuarial methodology that places the emphasis exclusively on the early and prompt identification of risks and their continuous monitoring. Known as the new penology, actuarial justice or managerialism (Feeley and Simon 1992 [2013]; Garland 2001: 18–19), the late modern approach to today's risks mirrors their conflated nature and the ever-expanding identities of their bearers. In employing a wide range of surveillance techniques and incapacitation measures in the name of security, it blurs the boundaries between criminal and administrative punishment, state welfare and regulation and state support and penalisation.

With regard to the politicisation of the above risks, it stems, on the one hand, from our increased existential insecurities following from the breakdown of informal social controls, the demise of the nuclear family, the precariousness of today's employment and the heterogeneity of social life and culture (all by-products of globalisation and free market capitalism), which are accentuated by the state's limitations in soothing them (Young 1999: 8, 14–15; Garland, 77–78, 81–85, 154–157). On the other hand, it derives its strength from our contradictory expectations of living our lives in a 'safety utopia' (Boutellier 2004: ix), a safety utopia in which we, as citizens, expect and demand from the state to protect us against the uncertainty and risks of our times in order to be able to enjoy without interference the seemingly unlimited freedoms and boundless experiences that the very same fluidity of the times generates and promises us (ibid.: 31–43). The implications of this schizoid mentality, which is aided and abetted by the media, are the othering and demonisation of anything and anybody that may seem to threaten or challenge its assumed prerogative to freedom, autonomy and individuality (Young 1999: 96–120; Garland 2001: 135–137). In seeking optimum security to enjoy the opportunities for a better and more fulfilling life opened up by globalisation and free market capitalism, it resorts to the very essentialism it rejects.

Boutellier's concept of a 'safety utopia' (2004) and the evolution of terrorism, immigration and crime into dominant risks are evidenced, inter alia, in recent Eurobarometer surveys. For example, in 2012, while European citizens identified democracy, human rights, the rule of law, respect for other cultures and solidarity as the most representative values of the EU and Europeans, they ranked social policy and human rights in the fifth and seventh places in terms of EU priorities behind economic and monetary policy, healthcare, immigration and crime (European Commission 2012a). Moreover, 84% of Europeans thought that the punishment of offenders was not severe enough, a finding that has been recorded since 2008 (European Commission 2012b). In addition, in 2014, while 'the freedom to travel, study, and work anywhere in the EU, peace, and cultural diversity' were among the most commonly cited attributes of the EU, references to negative attributes, such as 'not enough control at external borders' and 'more crime' increased, with immigration occupying the third place as a national concern (European Commission 2015a). In 2015, immigration continued to dominate the concerns of European citizens at both European and national levels (found in the first and second places, respectively). The ongoing refugee crisis witnessed at European sea borders and in individual European countries, such as Greece, Italy, Germany and France, and the terrorist incidents in France and Belgium in 2015–2016 have arguably contributed to the dominance of immigration and terrorism among the concerns of European citizens at European and national levels (European Commission 2016). By way of illustration, in the two countries under investigation in this book, immigration topped the concerns of both Dutch and British citizens at 46% and 38%, respectively, with terrorism being the third most commonly cited issue by both at 22% and 23%, respectively. Interestingly, only 6% of Dutch citizens and 7% of British citizens identified crime as a concern (ibid.: 11), a finding that is fundamentally at odds at least with the current public and governmental rhetoric on criminal justice issues in England and Wales (see Chap. 4).

In the context of late modernity and its challenges, human rights values appear to run parallel to considerations of risk identification and control, without being seen as part of the agenda when safety and security issues arise. Their treatment as an embodiment of democracy and the rule of law whose observance increases a state's democratic credentials and thus its political standing stands in marked contrast to their treatment as impediments to state security and public safety. Kalin (2013), Kunz (2013), Lacey (2013) and Baker (2013) illustrate well this ambivalence towards human rights and their precarious existence in late modernity.

Kalin (2013) highlights the pressure which human rights are internationally under by using as examples the inroads made by Western states post 9/11 to the once categorically absolute freedom from torture and the institutionalisation of torture in states plagued by internal conflict and corruption. Identifying practices and attitudes encountered in the 'new penology' (Feeley and Simon 1992) and 'safety utopia' (Boutellier 2004) concepts, he attributes this pressure to the present dominance of a utilitarian response to the threat of international terrorism and the contemporaneous dissipation of public sympathy to the pain of those who are perceived as a danger to public safety (2013: 405–408).

In his critical assessment of the evolution of the German concept of Rechtsstaat, Kunz (2013) similarly identifies the ascendancy of risk and security discourses and their embeddedness in German laws, documenting their corrosive effects on the state's legal, political and social fabric. In relation to the Rechtsstaat, Kunz notes its transformation from a guardian of individual freedom and dignity, and thus a protective shield against state abuses of power, into a flexible mechanism of unbounded state interference with fundamental rights and freedoms in the name of public safety and national security, a transformation that has crucially the public's seal of approval. In late modernity that is crazed with risk identification and security management, public tolerance, understanding and forgiveness are consigned to the past, to less troubled and more innocent (the assumption is) times (2013: 387–390).

In addition, Lacey (2013: 355, 358) draws our attention to the powerful re-emergence of 'character-based criminal responsibility-attribution' in neoliberal countries, such as England and Wales, which she cites as further evidence of the primacy of risk management in state expressions of its authority and exercise of control, as well as of public punitiveness (ibid.: 355–356). In a Kleinian vein, the state' and the public' splitting of behaviours, vulnerabilities and entire social groups into intrinsically good and bad in order to assuage their respective limitations and insecurities render scores of people incorrigible, (potentially) dangerous and unworthy of sympathy and support. The anti-social, the mentally disordered, the (suspected) terrorist, the migrant, the refugee and the sex offender (to mention a few) become diagnostic labels at the service of risk control and management of public insecurities that come to define single-handedly the very essence of the person, pointing to their intrinsic lack of worth. This revival of essentialism and its bearing on the development of social and criminal justice policies enables both political action and inaction that disregards human rights values with minimal public opposition and political reflection regarding the implications for public safety, national security and prosperity in the world in the long term.

Criminal justice developments at national and European levels provide incontrovertible evidence of the criminalisation of poverty (Wacquant 2012), the exclusionary and marginalising effects of European states' foreign policies (Melossi 2013) and the indelible stigmatisation of specific offender categories, which are perpetuated by the transformation of law into 'risk law' (Kunz 2013: 388–389).

For example, prison remains a popular punishment in many parts of Europe. Between 2002 and 2011, the European prison population rate increased in 36 out of the 51 countries covered by the CoE Annual Penal Statistics survey, with 34 countries showing more than 100 prisoners per 100,000 in 2011 (Aebi and Delgrande 2013). In 2014, the European prison population rate was up by 4% compared to 2012, at 124 prisoners per 100,000. Since 2009, the European penal system operates at full capacity, with 91 prisoners per 100 places in 2014. In 2011 and 2012, almost half of the penal systems surveyed by the CoE were overcrowded, with the figure being 27.5% in 2014 (Aebi and Delgrande 2013: 2; Aebi et al. 2015).

The unwavering popularity of the prison has seen not only an overrepresentation of foreign nationals in Southern and Western European penal systems (Melossi 2013: 126–128; Aebi and Delgrande 2014) but also a rise in preventive detention, targeting mentally disordered and repeat offenders. As we shall see in more detail in Chaps. 4 and 5, both England and Wales and the Netherlands have relied heavily on selective incapacitation measures (e.g. indeterminate sentences for public protection; TBS, SOV and ISD measures) to take out of circulation dangerous and recalcitrant offenders for public protection and for the offenders' own welfare, promising the provision of treatment and rehabilitation. A string of human rights violations in both countries emanating from prisoners' lack of access to this officially promised state-sponsored rehabilitation and treatment point, among other things, to the essentially secondary position of human rights and their selective application, distinguishing in effect between those who are seen as deserving of human rights and those who are not.

Lastly, in certain respects, the promotion of the 'free movement of criminal justice' (Baker 2013: 88) privileges the security of the free movement of people, goods and services (in essence of the trademark characteristics of the European project) at the expense of human rights. States are given little leeway regarding the circumstances in which they can refuse to implement a sanction against a person whose activities and behaviour are seen to threaten the archetypal EU freedom of movement, state security and society's morals. The state's limited discretion in such cases can result in their implementing a penalty that is at odds with their domestic criminal justice provisions, such as proportionality and legality of penalties. Conversely, the implementation of a custodial measure in another member state may well entail worsening conditions of detention for the person subject to it, giving rise to human rights concerns (ibid.: 89–90). Existing differences between European penal systems with reference, for example, to their levels of overcrowding, material conditions and the provision of rehabilitation and resettlement support already entail divergent experiences of imprisonment, with some penal systems being better situated and resourced than others to promote the European punishment aims of rehabilitation and reintegration.

In this climate of public insecurity and intolerance and state preparedness to bring in laws and procedures encroaching on civil liberties and human rights in the name of public protection, prison reform and prisoners' rights are not topical issues enjoying public support. Lack of informed knowledge about sentencing laws and the criminal justice system coupled with the exploitation of crime by politicians and the media is commonly cited among the reasons for public perceptions of official responses to crime and offenders as too lenient (Feilzer 2009; Hough and Roberts 2012; Indermaur et al. 2012). As the case of England and Wales shows, the politicisation of human rights and their trivialisation in the press only add to such public misperceptions, fuelling public hostility towards socially marginalised groups and publicly distorting the value of human rights (McNulty et al. 2014).

ECtHR Judgments and Procedure

ECtHR judgments are reactive in the sense that they cannot undo the victims' suffering; instead, they are consequent upon it. Although they have an inbuilt preventative function, this is at group level—not at individual level. Legal and policy changes in the aftermath of proven human rights breaches strengthen the protection of those who may or are likely to be in the future in a similar situation to that of present victims. Furthermore, the impact of litigation in general on prison policy and procedure can be notoriously slow to realise. Suffice to mention here two examples from the English jurisdiction.

The overhaul of the English official disciplinary system started with *St. Germain* in 1978 and was not completed until 2003 with *Ezeh & Connors v UK*. Recognition of the application of Article 6 and of its procedural rights to disciplinary adjudications was put on a drip, with the authorities granting rights and amending the arsenal of disciplinary punishments, the powers of the adjudicators and their background when a legal challenge came and was successful. In addition, nearly a decade after *Hirst v UK* (2005), which found that the practice of blanket prisoner disenfranchisement contravened Article 3 of Protocol 1 to the ECHR (right to vote), and four years after *Greens and M.T.* (2010), which criticised the UK government's procrastination in implementing a change in law, prisoners in England and Wales are still barred from voting. In the aftermath of the *Hirst* ruling, a two-stage consultation that commenced in 2006 ended in dead water when the much more pressing priorities of the 2010 general election began to dominate the country's domestic affairs. Then, when in winter 2010 the coalition government was forced to pick up the issue from the back burner in response to the deadline framework for the implementation of the *Hirst* ruling given by the ECtHR in *Greens and M.T.*, the debate on which prisoner categories would be granted voting rights was lost in a forcefully promoted argument by politicians and the media alike over the UK's relationship with the EU, the erosion of the UK sovereignty by its EU membership and the need for a tough renegotiation of its terms and conditions. Once again, the opportunity for a public discussion of prisoners' right to vote informed by the relevant principles—that is, human rights, social justice and penological knowledge—was missed before it presented itself, damaging publicly along the way the value of human rights (McNulty et al. 2014).

Regarding the ECtHR procedure, in response to the continuing backlog of cases before the ECtHR (ECtHR 2010: 4–5), controversial reforms have been made and have been adopted for implementation. Protocol 14 to the ECHR that came into force on the 1st of June 2010 introduced, inter alia, a new admissibility criterion. Applications can be ruled inadmissible 'where the applicant has not suffered a significant disadvantage provided that 'respect for human rights does not require the Court to go fully into the case and examine its merits (Protocol 14, Article 12)'. Its controversial nature lies in its very interpretation. It raises the question of how a finding of a 'not significant disadvantage' can be objectively reached, taking into account national differences in the administration of imprisonment, the cultural and political context in which the execution of prison sentences takes place, and in the implementation of the Convention. This very important question becomes even more urgent, considering that it is decided by a single judge instead of seven whose decision is final (another of the changes brought in by Protocol 14 (Protocol 14, Article 27).

The UK Joint Committee of Human Rights has expressed similar concerns. In its opinion, unless there were domestic implementation mechanisms in place, the new admissibility criterion could not be seen as 'acceptable'. CoE acceptance of these concerns is seen in the contemporaneous adoption of three Recommendations (on the Verification of the Convention Compatibility of Draft Laws, Existing Laws and Administrative Practice; on the Improvement of Domestic Remedies; and on the ECHR in University Education and Professional Training) with a view to strengthening the protection of ECHR rights at domestic level (Livingstone et al. 2008).

On the 24th of June 2013, Protocol 15 was opened for signature, and Protocol 16 was opened for signature on the 2nd of October 2013. While both Protocols aim to drive forward the process of the Court's restructuring in order to increase its efficiency and therefore its effectiveness in enforcing the Convention, Protocol 15 contains provisions that make further inroads to the individual right to petition and consequently put at risk the protection of people's rights and freedoms under the ECHR. Specifically, its Article 4 reduces the period within which an application can be lodged before the ECtHR from six to four months, and its Article 5 removes the safeguard 'provided that no case may be rejected on this ground which has not been duly considered by a domestic tribunal', which accompanied the new admissibility criterion created by Protocol 14. In respect of other provisions introduced by the Protocols, in Article 1 of both, attempts are evident to involve proactively national authorities and organisations in the implementation of the Convention, and thus to strengthen the recognition and protection of the ECHR on their soil, reducing the number of applications to the ECtHR. Article 1 of Protocol 15 amends the preamble of the ECHR, with the insertion of the principles of subsidiarity and margin of appreciation, and Article 1 of Protocol 16 allows domestic courts to seek the Court's advice on matters of interpretation and application of the ECHR.

At the moment we will have to wait to see what impact the renewed emphasis on the principles of subsidiarity and margin of appreciation will have on prisoners' rights. How the Court will interpret these principles will be hugely significant considering the diversity of CoE penal systems in the wake of the Council's considerable enlargement in the last years and the time that it understandably takes for the harmonisation of systems, even more so when these are heavily influenced by cultural and political factors peculiar to their geography.

Conclusion

In light of the above, the question is what more we can do or do better to maximise the contribution of the legalisation of human rights to prisoner treatment. Drawing on comparative data on English and Dutch prisoners' views on human rights in prison, the book aims to explore what lessons we can learn in this respect with a view to maximising the potential of human rights for penal reform.

Chapter 2 'English and Dutch Prisons: 'Contrasts in Tolerance' introduces the English and the Dutch prison systems and describes the social, cultural, political and legal factors that impacted on their respective penal policies and prison practices. Being described as 'Contrasts in Tolerance' (Downes 1988), for long time they were treated as polar opposites in their use of imprisonment, treatment of offenders and recognition and protection of prisoner rights. The Dutch decarcerative penal policy and practice of humane containment contrasted with the English incapacitative penal policy and its practice of less eligibility. Whereas the idea of prisoner rights was recognised in Dutch official policy and practice as early as the 1950s, it was not until 2000 that prisoners' rights received formal recognition in the English penal policy. Differences in the two countries' political economies and legal traditions are cited as the reasons behind their contrasting approaches.

Chapter 3 'English Penal Policy and Prisoners' Human Rights' provides an account of the developments that have taken place in English penal policy and their impact on prisoners' human rights since 'Contrasts in Tolerance' was published. Developed in an environment where crime and punishment are heavily politicised, English penal policy has been resolutely incapacitative through the years. After a short-lived experimentation with decarcerative measures in the early 1990s, successive governments have adopted a penal populist rhetoric that is fuelled by a risk discourse. The concept of less eligibility survives earlier times, resulting in hostile resistance to prisoner rights, with related developments driven exclusively by the courts and prison crises. Cuts in public spending from 2010 onwards, coupled with tougher sentencing, have resulted in an overcrowded, overstretched and understaffed prison system with increased levels of violence and numbers of prisoner deaths. In this context, particular attention is paid to prisoner deaths and life sentences.

Chapter 4 'Dutch Penal Policy and Prisoners' Human Rights' provides an account of the respective developments in Dutch penal policy over the years and their impact on prisoners' human rights. In the space of 20 years, Dutch penal policy has undergone major transformations. From being a beacon of humanity and the envy of other Western European countries, it took a punitive turn towards incapacitation and harsher punishment before it returned to more pragmatic penal politics. Its twists and turns and their impact on the prisoner's treatment and human rights offer valuable lessons to other European prison systems. The return to decarceration has not been accompanied by a return to the formerly practised penological aims of rehabilitation and resocialisation for all. These have been replaced by selective rehabilitation and selective incapacitation for the purposes of public protection. This selective approach has resulted in no-frills prison regimes and increases in preventive detention.

Chapter 5 'Human Rights in English Prisons: Prisoners' Views' presents English prisoners' views on human rights in prison. Findings highlight the inextricable link between human rights and the legitimacy of prison as punishment. Based on English prisoners' views human rights recognition and protection contributes to the normalisation of the prison environment, which allows for rehabilitation opportunities to flourish, empowering and supporting prisoners in their resettlement efforts. Informed by human rights principles, English prisoners built a picture of the prison as a place that can facilitate personal empowerment, independence and autonomy so as to prepare prisoners for release and increase their reintegration prospects.

Chapter 6 'Human Rights in Dutch Prisons: Prisoners' Views' presents Dutch prisoners' views on human rights in prison. Findings highlight the instrumental contribution of human rights to the legitimacy of imprisonment as punishment in a democracy governed by the rule of law. Like English prisoners, Dutch prisoners credit human rights recognition and protection with normalising the prison experience. A normalised prison life gives imprisonment a purpose as it creates conditions that promote prisoners' social and civic emancipation. As a result, human rights civilise the prison experience and connect the prison as a social institution to the wider social environment in which it operates.

Chapter 7 'Embedding Human Rights in Prisons' sets out how the positive developments emanating from the legalisation of prisoners' human rights can be maximised so as to embed human rights in prisons. It draws on English and Dutch prisoners' views that highlighted the need to tap the proactive function of human rights, which is currently found in soft human rights law. Human rights recognition demonstrates the primacy of rehabilitation, resocialisation and reintegration as prison aims which are enabled through effective human rights protection. Drawing on negative and positive rights, as well as negative and positive state interference in respect of their protection, prisoners credit the proactive function with an educative, a psychotherapeutic, a humanising and an emancipatory potential. The chapter concludes with the observation that the realisation of this all-important proactive function of human rights rests ultimately on states' commitment to a decarcerative penal policy.

2

English and Dutch Prisons: 'Contrasts in Tolerance'

Introduction: Contrasts in Tolerance

In 1988 Downes published *Contrasts in Tolerance*, the first-of-its-kind (in the twentieth century) comparative analysis of the post-war English and Dutch penal policies. The impact of his publication was twofold. It kick-started an interest in comparative penology and criminal justice in general,[1] and led to an enduring fascination with the Dutch approach to punishment and treatment of offenders.[2] Specifically in relation to prisons, *Contrasts in Tolerance* succeeded at fostering, despite dissenting voices (Franke 1990), a reputation for the Dutch prison system as a beacon of humanity in Western Europe and the very antithesis of the English one. Thus, we came to know that not only did Dutch prisons imprison far less people and for shorter periods of time but also cared far more for their welfare and rehabilitation whom they treated and detained humanely. In comparison, English prisons incapacitated far more people

[1] See e.g. Cavadino and Dignan (2006b), Pratt (2008), Green (2008), Lazarus (2004).

[2] See e.g. Resodihardjo (2009), King and Resodihardjo (2010), Kruttschnitt and Dirkzwager (2011), Pakes and Holt (2015).

A. Karamalidou, *Embedding Human Rights in Prison*,
DOI 10.1057/978-1-137-58502-8_2

and for longer periods in squalid and overcrowded conditions whom they treated antagonistically and harshly.

Downes attributed the divergent paths of the two prison systems to a distinctive culture of tolerance and a politics of accommodation that permeated Dutch society, politics and state governance, and stood in contrast to the English state of affairs.

Rooted in the country's history, Dutch tolerance translated into receptiveness to new things and toleration of 'deviants, minorities, religious dissent and extreme or eccentric views' (Downes 1988: 69). It was enabled by the system of pillarisation which referred to the organisation of Dutch society into distinct pillars[3] that represented the interests of predominantly religious groups. Although the pillars did not intermingle in their daily lives, they were successfully integrated into the social body through their participation and representation in political governance by forming coalition governments. For purposes of social and political stability, coalition governments adhered to a 'politics of accommodation', the working principles of which were deliberation, negotiation, and pragmatism (Lijphart 1967; cited in Downes 1988: 74–75). A willingness to mutually accommodate each pillar's interests was seen as the unavoidable price that all had to pay for their members' welfare and, ultimately, for the common good. Such a culture of tolerance was lacking in England and Wales. Also, there was no need for a similar politics of accommodation since in British politics a single political party would typically secure a majority vote in elections and thus be able to pursue its own ideologically informed policies without the need for compromises deemed necessary in coalition governments.

In relation to criminal justice policy, the influence of this Dutch tolerance and politics of accommodation could be seen inter alia in the availability and actual use of non-custodial sanctions, the practice of beleid[4] by the Prosecution Service by the means of prosecutorial waivers,

[3] There were four pillars that comprised Liberals, Catholics, Protestants and the socialists who had their own educational, recreational and healthcare facilities (Pakes 2004: 149). Based on van Dijk (2010) 'many lived from cradle to grave in the splendid isolation of their own column'.

[4] Described as 'a spider in the web of the criminal justice system because of its wide discretionary powers, prosecution waivers rose from 34% in 1960 to 54% in 1970, and reached 57% in 1981 (Blakenburg and Bruinsma 1994: 53–54). The high number of prosecutorial waivers is seen as an

a uniform judicial culture with penal abolitionist views, and a media culture that refrained from a populist crime reporting. All this contributed to sustaining a low prison population by diverting offenders away from prison and imposing, when unavoidable, short sentences. Again, these elements were absent in the English context. Increases in crime from the early 1950s onwards were met with harsh sentencing across the spectrum of offences which, coupled with the abolition of the death penalty in 1965, resulted in more and longer sentences, with prison overcrowding problems emerging as early as the 1960s (Morgan 1997). Despite the availability of alternative sanctions (e.g. probation order and community sentence), the perception of the probation order as a soft punishment, confusion over the aims of the community sentence, and their application to minor offences undermined their potential to reduce prisoner numbers (Mair 1997). Crucially, the politicisation and racialisation of crime along with the criminalisation of youth subcultures and civil disobedience from the 1960s onwards were not conducive to restraint in punishment and the use of prison for that matter. The strong presence of populist media reporting was a great enabler in this respect, creating moral panics of varying intensity and calling for thorough punishment in the name of a righteous public (Downes and Morgan 1997: 89–92, 98, 2007).

Moreover, Dutch tolerance, compromise and pragmatism also characterised the execution of imprisonment. Dutch prisons had more humane living conditions and less oppressive regimes geared more towards the normalisation of prison life. Prisoners in Dutch prisons were on much friendlier terms with officers, spent more time out of the cell, were paid substantially more for prison work and had much greater access to outside world through more visits, calls and mail, as well as to rehabilitation schemes. Additional normalising and humanising aspects that differentiated Dutch prisons from English prisons were

---

expression of the Dutch concept of *beleid*, being itself another example of Dutch pragmatism. Beleid refers to public authorities' rules, policies, procedures and standards, and is concerned with maximising their effective implementation. In this respect, to achieve optimum results, the Dutch approach would be to strike a balance between the letter of the law and its application through a less formalistic and rigid interpretation of its provisions. For instance, in case a rule was judged not to benefit the parties concerned in the long term, a way to circumvent it without giving rise to unlawfulness would be the preferred option (Blakenburg and Bruinsma 1994: 63–66).

the one prisoner to a cell rule,[5] the provision of conjugal visits, female staff presence in male prisons (e.g. as governors, officers, social workers etc.) and the lack of a tyrannical and/or arbitrary application of prison rules (Downes 1988: 163–188), whereas English prisoners would be customarily doubled up and locked up to 23 hours a day in cells that lacked sanitation facilities. Their visits were restricted in number and duration and were difficult for relatives to make due to the distance of prisons from prisoners' hometowns. Prisoner mail was not unlimited, legal correspondence was scrutinised, the procedure for making calls was bureaucratic, prison wages were substandard, conjugal visits did not exist, and rehabilitation was sidelined by security considerations. Last but not least, interactions with staff were far from amicable. Prisoners felt that staff attitudes were judgemental and discriminatory, and their relationship with staff was further strained by a highly discretionary use of prison rules (ibid.: 166–167, 173–177).

In short, the Dutch prison experience was heavily influenced by the concept of humane containment, the paternalistic undertones of which (van Swaaningen and de Jonge 1995) were still superior to the principle of less eligibility that characterised the English prison experience; that is, the belief that prisoners' living conditions and, implicitly, treatment ought to be of a lesser standard than those experienced by the lowest (law-abiding) socio-economic strata for purposes of retribution and individual deterrence.

In the years that followed scholars would revisit *Contrasts in Tolerance* in a renewed interest in Dutch penal affairs. What reignited the interest were the contrasting and contradictory developments in the Dutch approach to the punishment and treatment of offenders that have produced twists and turns, which some are challenging to understand (Pakes 2004, 2005; van Swaaningen 2013). By the time *Contrasts in Tolerance* was published, the Dutch prison population had already been

[5] The rule of one prisoner to a cell was introduced in 1947 (Franke 1990: 86). It is worth noting that what underpinned the introduction of this humane indeed measure was pragmatism and custom rather than humanism. For Franke (1990: 87), it was a continuation of the long-established practice of solitary confinement, 'the unintended result of historical developments and not of humane principles, stated explicitly'. Whereas Blakenburg and Bruinsma (1994: 50) argue that it aimed to reduce the risk of disorder and the spread of communicable diseases.

on the rise and continued to increase up until 2005. From an incarceration rate of 23 per 100,000 in 1980 and 33 in 1985, it passed the 100 mark in 2001, reaching 124 per 100,000 and 134 in 2004 and 2005 respectively (van Dijk 2010). From being one of the least incapacitative countries, the Netherlands experienced 'one of the steepest rates of increase in the world' (van Swaaningen 2013: 342), with its prison rates quadrupling since 1985. The quantitative increases were accompanied by qualitative changes which saw regimes being toughened up in terms of security and the degree of freedom and autonomy, as well as access to rehabilitation afforded to prisoners (Boone and Moerings 2007). This break from tradition, a parsimonious use of imprisonment and liberal prison regimes, alarmed scholars who lamented what they saw as the gradual shaping of a 'dystopian' state in Dutch penal affairs (Downes and van Swaaningen 2007). The culture of tolerance, which Dutch society and politics were distinctive of and had underpinned the hitherto penal mildness, was in decline, and consequently, Dutch penal reductionism had to be assigned firmly to the past (Pakes 2005: 148–150, 155–158).

Contrary to scholars' expectations, the ensuing pessimism brought about by the loss of an exemplary progressive penal policy, which resisted emulating other comparable countries' reliance on prison as punishment and response to social ills, has been replaced at the time of writing by incredulity and cautious optimism (van Swaaningen 2013: 339, 349, 351, 354–357; Boone and van Swaaningen 2013). Since 2006 prisoner numbers are declining without a cultural shift in tolerance taking place, and eight prisons have closed down. With an imprisonment rate of 69 per 100,000 in 2014, down from 134 and 92 in 2005 and 2010 respectively, the Netherlands finds itself well below the Western European average rate of 84 per 100,000 (van Swaaningen 2013: 349; Walmsley 2015). Moreover, the freed-up space in its prison capacity has led to rather interesting developments. Two of its prisons are being rented out to Belgium and Norway, which experience capacity pressures of their own (Pakes and Holt 2015).

While Dutch prisons have gone through unprecedented changes, despite improvements in material conditions and prisoners' human rights, English prisons have continued on the same path. In the intervening years, they have been shaken by widespread riots in the 1990s; have been plagued by overcrowding, self-harm incidents and suicides to the present day; and have witnessed in the last years a return to violence among prisoners and against staff (Cavadino et al. 2013; EHRC 2015; HMIP 2015, 2016). Unlike the Dutch prison population, the English prison population has been increasing year on year, having reached 85,843 in 2015. With an incarceration rate of 148 per 100,000, England and Wales is in the infamous position of having the highest rate in Western Europe (Walmsley 2015: 10). Despite a shift in governmental policy from *Getting Tough on Crime* in the late 1990s and 2000s to promising a *Rehabilitation Revolution* from 2010 onwards, English prisons are still struggling to find their pace.

The Research Context

It is in the context of the convergence between the two national prison systems that my comparative study on human rights in English and Dutch prisons took place. Unlike Downes (1988) and Kruttschnitt and Dirkzwager (2011) who interviewed Dutch nationals detained in English prisons and vice versa on how they experienced imprisonment in each other's countries, I interviewed Dutch and English prisoners serving sentences in their own countries between 2004 and 2008. In seeking their respective views and conceptualisations of human rights in prisons, I aimed to shed light on the impact (if any) of key changes in the two systems on the recognition and protection of prisoners' human rights from the prisoner perspective. Drawing on the prisoner voice, my objective was to build a prisoner account of the contribution of human rights to their lives that went beyond the official picture painted by the legalisation of human rights. With the comparative data as an aid, my goal was to explore what lessons we can learn with a view to maximising the potential of human rights for penal reform.

In 2008, when I interviewed the Dutch prisoners, prisoner numbers were decreasing from their peak in 2005 (van Dijk 2010), but the prison experience had already permanently changed after taking a regressive turn that has yet to be reversed (Boone and van Swaaningen

2013: 21; Struijk 2015). On the other hand, when I interviewed the English prisoners between 2004 and 2007, the state of affairs can be described as business as usual irrespective of structural changes in prison management.[6] Overcrowding and prisoner numbers remained (and have continued to be) high, straining material resources and rehabilitation provision before and after the fieldwork (see Chap. 4), with the most game-changing development being the partial incorporation of the ECHR into domestic law in 2000 through the 1998 Human Rights Act (HRA).

Prisoners' Rights in English and Dutch Prisons: Background

Before we explore the trajectory the English and Dutch penal policies have taken since their characterisation as *Contrasts in Tolerance*, it is necessary to document the two countries' approach to prisoners' rights. This is necessary for the following reasons. First, we will be able to contextualise the impact of the legalisation of prisoners' human rights at European level on the two prison systems and, importantly, prisoners' respective views on and conceptualisations of human rights. Second, we will be able to reach conclusions on what steps to take and what steps to avoid for successfully embedding human rights in prison.

It can be argued that the two countries' approach to the idea of prisoner rights in general adds another contrast to those identified by Downes. In terms of both recognition and protection of prisoners' rights, there have been substantial contrasts between the two prison systems. These emanate as much from their differing interpretation of human rights protection due to their legal traditions as from their differing cultures of punishment.

[6] In 2004 the National Offender Management Service (NOMS) was created. NOMS is responsible for the running of prisons and the delivery of punishment in the community by the probation service. It introduced the concepts of offender management and of an 'end-to-end' practice whereby the supervision of the offender and treatment of their needs is delivered in an uninterrupted and consistent manner through the different stages of their punishment through inter-agency work.

The Dutch Concept of Moral Rights

Dutch recognition of prisoner rights can be traced back to the late 1950s and 1960s where the notion of granting prisoners' rights came to be seen as morally justified. According to Franke (1995) the concept of moral rights was borne out of post-war penal reform efforts by experts and politicians, who had been affected by imprisonment themselves during the war. These were intensified from the 1960s onwards when the government and society alike were confronted with high prison re-offending rates and emerging research evidence on the wide range of afflictions caused by imprisonment. Both forced an acknowledgement of the limitations of imprisonment in rehabilitating and resocialising offenders and a gradual recognition 'that societal reform, education and improved living conditions could be more instrumental in the battle against crime than judicial reactions (ibid.: 248)'. This led to an emphasis on humane containment and the normalisation of prison life, which via the recognition of prisoners' moral rights aimed at minimising the corrosive effects of imprisonment on an already socially disadvantaged population (ibid.: 255, 258–259). For example, the 1953 Prison Rules recognised prisoners' moral rights to work, education, medical and social care, to religious instruction, and to rest (!) (Vagg 1994), with the moral right to 'contact with a woman' becoming policy in the 1980s with the introduction of conjugal visits[7] (Franke 1995: 258–259).

The concept of prisoners' moral rights is simply not found in English prisons, where rights were typically understood and translated into either privileges or legitimate expectations at best (especially prior to the 1998 HRA) (Vagg 1994: 170). Notably, the rights, which are covered by the

[7] Dutch male prisoners' accounts on the distortion of their gender identity and resultant sexual disorientation due to the deprivation of sexual contact with the opposite sex began to surface from the early 1950s. By the end of the decade the liberalisation of morals in society at large brought this intrinsic pain of imprisonment (Sykes 1958: 289–290) to the spotlight. In the early 1960s, research by the Dutch Society for Sexual Reform focused on the 'sexual need in judicial, penal and health institutions' and a Ministerial Committee was set up to look into 'conjugal visits in prisons' (Franke 1995: 258–259). Dutch consideration of this important human rights issue for prisoners in terms of its early timing and actual implementation contrasts sharply with the state's inattention to and inactivity in this aspect of prison experience in England and Wales.

English Prison Rules, have nearly always been a by-product of a court ruling or of an official inquiry in the aftermath of a prison crisis (see e.g. the 1995 introduction of the Incentives and Earned Privileges scheme). It is also worth noting that there exists no provision of conjugal visits yet, which, as we will see in Chap. 5, English prisoners called for their being recognised as their human right.

The Dutch Legal Right to Complain

In addition to the concept of prisoners' moral rights, the 1976 Legal Status of Prisoners recognised prisoners' legal right to complain and appeal against decisions taken by or on behalf of the prison governor[8] (Tak 2008). Its importance cannot be stressed enough considering the typically wide discretionary powers of prison staff. It had an immediately positive effect as a number of restrictions on moral rights were lifted (Franke 1995: 249). In a way, this was anticipated following the recognition of the right to appeal one's placement in a particular prison or wing in the 1953 Principles of the Prison Administration Act (PPA) (Kelk 1983).

What further merits attention is how embedded in the prison system the legal right to complain has been, being exercised through a tripartite complaints system based on clearly demarcated hierarchical levels and subjects of complaint. The complaints system involves an informal and a formal process in making and dealing with prisoner complaints.

On the lowest level, by virtue of the 1953 PPA, every prison has a Supervisory Committee, whose role is to ensure that prisoner treatment meets the required standards of care (Art 7(1&2a), 1999 PPA) by being tasked, among other things, to receive prisoner complaints. At this stage, these are dealt with by the means of informal mediation, and complaints of serious nature are discussed in the first instance with the prison governor at the Committee's monthly meetings (Art 63(4), 1999 PPA; Art

[8] Based on Art 60 of the 1999 PPA this includes 'an omission or refusal to take a decision. The taking of the decision shall be deemed omitted or refused if a decision is not taken within the statutory term, or, if this is lacking, within a reasonable term'. The Prison Rules and the behaviour of the governor and their representatives cannot, however, give rise to a complaint (Tak 2008: 167).

16(5), 1999 Penitentiary Order). The Committee has unrestricted access to the institution, its prisoners and their files at any time unless the latter object (Art 15(1&2), 1999 Penitentiary Order).

At the next level, by virtue of the 1976 Legal Status of Prisoners Act, every prison has a Complaints Committee, which, in contrast to the Supervisory Committee, is part of the formal complaints procedure and has a judicial capacity. Prisoners can formally lodge a complaint with the Complaints Committee upon an unsatisfactory outcome from the Supervisory Committee. At this stage, governors are required to provide information and their views on the complaint, which are made available to complainants (Art 61(2&3), 1999 PPA). In the hearing, the prisoner and the governor can be requested for questioning (Art 64(3), 1999 PPA). If the complaint is found valid, the Committee is empowered to annul the decision that gave rise to it, and to either request the governor to amend it or decide the matter itself. In some instances, an annulment can be regarded a sufficient remedy in itself. When the effects of the nullified decision cannot be redressed (e.g. a disciplinary punishment has already been served), the Committee can order compensation. Compensation can be monetary or in kind, such as extra visits, phone calls or more association time (Art 68(2&3, 6&7), 1999 PPA).

The Complaints Committee's decisions are not final, with governors and prisoners having the right to appeal before the Appeals Committee (Art 60, 69, 1999 PPA). At both levels of the formal procedure, prisoners have a series of procedural rights: to legal aid and assistance (e.g. from a qualified lawyer, a social worker or even a fellow prisoner) (Art 65(1), to the service of an interpreter if they do not command the Dutch language (Art 61 & 65(1&2)), to make written or oral representations (Art 64) and to call and cross-examine witnesses (Art 64(4)) (1999 PPA). Moreover, the prisoner can request partial or whole suspension of the decision, which forms the subject of their complaint, in anticipation of the Complaints and Appeals Committees' findings (Art 66(1), 70(2), 1999 PPA). It is also worth noting that irrespective of the nature of the complaint, Art 75 (1999 PPA) recognises prisoners' entitlement to a proxy if they are under restraint, are of minor age or if their relationship with the proxy has been beneficial to them. In such cases, all the rights just mentioned are transferred to the prisoner's proxy. The Complaints

Committee's decisions must be reasoned and dated, and are made public (Art 67(7), 71(4), 73(4), 1999 PPA).

As mentioned earlier, since 1953 prisoners have the right to appeal against prison/wing placements or transfers (Kelk 1983: 170). These are heard by the Admission and Transfer Appeals Committee, whose remit includes withdrawal from penitentiary programmes since 1999, as well as decisions on leave and interruption of sentence. The above procedural rights apply here, with prisoners having also the right to make a fresh appeal six months after the first appeal is rejected (Art 18(3), 72–73, 1999 PPA).

Lastly, by virtue of Art 30 of the 1999 Penitentiary Order, a Central Medical Appeals Committee is tasked with hearing medical complaints. The medical complaints procedure is quite similar to the generic one in terms of stages and prisoners' procedural rights (Art 29, 131, 1999 Penitentiary Order). Before an appeal is made, prisoners have to communicate their grievances either to the establishment's medical practitioner or the Medical Adviser of the Ministry of Security and Justice. Like the Supervisory Committee, the Medical Adviser acts as a mediator. If mediation fails or the complaint is serious, they have to inform the prisoner of their right to appeal and can refer the case to the Complaints Committee (Art 29(1, 7), 1999 Penitentiary Order). The Medical Appeals Committee has the authority to order compensation, which may be monetary, if it judges the complaint valid (Art 33(2), 1999 Penitentiary Order).

In comparison, respective arrangements in English prisons have lacked structure, coherence, procedural guarantees for prisoners and accountability, being identified in the 1990 Woolf Inquiry into the prison disturbances of the 1990s among the dominant sources of prisoners' frustration and widespread feeling of injustice against them (Tumim 1996). While prisoners' right to 'pursue a request or complaint connected to or arising from their imprisonment' was recognised by Rule 7 of the 1964 Prison Rules, in practice prior to 1990 an internal complaints system was virtually non-existent (Livingstone et al. 2008: 42–43). 'Developed piecemeal over the previous 100 years' (ibid.: 43), prisoners could lodge a complaint with the governor or the Board of Visitors (BoVs), which could hardly be perceived as an independent and accountable means of resolution. First, the governor was in the position of both an adjudicator and a defendant since complaints rose out of decisions they or their representatives made. Second, the BoVs acted both like the Dutch Supervisory Committee and as an adjudicator in disciplinary hearings for serious offences (ibid.: 44).

Attempts to address the above deficiencies led to the introduction of a new system in 1990, with further changes being made by 2002 following its review in 1999–2000 (ibid.). Based on the 1990 system prisoners first would make a request or complaint locally in their holding institution, the outcome of which they could appeal against at the level of the Prison Service Headquarters. If the dispute involved a reserved subject, it was dealt with from the start by the Prison Service Headquarters. Reserved subjects are those which the prison does not have the authority to resolve. These involve "allegations against the governing governor, parole for determinate sentenced prisoners, litigation against the Prison Service, artifical insemination, repatriation, transfer to Scotland or Northern Ireland, Mother and Baby Unit placement appeals, special remission, and all complaints relating to category A or life sentence prisoners" (Livingstone et al. 2008: 48–49).

Moreover, by the 1990s the BoVs' dual role as a monitoring and informal complaints mechanism and as a disciplinary adjudicator had become untenable. The 1990 Woolf Inquiry and prisoner litigation at home and abroad revealed systematic bias and discrimination against prisoners and found the BoVs acting in a judicial capacity without affording prisoners the right to a fair trial (Karamalidou 2010). As a result, since 1992 the role of the BoVs is to only monitor prisoner treatment through regular prison visits and to hear prisoners' requests/complaints (Livingstone and Owen 1999).

Further changes have seen the exclusive use of Prison Service Headquarters for reserved subjects only and the adoption of differing procedures for requests and complaints. In respect of the latter, it was judged necessary as it was found that 'failing to distinguish between the two can create a sense of grievance where none exist. A complaints system should be a means of redressing grievances, not of meeting everyday needs' (PSO 2510; cited in Livingstone et al. 2008: 46). Under the new framework, the generic complaints procedure has three stages, at wing level, middle management level and finally before the governing governor. Requests can be first made informally at wing level and formally followed up at wing and management levels. Upon an unsatisfactory outcome, the prisoner can appeal to the governing governor. Additionally, prisoners can lodge a complaint with the governor, the Chair of the BoVs and/or the Area Manager through the confidential access route, and have the right to make an oral or written complaint to the BoVs. When all the above options fail to deliver a satisfactory outcome from the complainant's perspective, staff must inform prisoners of the available options they have (ibid.: 46–47).

Human Rights in Dutch and English Prisons

In addition to their differing approach to prisoners' rights, the two systems have interpreted differently the idea of prisoners having human rights, as opposed to merely rights. While this was to be expected considering their socio-cultural differences in their tolerance levels and ways of governing, their different legal traditions have also played a major role.

Both countries are signatories to the ECHR. The UK government was among the first to ratify the Convention in 1951, which it followed up with the ratification of Art 34 in 1966 (the right to individual petition). The Netherlands ratified the ECHR and its Art 34 in 1953 and 1956 respectively. As a result, they share the same human rights obligations under the ECHR, but they have interpreted these differently, which, as we will see in Chap. 3, has proved particularly troublesome for the English authorities.

The source of the difference and trouble lies in that the Netherlands has a civil law system, which the ECHR also originates from, whereas the UK has a common law system. This entails two important things. First, in sharing the same legal tradition with the ECHR, the Dutch follow the same principles with the ECHR regarding its protection[9] and interpret these principles in a similar fashion. This has not been the case for the UK. This is especially with reference to the principles of the positive duty of care and, to a lesser extent, of proportionality (Wadham and Mountfield 2000).

The English conception of human rights, known as the Diceyan interpretation of human rights, has traditionally been cast in negative terms, laying emphasis on limited state intervention with people's lives

[9] These are the positive duty of care, proportionality, legality, legitimate aims and the margin of appreciation.

to the exclusion of a proactive state interference for the purposes of an effective human rights protection. Based on the Diceyan interpretation people are free to do anything they want unless it is legally prohibited, thus privileging negative rights over positive rights (ibid.: 6). The added importance of the positive duty of care lies in that in its application it does not distinguish between negative and positive human rights, thus invalidating its long-held association only with the protection of the latter. This bolsters human rights protection through a more encompassing enforcement methodology. Regarding the principle of proportionality, the English interpretation has been traditionally loose, thus widening the scope of state interference with human rights. Under the Convention a proportionate interference is necessary in a democratic society in the interests of state security, public safety and crime prevention that is rendered unavoidable in the absence of an alternative solution. In contrast, under English law a proportionate interference is one that is rational to the legitimate aim it seeks to serve (ibid.: 19).

Second, constitutionally, the Dutch (written) Constitution is the supreme authority in the Netherlands, whereas in the UK it is the Parliament. The UK does not have a codified written constitution. Of course, this does not mean that there are no constitutional principles to abide by. There are but are scattered across unwritten customary laws, legislation and case law (Heringa and Kiiver 2007). Under each country's constitutional arrangements, ratified international law, such as the ECHR, is treated differently. In the Dutch context, following amendments to the Constitution of the Kingdom of the Netherlands in 1953 and 1956, international law is set above domestic legislation, and its provisions are directly applicable to the national sphere without the need for additional domestic legislation to give effect to them. Although Dutch courts cannot invalidate an act of Parliament on the grounds that it is unconstitutional, they can refrain from applying an act judged to be in contravention with international law (ibid.: 28, 112). The treatment of national and international law as a single unitary authority is known as the doctrine of monism that stands opposite the doctrine of dualism the UK follows. This means that ratified international law is not directly applicable to the national setting and cannot be directly invoked before national courts unless the Parliament (on account of its sovereignty) incorporates the relevant law into the domestic legal order by passing an Act (ibid.: 108).

The UK incorporated the ECHR into domestic law through the 1998 HRA that entered into force in 2000. It needs to be noted that this is a partial incorporation that has seen all ECHR substantive rights and freedoms (Art 2–14)[10] becoming actionable except for Art 1 and 13 (the obligation to respect human rights and the right to an effective remedy). For the first time, the Act imposes on the state, its public and quasi-public authorities the statutory duty to comply with the ECHR. For example, Sect. 19 of the 1998 HRA requires a public ministerial statement on the compliance of a legislative proposal with the Convention, as well as on the reasons for its consideration when it is not compliant. Section 2 of the Act requires domestic courts to pay due regard to the ECtHR case law when they adjudicate on matters that invoke directly the Convention. Section 3(1) also places upon the courts the requirement to 'read primary and subordinate legislation, so far as it is possible to do so, in a way which is compatible with the convention rights'. This means that judges are obligated to not only take into account the substantive ECHR content but also employ the five interpretative principles of the convention (see note 9 in this chapter). This contrasts with the hitherto practice based on which the ECHR was used as guidance on resolving legal ambiguities, clarifying the scope of the common law, and determining judicial discretion (Wadham and Mountfield 2000: 1). As a result, legal and financial hurdles standing in people's way are removed, and a less expensive and speedier legal avenue of redress is created.

Although domestic courts cannot strike down legislation on grounds of incompatibility with the ECHR, they can issue a declaration of incompatibility (Sect. 4, 1998 HRA). Such a declaration, which can be seen as an English example of the Dutch *politics of accommodation*, entails that incompatible legislation returns to Parliament for reconsideration. If the sovereign Parliament reaches the view that 'there are compelling reasons' to remove the incompatibility, amendments to the legislation are made. Throughout this process, and in the absence of compelling reasons, the legislation retains its legal effect (Wadham and Mountfield 2000: 3).

In relation to prisoners' human rights, the respective impact of the above has been as follows:

[10] These are supplemented with the incorporation of Art 1 (protection of property), 2 (right to education) and 3 (right to free elections, involving the right to vote) of the First Protocol to the ECHR, as well as of Art. 1 of the 13th Protocol (abolition of the death penalty).

Starting with the Netherlands, in Chap. 1 the Dutch Constitution recognises a number of fundamental rights 'for all persons in the Netherlands',[11] with Art 15 being directly relevant to people deprived of their liberty. It recognises their right to a prompt trial for determining the charges against them and to an immediate release from custody following a ruling on the unlawfulness of their detention.

The effect of Dutch constitutional principles and the influence of European human rights soft law, such as the positive duty of care and the European Prison Rules (EPRs),[12] are evident in prison legislation. The 1999 PPA, which replaced the 1953 PPA, identifies a number of rights and, occasionally, freedoms and recognises the prison service's duty of care on numerous occasions. This duty of care, which ultimately rests upon the governor (Art. 3(3), 1999 PPA), pertains principally to the active protection of prisoners' procedural rights in complaint procedures and, to a second degree, to the facilitation of prisoners' rights to care, social assistance, and to know of impending restrictions on calls, visits, mail, and media contact. Active protection and facilitation mean that the governor is expected to act proactively so as to ensure that inmates are able to exercise their rights and benefit from them in practice.

For example, Art 57 and 58 (1999 PPA) require that the governor issues a prompt, 'reasoned, dated and signed written notification' to the prisoner regarding matters that fall within their decision-making powers and can consequently become grounds for complaints. Both articles refer to these matters by name, listing 12 in number. These range from declining a request for or interrupting a child's stay in prison to being placed in solitary confinement, and being subjected to an internal physical examination. Also, Art 56 unequivocally declares that upon their arrival at the institution prisoners are to be informed of their rights and duties under the 1999 PPA, including ways to complain about their treatment in a

[11] Based on the Constitution of the Kingdom of the Netherlands, these are the rights to equality and equal treatment, to association, assembly and demonstration, respect for one's privacy, the inviolability of one's person, petition, access to courts, legal representation and aid, and the right to property. In addition, it recognises the freedoms of expression and religious belief, the rights to vote and stand for elections, to education, medical care, and employment.

[12] The 1973 version of the EPRs and the 1955 UN Standard Minimum Rules for the Treatment of Prisoners informed prisoner entitlements stipulated in the 1951 Dutch Prison Act and 1953 Prison Rules (Franke 1995: 257).

written and oral form. Notably, it makes reference to foreign nationals' right to contact their consulate regarding their status, which is especially important considering that foreign nationals represent over 20% of the Dutch prison population (World Prison Brief: Netherlands, 2014).

The respective status of human rights in English prisons could not have been more contrasting. Prior to the 1998 HRA, which placed on the Prison Service as a public authority the duty to comply with the ECHR, in theory prisoners' human rights were protected through relevant prison legislation and common law values. So, if prisoners wanted to know what their human rights were, they had to look up in prison legislation; and, if they felt that their human rights were infringed or unnecessarily limited, they could pursue a case before the courts.

The 1952 Prison Act is silent on the issue except for a brief and general reference to the prisoners' right to 'be given a proper opportunity of presenting his case' for the purposes of disciplinary adjudications (Sect. 47(2)). As mentioned earlier, the rights covered by the Prison Rules are the outcome of an enforced evolutionary process that has seen amendments to the Rules following successful prisoner litigation and/or an official inquiry into a prison issue. For example, the overhaul of the official disciplinary system started with *St. Germain* (1978) and was not completed until 2003 with *Ezeh & Connors v UK* (2002). Moreover, it was not until 1978 with the aforementioned case of *St. Germain* that the UK courts began to show willingness to intervene in prison matters. Prior to 1978, the judicial attitude towards prisoners was overwhelmingly unsympathetic, exemplified in *Becker v Home Office* (1972) where in Lord Denning's words, 'If the courts were to entertain actions by disgruntled prisoners, the governor's life would be intolerable. The discipline of the prison would be undermined' (Treverton-Jones 1989: 32).

Conclusion

The geographically strategic trade position of the Netherlands, which has brought the country in closer contact with people from all over the world, and its composition of minority groups have arguably contributed through the centuries to the development of a more pragmatic and tolerant approach to life, its social organisation, political governance and management of its challenges (Andeweg and Irwin 2005). Dutch pragmatism, following from the need for *a politics of accommodation* in a country of minorities where each had their own interests to protect, has arguably been a driving force behind its decarcerative post-war penal policy. As the one prisoner to a cell rule testifies, the humanity of the Dutch prison system may have been more a by-product of pragmatism, rather than the outcome of pure humanitarian considerations.

Whether its humanism was heavily informed by pragmatism or it was a mixture of both, the fact remains that compared to the English prison experience the Dutch one was more humane, adopting a more progressive stance on prisoner rights. The absence of the Dutch cultural and political ingredients of tolerance from the English setting led to an incapacitative penal policy that viewed prisoners as less deserving of the state's attention and care, as well as rights on account of their law-breaking. Differences in the two countries' legal traditions and legal interpretation of human rights protection have exacerbated the differing level of recognition and degree of protection they have afforded those in their custody and care.

In this context, the two countries' political economies,[13] represented by their socio-cultural and political differences upon which their 1988

[13] In their examination of the association between penal policy and political economy, Cavadino and Dignan (2006a, b) developed a typology of political economies with reference to a number of socio-economic and penal measures, such as a country's political and economic orientation, social and economic levels of (in) equality and in/exclusion, and approach to punishment in terms of its aims, methods and administration. They argued that a country's political economy impacted on the nature of its penal policy and subsequently its imprisonment levels. They identified four main political economies: neoliberal ones represented, for example by England and Wales and the United States; conservative corporatism followed by Germany and the Netherlands; social democratic corporatism exemplified by Sweden; and oriental corporatism represented by Japan (2006b: 15). The argument has been that the high prison population in England and Wales is principally the combined outcome of a neoliberal economic policy (free market capitalism) and law and order politics. Unrestrained economic competition, the privileging of private-led initiatives over state involvement in important spheres of social life (e.g. health, education and employment) and reduced state welfare have exacerbated socio-economic inequalities, thus engendering the marginalisation and exclusion of increasing numbers of people. In the highly and ruthlessly individualistic, consumerist and competitive neoliberal economic culture, those left behind by the unrelenting force of capitalism are labelled failures and are seen as personally responsible for their lack of economic and thus social success. Law and order politics help cementing such views, creating a platform for the expression and practice of retributive sentiments and attitudes to the treatment of all those who are not

description as *Contrasts in Tolerance* was qualified, help us understand the post-war trajectory of their penal policies, however, only to a certain degree as the twists and turns of the Dutch penal policy from the late 1980s to the mid-2000s show.

(seen) productive actors in the neoliberal capitalist order. In contrast, the low prison population in the post-war Netherlands can be seen as the outcome of a capitalist economic model that for the purposes of the national interest has tried to accommodate the competing interests of different social groups. Acting as a restraint on the excesses of a free-for-all capitalism, this state-driven accommodation of interests has enabled the development of more inclusive and caring social policies, shaping along the way societal expectations of the state's role in relation to its citizens and attitudes to punishment. In this environment, the state has a responsibility to care for the less fortunate and the vulnerable through an adequate provision of state welfare, and thus to rehabilitate and reintegrate into society those who find themselves at its margins.

3

English Penal Policy and Prisoners' Human Rights

Introduction

In Chap. 2, reference was made to the punitive turn the Dutch penal policy took from the mid-1980s to the mid-2000s, which led to substantial increases in the prison population, and its return to decarceration from the mid-2000s to the present day. Like the Dutch penal policy, the English penal policy has had its own twists but these have not had an impact that would allow us to talk about turning points being made. Lest I be misunderstood, I do not mean that no positive developments in English penal affairs have taken place, quite the contrary. Pertinent to the subject of this book, major strides have been made in the sphere of the legalisation of prisoners' human rights, which the 1998 HRA has further enabled. As we shall see, specific prisoner categories, such as lifers, have secured formidable gains in matters pertaining to their release and treatment. The prisoner group as a whole has also benefitted, seeing greater protection of their human rights in areas of prison life, such as disciplinary adjudications and contact with the outside world. Moreover, organisational and legislative changes in prison healthcare and investigations into prisoner deaths have recognised prisoners' right to equivalence

A. Karamalidou, *Embedding Human Rights in Prison*,
DOI 10.1057/978-1-137-58502-8_3

in healthcare, as well as that their families have rights in connection to their treatment while incarcerated.

The progressive force and potential of the above have been stalled though by an ever-increasing prison population that shows no signs of abating. Based on the Ministry of Justice (2015a) projections for 2015–2021 the prison population is estimated to reach 89,900 in 2021. After a drop in prisoner numbers from around 50,000 in 1988–1989 to around 45,000 between 1990 and 1993, the prison population has been on the rise since (Morgan and Liebling 2007). Between 1993 and 2014 there has been a whopping 91% increase, and with 148 people per 100,000 in prison in October 2015, England and Wales have the highest imprisonment rate in Western Europe. The scale of this increase has resulted in an overcrowded prison system year on year, with 70 of the 117 prisons being overcrowded in October 2015. Moreover, in the last six years, in the context of the wider economic crisis, the Prison Service had to accommodate big expenditure savings. As a result, it had to cope with far fewer prison officers, more prisoners and a revolutionary (it is promised to be) organisational facelift in respect of prisoner rehabilitation (Walmsley 2015: 2, 10; Bromley Briefings Autumn 2015: 4–5; National Audit Office 2013; Ministry of Justice 2013). Such conditions—overcrowded prisons with reduced budgets and human resources—are simply not conducive to a dignified, respectful and human rights-informed prisoner treatment.

A closer examination of the contextual background of this stubbornly upward trend of the prison population directs our attention to the socio-cultural and political aspects, which Downes (1988) identified as responsible for the comparatively tougher penal climate in England and Wales. It reveals that they have remained constant while crime rates have not.

More specifically, crime, punishment and the treatment of offenders are essentially politicised issues in England and Wales. The tabloid press has held onto its power, which has enabled it to continue with its tradition of sensationalist and populist reporting. Being constantly in the public eye, and in a principally non-consociational system, crime and punishment acquire an importance similar to that reserved for the economy and become the battleground of election campaigns. In this context, crime and punishment are law and order issues that call for tough and immediate action (Downes and Morgan 2007: 203–208, 213–222, 2012: 186–195). In the light of this, political pronouncements on prison reforms of a reductionist nature are a political suicide. They privilege (we are told) offenders' interests over those of the hard-working and law-abiding majority, and thus are inattentive to their needs and disrespectful of the victims' anguish. The politicisation of crime, its transformation into a law and order issue as early as the mid-1960s (Downes and Morgan 1997) and its dominance in political life have had a profound impact on penal policy.

English Decarceration: A Short-Lived Experiment

As mentioned in Chap. 2, just two years after Downes's publication, the Prison Service was thrown into a crisis, shaken by widespread riots and disturbances. The 1990 Inquiry into the events, headed by Lord Woolf, was categorical in its conclusion that a safe and secure custody was a humane, fair and just custody. Its message was unequivocal: prison conditions had to improve. For example, the inhuman and degrading practice of slopping out, as was described by the CPT in its first UK visit in 1990, had to stop. Also, the exercise of control had to be balanced with a respectful prisoner treatment. Integral to such treatment was that prisoners knew what rights and responsibilities they had, and how to enjoy their rights and meet their responsibilities. A heavy-handed approach to prisoner treatment was counterproductive to prison security and prisoner safety (Resodihardjo 2009: 100–101).

The Conservative Government accepted almost all of the Inquiry's recommendations,[1] which incidentally could be accommodated by the approach already followed. The so-called Hurd approach sought to

[1] Against the background of the chronic problem of overcrowding the prison system has been facing, it is worth noting that back then the government rejected the recommendation for a legally enforced limit on prisoner numbers per institution, which could only be overruled by Parliament (Livingstone et al. 2008: 215).

make punishment more effective, efficient and just, adopting as its point of departure that prison 'can be an expensive way of making bad people worse' (cited in Cavadino and Dignan 2006b: 66). To this end, it championed community involvement in crime prevention, promoted a managerialist work model in the criminal justice system and introduced through the 1991 Criminal Justice Act a punishment model under which offenders would get their just deserts. Just deserts entailed credible (=toughened up) community punishment for less serious offenders and imprisonment for the serious ones, with longer sentences in particular for violent and sexual offenders, including those who posed a persistent risk to the public. Notably, it was the Hurd approach that led to the reduction in prisoner numbers between 1989 and 1993 (ibid.: 65–66).

However, neither the reforming rays of the Woolf Inquiry were to shine long nor the Hurd approach and its decarcerative effects. A major economic crisis in 1992, heightened public concerns about youth offending that reached a climax in 1993 when two 10-year-old children killed a 2-year old boy, and high-security prison escapes in 1994–1995 effectively put a brake to decarceration. These were difficult times and thus not suitable to experiment with liberal ideas. The new but still Conservative Government under new leadership rediscovered its faith in prison and abandoned most of the reductionist provisions in the 1991 Criminal Justice Act that were not favoured anyway by the judiciary who regarded them as soft (ibid.: 67). They were replaced by the 1997 Crime (Sentences) Act, which introduced automatic life sentences for a second serious violent or sexual offence and minimum prison terms for third-time Class A drug traffickers and domestic burglars (Cavadino et al. 2013: 104). In addition, the 1994 Criminal Justice and Public Order Act increased the maximum length of custody in a Young Offenders Institution (YOI) for 15- to 17-year-olds from one to two years and introduced Secure Training Orders (STOs) of the same maximum length for 12- to 14-year-olds (Morgan and Newburn 2007).

With 'Prison Works' being the slogan of the times, the prison population (for both adults and youths) began to rise, regimes were tightened and prisoner treatment became harsher (Cavadino and Dignan 2006b: 68; Cavadino et al. 2013: 187). CPT Reports on its visits to the UK in

1994 and 1997 make an illuminating reading, prophesising the state of English and Welsh prisons in 20 years' time. The CPT Report on the 1994 visit noted that the increases in prisoner numbers exceeded the government's projection figures, the deadline for the abolition of slopping out had been extended and overcrowding remained a serious concern (CPT 1996). Tellingly, its Report on the 1997 visit dedicated a whole section to what was already seen as persistent overcrowding and called on the authorities to 'redouble their efforts to develop and implement a multifaceted strategy to bring about a permanent end to overcrowding' (CPT 2000, para. 67–77). Lastly, still very much relevant to the current situation in prisons, both reports highlighted the lack of purposeful activities for prisoners (CPT 1996: para. 77, 82, 2000: para. 73, 87).

The New Labour Years

By the time the 1997 general election brought into power a New Labour Government, the prison population had increased from around 44,000 in 1993 to over 60,000 (Cavadino and Dignan 2006b: 68; Bennett 2007). Having successfully reinvented itself as the party with the credible economic policy to move the country forward and with the resolve to take on the fight against crime and anti-social behaviour, New Labour went on to govern for 13 years. During that period, it both delivered on (some) promises made and grossly disappointed the hopes of many in other respects. On the positive side, in the first two terms the economy prospered and some measures to tackle inequality were taken, such as the launch of Sure Start in 1998, which targeted child poverty, and the introduction of a minimum wage in 1999. Moreover, as promised, Rights were Brought Home[2] with the enactment of the 1998 HRA, and the Youth Justice Board was set up in the late 1990s with the responsibility to monitor the youth justice sector.

Disappointingly though, New Labour reneged on its promise to be tough on the causes of crime and focused exclusively on being tough on

[2] 'Bringing Rights Home' was the title of the 1996 consultation paper that pledged the incorporation of the ECHR if the Labour Party came to power in the 1997 general elections (Wadham and Mountfield 2000: 10).

the criminal,[3] as well as those perceived to be anti-social among whom we would increasingly find young people. In a bid to shake off its past soft image on crime and establish itself as the party to be trusted with the country's security and the public's safety, New Labour espoused 'popular punitiveness' (Bottoms 1995) with religious fervour. This entailed a flurry of tough criminal justice measures that made substantial inroads into civil liberties. They were intensified after 9/11 and the 2005 London terrorist attacks (Downes and Morgan 2007: 215–217, 220–221; Sanders et al. 2010), which with the assistance of managerialism enabled actuarialism to be embedded into the fabric of criminal justice.

During the New Labour years managerialist practices, which had already begun to emerge under the previous Conservative governments, were adopted on a full-blown scale (Cavadino and Dignan 2006b: 69; Sanders et al. 2010: 38–42). The full-hearted adoption of managerialism fitted in with New Labour's Third Way in respect of the economy and greatly assisted the government to prove to the public its determination and ability to address safety concerns and security issues. Since, managerialism has impacted on the management and operation of every criminal justice institution (Sanders et al. 2010: 38–42) and is reflected in our language. We now talk about performance and contestability (especially but not exclusively in cases of underperforming public institutions) based on key indicators and standards that quantify processes and human contribution and turn them into targets so that we are able to measure and be confident about an institution's performance.

New Labour's 'popular punitiveness' and actuarialism are exemplified in the 1998 Crime and Disorder Act and the 2003 Criminal Justice Act.

The 1998 Crime and Disorder Act

The 1998 Crime and Disorder Act completely overhauled the youth justice system and steered it into actuarialism and utilitarianism in respect of the punishment of young offenders. Community safety and

[3]As a Shadow Home Secretary in 1993 Tony Blair famously spoke the words, 'tough on crime, tough on the causes of crime', setting the tone for New Labour's criminal justice policy.

order were of paramount importance for the public, and youth offending disturbed community peace and threatened public safety. Based on governmental thinking, as expressed in the 1997 policy paper *No More Excuses*, there was no 'conflict between protecting the welfare of a young offender and preventing that individual from offending again' (Morgan and Newburn 2007: 1032). Based on the above priorities, Sect. 37 of the Act explicitly identified prevention of youth offending as 'the principal aim of the youth justice system' and sent a clear message that no more excuses would be tolerated through the abolition of doli incapax (Morgan and Newburn 2007: 1036). The abolition of doli incapax, the presumption that children between 10 and 13 years of age do not have the capacity for mens rea yet due to their age-related emotional and cognitive immaturity, put effectively the age of criminal responsibility in England and Wales at 10, which is currently the lowest in Western Europe. Since, it has attracted strong criticism nationally and internationally (ibid.: 1037). In 2016 the UN Committee on the Rights of the Child (UNCRC) called on the UK 'to raise the minimum age of criminal responsibility in accordance with acceptable international standards'. For UNCRC an acceptable age of criminal responsibility is 12 or above (UNCRC 2016). Internationally, the average age of criminal responsibility is 12 (Penal Reform International 2013), which incidentally is the case in the Netherlands.

In order to achieve its principal aim of preventing youth offending, the 1998 Act promoted heavily the managerialist practice of multi-agency partnerships in a series of community-based interventions. Their aim was to identify early those at risk of offending and intervene promptly in their lives with a holistic and co-ordinated care plan, drawing on the expertise and co-operation of all relevant stakeholders (Morgan and Newburn 2007: 1034, 1036). These interventions have also drawn criticism. Experts have highlighted their net widening effect both in terms of the diffuse social control exercised over young people and, informed by the insights of Becker's labelling perspective (1963), the potentially greater numbers of them drawn into the criminal justice system as a result of their acting out the stigmatising labels applied to them. Also, they have pointed out the lack of robust evidence on their deterrent value (Morgan and Newburn 2012: 512, 517).

Additionally, the 1998 Act tapped the involvement of the community in the controversial anti-social behaviour order (ASBO). Here, the community's involvement served a double purpose. On the one hand, it aimed to craft a public image for both local communities and the criminal justice system as responsive to people's concerns and victims' needs whose voice and contribution mattered for building safer communities and ensuring an effective criminal justice response. On the other hand, it aimed to responsibilise the young offender by naming and shaming them.

Being introduced to tackle principally youth anti-social behaviour, the ASBO encompassed all sorts of public nuisance and youth mischief, with anti-social behaviour being defined as 'a matter that causes or is likely to cause harassment, alarm or distress to one or more persons not of the same household' (Morgan and Newburn 2007: 1037). Social landlords, housing associations, local authorities and the police could apply to the courts for an ASBO either on their own initiative or if they were requested by the public (Office of the Commissioner for Human Rights 2005: 36). If an ASBO application was successful, it could result, for example, in the person subject to it being banned from designated areas for a minimum two years. Despite being a civil order, failure to meet ASBO conditions was a criminal offence that could attract a prison sentence when the person was over 12, and it did for considerable numbers of young people (ibid.: 39). Moreover, as a result of the civil nature of the order, the young person's identity could be disclosed if the court judged that this was in the public interest, which compromised the young person' welfare interests under Sect. 39 of the 1933 Children and Young Persons Act, and their right to respect for private and family life under Art 8.

During the New Labour years the European Commissioner for Human Rights expressed grave concerns over the stigmatising, criminalising and disproportionately penalising ASBO effects on young people in 2005 and 2006. The Commissioner's reports make an uncomfortable reading, highlighting the dynamics of the politicisation of crime in England and Wales, as well as politicians' reluctance and/or unwillingness to be honest with the public about the effectiveness of punitive measures. In 2008, in response to the lack of change in the reporting of ASBOs, especially as applicable to young people, the Commissioner stated that 'It is difficult to comprehend why any civilised government would permit such a practice, let alone proactively pursue it' (Commissioner for Human Rights 2008: para. 30).

The 1998 Act also increased the sentencing powers of the youth courts. In the context of *No More Excuses* the availability of tougher youth sentencing powers and the ASBO-mania of the early 2000s (Office of the Commissioner for Human Rights 2005: 38) led youth custody numbers to soar, reaching their peak in 2008 when there were more than 3000 children under 18 in custody (Bromley Briefings 2012: 5). Between 1995 and 2005, the figures for the 15–17 age category increased by 86% and for those between 18 and 20 by 14%. Women were particularly affected. Statistics show that the numbers of young women aged 18–20 more than doubled, while there was a 181% increase in the numbers of girls aged 10–17 between 1996 and 2006 (Bromley Briefings 2007: 19, 21, 2009: 27).

The 2003 Criminal Justice Act (2003 CJA)

The 2003 Criminal Justice Act was both managerialist in its direction and punitive in its outcomes, leading to huge increases in the adult prison population as well as contributing to youth custody figures. The Act was one of a series of legislation that implemented the 2002 White Paper *Justice for All* that strived for 'strong, safe communities through tough action on anti-social behaviour, hard drugs and violent crime, by rebalancing the criminal justice system in favour of the victim, and by giving the police and prosecution the tools to bring more criminals to justice' (p. 11). These were important action points, being previously identified in two consultations on the criminal courts and sentencing (the 2001 Auld, and Halliday Reports (Fowles 2006). The reports had highlighted the need to maximise court efficiency and consistency in sentencing for the purposes of an effective and trusted criminal justice system. The process of bringing an offender to trial and giving them their just deserts was overly lengthy, and their punishment was mostly ineffective. Sentencing aims were unclear, unstructured and inconsistently applied. Knowledge of what and how different sanctions worked, and an effective management of their execution and offender supervision were lacking. All these issues were not only financially costly but also undermined public confidence and victim trust in the operation of the criminal justice system and its outcomes.

In response to the above, the 2003 CJA created inter alia a Sentencing Guidelines Council (SGC), as recommended in the Halliday Report, and identified for the first time in legislation the aims of adult sentencing for the English and Welsh jurisdictions. To facilitate greater consistency in sentencing, the SGC was tasked with the promulgation of sentencing guidelines in consultation always with the Sovereign Parliament that has been a statutory obligation since. The will of the people must be reflected in the guidelines, which in the context of the politicisation of crime arguably creates rather than solves sentencing dilemmas in a democracy governed by the rule of law and human rights.

Following amendments by the 2009 Coroners and Justice Act, which replaced the SGC with the Sentencing Council of England and Wales, the Council's functions have been bolstered to a degree. Since 2010 the courts have a statutory duty to follow its guidelines whereas before they only had to consider them. Also, among the new Council's functions are to monitor the application and impact of the guidelines on sentencing practice and to increase public understanding and confidence in the sentencing system (Sentencing Council 2016). While the jury is still out on the Council's success in promoting consistency in sentencing, the consistently high prison population is clear evidence of a widespread failure to honour its guideline to use prison as a last resort and for the most serious offenders (Ashworth 2007: 1006; Ashworth and Roberts 2012; Cavadino et al. 2013: 107–111).

One of the issues, which is directly related to the politicisation of crime and has arguably undermined the role and purpose of the Sentencing Council, is that the 2003 CJA adopted all possible sentencing aims-retribution, crime reduction, reform and rehabilitation, public protection, and reparation (Sect. 142). Deciding which aim to choose or in what combination becomes a rather complicated matter considering that they conflict with each other and their appropriateness must be assessed in relation to the degree of mens rea present and the harm caused/intended by the offence (Sect. 143(1)). In being encompassing rather than selective in its sentencing aims, the 2003 CJA overlooked the lack and poorness of evidence on the effectiveness of the aims of crime reduction, public protection and rehabilitation. This oversight is noteworthy and cannot be anything other than evidence of the lasting impact the politicisation of crime has on criminal justice policy. The Halliday Report, which informed the Act, explicitly referred to the limitations of these aims (Ashworth 2007: 997–998).

This unwillingness to be openly selective on an informed basis is evident throughout the Act's provisions. Driven by public protection and crime reduction considerations (even if their effects are temporary), it added to the arsenal of minimum sentences a five-year sentence for first-time possession of prohibited firearms, increased penalties for drug-related offences and sentences for offences where race, religion, disability and sexual orientation were aggravating factors (Sect. 145–146, 284, 287). It also introduced minimum starting points for mandatory life sentences and the disastrous indeterminate sentence for public protection (IPP) for both adults and those aged 18 or under (Sect. 255-28, 269). In a self-contradictory fashion it supplemented the principle of proportionality in sentencing with considerations of past convictions; the courts had to treat previous convictions as aggravating factors if they judged the nature and timing of the previous offence(s) relevant to the present one.

The contradictions did not end here. Rehabilitation, punishment and crime reduction merged together in new tougher community and suspended sentence orders, with 12 possible requirements that aimed to replace short sentences after being identified in the Halliday Report as 'one of the most serious deficiencies' in the sentencing system (2001: iv). Despite all this, two new variants of short sentences were introduced where the shock of a short prison spell was to be followed by an extensive period of supervision and rehabilitation in the community. These were *custody plus* for sentences less than a year and *intermittent custody* between 28 and 51 weeks for a single offence for those serious offenders who did not pose a risk to the public (Sect. 177–179; 181–186).

In addition, the Act sought to contribute to the streamlining of court processes, the cumulative effect of which was the erosion of defendants' right to a fair trial (Art 6). To relieve the pressure from the overburdened Crown Courts, it increased magistrates' sentencing powers for offences triable either way from 6 to 12 months (Sect. 282), while SGC guidelines embedded sentence discounts for guilty pleas at magistrates' courts; being part of the drive to modernise their 'often lengthy and arcane' proceedings (Falconer 2006: 9; cited in Morgan 2008: 11).

When we fast forward to the end of the New Labour years, we can say that the criminal justice policy did not escape the skilful political spin and communication of the times. How could it when it is an inherent emotive policy field that becomes a landmine if it is not managed smartly in an environment where crime and anti-social behaviour are law and order issues? In such an environment, political survival dictates that the noisiness of the tabloid press must be reduced, the public must be appeased and its anxieties dampened, and political opposition with tougher promises must be eliminated. Against this background we got a speedier and seemingly cheaper justice that was still biting. But, was this justice for all, creating strong and safe communities as it had been promised in the homonymous 2002 White Paper? A snapshot of imprisonment from these years leads us to conclude that offenders, victims and the public were all victims of mis-selling who were essentially short-changed, deceived and further disadvantaged.

New Labour's Prison Legacy

It is important to communicate that rising crime rates are not a foregone conclusion for the increase in the prison population during these years. Like in other comparable countries, crime in England and Wales did rise in the 1980s and first half of the 1990s, peaking in 1996. Since, we witnessed considerable yearly crime reductions until March 2005. From then onwards, the downward trend has continued, only less sharply and with some fluctuations (Chaplin et al. 2011; Bromley Briefings 2015: 74; ONS 2016).

Against this background, the 85,085 people in prison in 2010 (Bromley Briefings 2010: 4) are the outcome of harsher sentencing that saw a more frequent use of imprisonment and for longer periods. This was allowed through legislation, such as the 1998 Crime and Disorder Act and the 2003 CJA, and was encouraged by tough political rhetoric. Between 1991 and 2008 the number of people found guilty by the courts decreased, but a greater proportion of them were sentenced to prison, serving on average 9.3 months compared to 8.1 months in 2000 (a 14% increase in sentence length) (Bromley Briefings 2010: 13). Those recalled to prison and mandatory lifers also served longer time, and the high numbers of IPP prisoners and their prolonged stay in prison beyond their tariff helped clogging up capacity space. Recalls in particular contributed to the increase in the prison population between 1995 and 2009 by 16%. Moreover, 46% of adult prisoners had been sentenced to prison at least three times before (ibid.: 13–15, 19).

The most revealing aspect is that short prison sentences were not reduced. The courts kept sending people to prison on short spells, especially when they were persistent offenders. Sect. 143(2) of the 2003 CJA required them to consider the relevance of previous convictions. Contrary to the legislator's intentions, community and suspended sentence orders (SSOs) did not divert people from short sentences because they were inappropriately used and/or underused. Community orders (COs) were used as a toughened-up response to offenders who would previously be fined or discharged while SSOs were used as a substitute for COs. Their inappropriate use had an 'uptariffing' effect, increased the risk of imprisonment for those on SSOs due to their more demanding conditions, and provided no relief from the resource-intensive short prison sentences. As for Custody Plus, it was never implemented because there were (after all) no resources (House of Commons Justice Committee 2008). Intermittent custody was similarly ill-fated, coming to an end after a three-year trial period because in the words of the Home Office Minister Baroness Scotland, 'all our attention, energies and resources must go into protecting the public from the most and more serious offenders' (BBC News, 'Weekend prison' scheme scrapped, 2006).

The above cited 2008 Justice Committee Report on the implementation and effects of changes made to the sentencing policy since 2001 makes an uncomfortable reading. It further highlights the lack of a holistic assessment of the resources necessary for a fully fledged implementation of COs, and the absence of concerted efforts to raise public confidence in non-custodial measures. The importance of public education on the effectiveness of custodial and non-custodial sanctions, especially in the English and Welsh setting where crime is used to score political points, was noted (again) in a number of surveys on public and victim attitudes to crime. Like earlier and subsequent surveys, they attributed public misconceptions about crime and punishment and disproportionate levels of fear of crime among victims to the tabloid press and the 'competition to "talk ever tougher on crime"'. As a 2006 survey with the name *Crime Victims Say Jail Doesn't Work* points out, justice for victims, in victims' view, is not necessarily tautological with a 'lock them up and throw away the key' approach. This alternative message (to some) is, however, drowned out in public life (cited in House Of Commons Justice Committee 2008).

The Rehabilitation Years: 2010 to the Present Day

After 65 years 2010 ushered in a Coalition Government between the Conservatives and the Liberal Democrats, and difficult times. With the reverberations of the 2008 (and later 2011) banking crisis keenly felt by the British economy and a huge structural deficit to contend with, the focus was firmly on economic recovery and drastic deficit reduction. In order to achieve this, public spending cuts had to take place; the imprudence and carelessness of the past had got to end for a sustainable future for the next generations and a viable economic growth. This was the economic message (The Coalition: our programme for government 2010).

On a social level, the imminent sacrifices required a reconfiguration of the relationship between the state and its citizens. To increase public acceptance of the sacrifices to come, their painfulness had to be shared and thus the *Big Society* idea was born and sold hard. The Chancellor of the Exchequer famously said that 'we are all in this together,' and together we had to 'take responsibility for ourselves and our communities, to create active, sustainable communities' (Bowles 2010; cited in Ryan 2012: 22). The state could no longer afford to do this on its own. The repeated message was that communities could be resourceful if they were trusted and, importantly, were given incentives.

By way of Payment by Results (PbR) a whole array of organisations (private and voluntary based) were invited under contract to help the state and their own communities by delivering public and community services in creative ways, that is, ways that economise smartly so as to deliver a still good service. Based on the PbR model tariff-based payments were drawn and awarded reflecting the degree of success achieved, with underperformance leading to loss of contract and all sorts of potential financial consequences for the organisation concerned (Puddicombe et al. 2012).

In this new economic reality, the Prison Service, as a public organisation, was called to find ways to cut its own expenditure. This concerned though only the implementation of the Government's economic policy. The social message of the new economic direction had to be also incorporated into the prison reality. In 2010 the Green Paper *Breaking the Cycle* announced that prisons would 'become places of hard work and industry instead of enforced idleness' (p. 1) and that it 'will create a rehabilitation revolution that will change those communities whose lives are made a misery by crime' (p. 1, 5). In 2013 the Government's *Transforming Rehabilitation: A Strategy for Reform* set out its plan of action for the prison rehabilitation revolution. As with any kind of revolution, this revolution and the accompanying grandiose statements have proved costly and have also failed to deliver on the promises made. From the start, the chances of success were not high because of the government's default position. Like under the previous New Labour governments, under this government 'the safety and security of the law-abiding citizen was a key priority.' In this respect, the government had 'both radical and realistic' reform plans (Breaking the Cycle 2010: 1–2) to which we can add the words 'self-contradictory' and 'self-defeating'.

While the government acknowledged the high prisoner re-offending rates, especially of those on short sentences, it declared its unreserved support for short sentences, 'which remain an important tool for magistrates, particularly for recidivist criminals who have not responded to community punishments or fines' (Breaking the Cycle 2010: 1–2, 5). At the same time, while it criticised the previous government's penal policy, which 'was dominated by unstainable increases in the prison population rather than tackling re-offending', next to its support for short sentences it defended the imprisonment of 'the less serious offenders with mental illness and drug dependency when they endanger public safety'. In this context, it re-assured us that unlike the previous government, it 'will not allow our jails run out of capacity' (ibid.: 2, 5).

So, the Coalition Government set out to reform prisons, having no intention to take action against the unstainable (in its own words) prisoner numbers and with total disregard of recent major reports on sentencing and prisons (see, e.g. the 2001 Halliday Report, the 2007 Corston Review, and the 2009 Bradley Report). Its prison reform agenda was driven by four principles: public protection, effective offender punishment and rehabilitation, transparency and accountability, and decentralisation. The last two principles denoted the nature of the delivery of reform, which was to be smart in its use of resources and innovative; in short reform was to be delivered based on PbR (Breaking the Cycle 2010: 5, 7, 10), employing the crude measure of re-offending rates that does not take into account the dynamic nature of the offenders' rehabilitative journey.

The prison reform package involved the following innovations. With the help of the 'private, voluntary and community sectors', institutions would become *working prisons*, with the aim to instil in prisoners a work ethic, discipline and a sense of personal responsibility. Prisoners would have to work a full 40-hour week and make reparation to their victims and communities through wage deductions under the 1996 Prisoners' Earnings Act (ibid.: 14–16).

Under its *Transforming Rehabilitation Strategy* (2013), offender rehabilitation becomes the means of reducing re-offending and thus increasing public safety. Informed by the principles of consistency and accountability in the administration of punishment, as well as by an 'an end-to-end practice in offender management', rehabilitation is to be delivered 'through a prison gate' service (TTG). While in custody and following their release prisoners would be receiving rehabilitation and resettlement support by one service provider in order to ensure continuity and consistency in service provision. In order to increase the effectiveness and efficiency of the rehabilitation and resettlement support services, service providers would be diverse, ranging from public and private sectors to voluntary and community organisations. To ensure providers' accountability both to the service users and the taxpayer, their work would be assessed on a PbR basis, that is, in terms of reductions in re-offending rates (pp. 6–7, 9–16). For the first time, statutory rehabilitation would be at least a year and would include prisoners serving sentences of less than 12 months and young offenders who are 18 at the time of their release (two of the groups with the highest re-offending rates). Moreover, all female prisons and the ones located close to major court committal areas would become resettlement prisons (Westminster Legal Policy Forum Keynote Seminar, 2014).

Once again the combined effect of the impact of the circumstances in which the Rehabilitation Revolution was to occur, the quality of its proposed reforms and their pace were not properly assessed. During the course of the Parliament between 2010 and 2015 and until the Brexit decision in June 2016 across the public sector the overarching priority has been deficit reduction. The Prison Service had no other option than to make savings quickly. The modernisation of the prison estate and staff cuts have been the two sources for its cost reductions. The modernisation of its estate saw the replacement of existing institutions with ones that have a longer lifespan and better accommodation, as well as greater inbuilt flexibility, for example when there is a need for a re-categorisation of a prison's security status. Since 2010, 23 prisons have closed and prison officer numbers have declined by 30% against the backdrop of a high prison population (National Audit Office 2013; The Howard League for Penal Reform 2014; Bromley Briefings 2016: 5).

The 2013 National Audit Office (NAO) Report on the impact of the Prison Service's cost-cutting measures on institutional quality and performance is worrisome while the state of prisons six years into the cuts, as documented by HM Chief Inspector of Prisons Reports, is distressing. The NAO paints a picture of constrained choices and rushed actions that have compromised quality and performance in order to deliver substantial savings quickly. The modernisation offensive went ahead without taking into account or conducting quality and performance assessments; it was driven exclusively by efficiency considerations. As a result, high-performing prisons with a good quality and number of offending behaviour programmes (OBPs) were closed down. This hastiness has reduced overall performance across the sector as it takes time for new institutions to build up quality and has further dented the provision of OBPs. This has had a domino effect on lifers' and IPP prisoners' access to such programmes (NAO 2013: 5, 7). Although the new accommodation is materially superior and safer in terms of inbuilt suicide prevention features, shared accommodation is still a standard practice in some of the new establishments. Their large size also militates against improved prisoner safety and rehabilitation as evidence shows that smaller establishments are easier to manage and better at creating and maintaining custody environments conducive to rehabilitation. Rehabilitation opportunities are further negatively affected by the structural non-availability of space dedicated to purposeful activity as this aspect of the prisoner experience was not factored into the modernisation plans (NAO 2013: 6–7).

Annual Reports by HM Inspectorate of Prisons are disturbing. The Annual Report 2014-15 (2015) documents that violence among prisoners and against staff has been on the increase. The violence is interlinked with the widespread availability of new non-detectable psychoactive drugs, which gravely affect prisoner safety and mental health. There is currently no policy on what steps are needed to effectively respond to this drugs crisis. Overcrowding remains hopelessly high, contributing to indecent living conditions and prisoner insecurity, as well as limiting prisoner access to rehabilitation and time out of the cell. Related to this, the provision of purposeful activity is described as 'dismal', showing the worst performance since measurements began in 2005–2006. Working prisons are not reported. One in five prisoners is locked in their cells 23 hours a day, with only 16 out of 42 male prisons inspected offering some kind of purposeful activity the quality of which is not good, with education showing the worst outcomes. In two-thirds of prisons, education is assessed as in need of improvement or as inadequate. Like purposeful activity, resettlement support shows the worst performance since measurements began despite the rolling out of the TTG service. Only 45% of male prisons returned reasonably good or good assessment scores. As the report states, we are 'still waiting for the rehabilitation revolution', and it identifies the negative impact of staff shortages on safety and rehabilitation in prisons (ibid.: 10–11, 13–14).

The latest HM Inspectorate of Prisons Annual Report 2015-16 (2016) does not register improvements. It is worth quoting, 'There is a simple and unpalatable truth about far too many of our prisons. They have become unacceptably violent and dangerous places' (p. 8).

Impact on Prisoners' Rights

Mental Health and Deaths in Prison

The result of successive governments' insistence to ignore the real causes of offending, to create a hyperbole around public safety, and to encourage false expectations about the measures employed to deal with an exaggerated picture of crime and disorder has been very costly. The taxpayer is billed 45,000 per prisoner and 13 billion per year for their re-offending. The figure for sentences of less than 12 months is in the region of 286 million, without education and healthcare being included in the calculations. To accommodate the penal capacity demand, since 1997, 2700 prison places have been created, with 6700 of them between 2007 and 2010 at an average price of 170,000 per place (Bromley Briefings 2010: 4). The 49% of adult prisoners who re-offend within a year of their release are not only costly in terms of their burden on public finances but also in terms of their impact on their victims' lives (Bromley Briefings 2010: 5). Their high re-offending rates harm other people, and we keep sending them to prison in full knowledge of what the most likely outcome will be.

Next to their victims' lives, prisoners' and their families' lives are also greatly impacted upon, to the point of being endangered. In our watch, increasing numbers of prisoners die of unnatural causes. In their majority, these deaths are suicides, and in a minority of instances they are the result of prisoner-on-prisoner homicides, or of excessive force or restraint employed by staff (JCHR 2004). Ill mental health is responsible for the vast majority of prisoner deaths, and it has been widely known that prisoners suffer disproportionately from a range of mental health conditions. For example, the government's own Exclusion Unit highlighted the association between ill mental health and (re)offending in its 2002 Report on *Reducing Re-offending by Ex-prisoners*. 72% of male prisoners and 70% of female ones have one or more mental health disorders. 75% of the prison population have a dual diagnosis and 20% of prisoners have four of the five main mental health disorders. Women, in particular, have an increased risk of self-harming, making up 47% of all self-harming incidents while representing 5% of the prison population. Between 1997 and 2010 there were 1032 prisoner suicides of whom 81 were women, 117 were young people aged 18–20, and 17 were children (Ministry of Justice 2011).

In this context, *Keenan v UK* (2001), *Edwards v UK* (2002), *McGlinchey & Others v UK* (2003) and *Amin* (2004) have all demonstrated the life-threatening and life-changing consequences the inappropriate use and careless execution of imprisonment have for prisoners and their families, as well as the reduced accountability on the part of the authorities. In doing so, they highlight the lingering negative effects of the Diceyan approach to human rights protection on the prevention and investigation of prisoner deaths, which imperilled, to the point of violation, prisoners' rights under Art 2 and 3, as well as their relatives' rights under Art 13.

In *Keenan v UK* (2001), which concerned the suicide of a mentally ill prisoner with suicidal tendencies, the ECtHR found a violation of Art 3 and 13. In relation to Art 3, it concluded that the authorities had failed to protect the deceased against inhuman or degrading treatment. Although he was known to be a danger to himself, his assessment and treatment were not led by psychiatric professionals and were insufficiently monitored. His subjection to a serious disciplinary punishment, which run the risk of impacting further on his poor physical and mental health, did not accord with the required standards of treatment for the mentally ill. Importantly, the ECtHR ruled that 'proof of the actual effect' a measure has on a person's physical and mental state may not be always required for an Art 3 violation. This was particularly pertinent to mentally ill people who could experience greater difficulties in articulating physical and mental health complaints (Keenan v. The United Kingdom Judgment 3 April 2011: para. 113, 116).

In respect of Art 13, at the heart of the matter was the inability of the deceased's mother to pursue a civil law action against the authorities for negligence as this was only an option for spouses, dependent children, and parents of children under 18. This lack of available remedies was compounded by the operation of the coroners' inquest system. The practice was for the inquest to examine only 'who, where, when, and how' the deceased was and died (Sect. 11(5)b, 1988 Coroners Act; Rule 36, 1984 Coroner's Rules). Considerations of liability fell outside the remit of the inquest, which entailed that coroners were not legally empowered to establish whether there was negligence involved and to direct the prosecution of those identified as responsible. Regarding relatives' rights in the inquest process, Rule 20 of the 1984 Coroner's Rules recognised their right to cross-examine witnesses either in person or through a legal representative, but then non-availability of legal aid except in exceptional circumstances rendered the right redundant.

Overall, *Keenan* highlighted five defects in the treatment of disruptive (as a result of their condition) mentally ill prisoners. These were an absence of an 'automatic' re-evaluation of mentally ill prisoners' ability to cope with disciplinary punishments; a lack of a speedy resolution of disciplinary punishments when evidence pointed to prisoners' inability to cope; the limitations of the coroner's system; and a lack of consultation with prisoners' families when a prisoner was identified at risk of suicide and this risk materialised (Keenan v. The United Kingdom Judgment 3 April 2001: para. 125–128).

Similar deficiencies were found in *McGlinchey & Others v UK* (2003). The case concerned the death of a chronic heroin addict from drug withdrawal, who was serving a four-month sentence for theft 'despite an alternative proposal for a probation order with a condition that she be treated for addiction' (McGlinchey and Others v. The United Kingdom Judgment 29 July 2003: para. 11). In respect of Art 3, the Court concluded that the prison failed to protect Ms McGlinchey against inhuman or degrading treatment. Her physical complaints and drastic weight loss had not been adequately and consistently monitored, and her hospital transfer had taken place too late; the deterioration in her health had been irreversible (ibid.: para. 57). In respect of Art 13, the Court reiterated that the remedy required had to be 'effective' in practice and in law, and that 'compensation for the non-pecuniary damage flowing from breaches of Art 2 and 3 should in principle be part of the range of available remedies' (ibid.: para. 62–63). The internal prison complaints mechanism did not provide for compensation while a finding of negligence was required for the award of compensation in a civil law action or a judicial review (ibid.: para. 65).

Edwards v UK (2002) and *Amin* (2004) revealed another instance of the authorities' failure to comply with their statutory duty of care. Both cases concerned prisoner-on-prisoner homicides perpetrated by the victims' cellmates. In *Edwards v UK* (2002) the Court found a violation of Art 2 and 13, pointing out the considerable lapses in inter-agency communication regarding prisoners' medical records (both Mr. Edwards and his cellmate were mentally ill, with the latter being identified as a danger to others) and the prison service's ineffective screening of prisoner compatibility for the purposes of cell sharing. Like Mr. Keenan's mother, the parents of Mr. Edwards could not seek relief for non-pecuniary damages or determine the prison service's liability for their son's murder (Edwards v. The United Kingdom Judgment 14 March 2002).

Equally disturbing was the racist murder of the 19-year-old Mubarek by his cellmate of a similar age, Mr. Stewart. Mr. Mubarek was in prison for the first time, serving a three-month sentence for theft. In contrast, Mr. Stewart had previous sentences for violence, was (belatedly) identified as a white supremacist and had a personality disorder, all of which rendered him highly dangerous to others, especially people of non-white background (Casciani 2006). The case attracted great publicity as it woke up distressing (for the victim's families) and embarrassing (for the authorities) memories of another highly publicised racially motivated teenage murder, that of Stephen Lawrence in 1993. Back in 1999, the MacPherson Inquiry Report into the police investigation and handling of the Lawrence case had made huge headlines, not least because of its finding of institutional racism in the Metropolitan Police (Ellison 2013). After only one year, another criminal justice institution, HM Prison Service, was facing similar criticism amid allegations that the two young people had been placed together deliberately.

The two-part investigation by the Commission for Racial Equality (CRE) confirmed the criticism of institutional racism but not the allegation of foul play by staff (Livingstone et al. 2008: 91–93). In relation to the Prison Service in general, the CRE found 14 'failure areas' that involved, inter alia, lack of action to amend the haphazard implementation of race equality policies as applied to both prisoners and staff, failure to effectively investigate race discrimination due to insufficient staff training in race equality, and unfettered exercise of discretionary power, leading to widespread racist attitudes and behaviour that went unchallenged. Like in the case of the Metropolitan Police, institutional racism in the Prison Service manifested itself in a bold and subtle, subterranean way, and thus deeply affected the lives of ethnic minority prisoners on a daily basis (ibid.: 92). The CRE attributed Mr. Mubarek's preventable death to 11 out of the 14 identified failure areas, two of which 'concerned the fact that staff at HM Prison Service had knowledge of Mr. Stewart's racism but failed to act properly upon that knowledge' (cited in ibid.: 91). Like the ECtHR in *Keenan* and *Edwards*, the CRE highlighted the lack of communication between individual prisons, which impeded a timely exchange of information on prisoners' vulnerabilities and risks posed, and the absence of robust monitoring procedures, involving in this case regular cell searches (ibid.).

In addition to the CRE findings above, the legal battle by Mr. Mubarek's parents, *Amin* (2004), led to a verdict of a violation of Art 2. The finding was important for two reasons: First, it clarified the procedural requirements necessary for the authorities' compliance with Art 2. There had to be a public and independent investigation into the Prison Service's role in the fatal incident and the parents had to be given the opportunity to actively participate in such an investigation. The two conducted investigations fell short of these requirements. The Prison Service had conducted an internal investigation in which the family could not participate, and its findings were private. Neither could the family participate in the CRE investigation that was additionally restricted to race-related issues (Livingstone et al. 2008: 123–124). Secondly, *Amin* led to a public inquiry, known as the Mubarek Inquiry. Identifying 186 individual and systemic failings, the Inquiry's conclusions were illuminating of the combined toxic effects of overcrowding, which forces upon institutions, staff and prisoners the practice of cell sharing, institutional failures to take action and racism, and lack of effective leadership and staff management (Report of the Zahid Mubarek Inquiry, 2006).

The above cases had some impact that culminated in a number of welcoming legislative and policy changes in the areas of prison (mental) healthcare, investigations into prisoner deaths, the coroner's system, and race equality. Before we take a look at some of them, it must be said that such changes tend to take place in a piecemeal fashion and usually in the aftermath of scandals, court rulings and official reviews (with the latter being often the product of the former), without being consistently supported by adequate investment in resources for their effective implementation. Subsequent Reviews and Inquiries are a testament to this. This essentially reveals a reactive rather than a proactive approach to the development of prison policy that is counterproductive for prison work and prisoner treatment as it drip-feeds long-overdue changes.

In this context, a momentous development in prison (mental) healthcare was the transfer of responsibility for its provision from HM Prison Service to the Department of Health and the NHS. The handover commenced in 2003 and was completed in 2006. With the NHS in charge, mental healthcare received more focused attention, informed by practices followed in the community (Livingstone et al. 2008: 266-269). For example, building on the past suicide strategy, an Assessment, Care in Custody and Teamwork (ACCT) procedure was introduced in 2005–2006 that aimed at early identification of suicide risks and self-harming behaviour so as to prevent and better manage such risks. The ACCT framework reaffirmed that the prevention of suicide and self-harm is the responsibility of all staff and recognised the importance of linking prison care and resettlement support in order to achieve continuity of care. In doing so, a team of trained staff of different specialisations and roles jointly develop, administer and supervise (with clearly defined lines of responsibility) 'flexible and individualised care and management plans' for vulnerable prisoners (Prison Service Instruction 18/2005).

In addition to ACCT, mental health in reach teams were introduced whose primary focus was the treatment of people with severe and enduring mental illness (SMI). An important feature of these teams has been their working model. Like mental health community practice, they follow a Care Programme Approach (CPA). The CPA recognises the vital role established communication channels and partnerships between different agencies and stakeholders have in the seamless delivery of a mental health service. In the carceral environment, this translates in prison and community mental health teams working together so that release plans are reflective of the individual prisoner's needs and actionable once they are released into the community (The Bradley Report 2009). In this way, continuity of care becomes a more likely outcome and is easier to maintain.

To those who had called for control of prison healthcare to transfer to the NHS, such as the Royal College of Psychiatrists and HM Inspectorate of Prisons, prisoners' right to equivalence in healthcare was at last recognised. The expectation was that under the NHS wing, prisons would become healthier places, driven by the higher NHS care standards, its wider treatment provision, its more transparent and effective operational and managerial framework, and greater availability of staff training (Livingstone et al. 2003: 224–225, 2008: 281).

Ten years later, this expectation is yet to materialise. In 2009, the Bradley Report on people with mental health problems or learning disabilities in the criminal justice system was published. Its assessment of the quality of mental healthcare in prisons painted a picture of overstretched and ill-integrated resources with limited mental health awareness against a backdrop of an ever-increasing prison population with increasingly complex needs. From the crucial stage of reception into prison all the way through to resettlement, the Bradley Report found inadequate monitoring procedures and care standards, as well as a lack of co-ordination between different services (pp. 101–118).

In spite of the well-known fact that the risk of suicide and self-harm is exceptionally high in the first week and month of one's arrival in prison (Livingstone et al. 2008: 291), relevant screening and assessment at the reception stage were inadequate due to poorly implemented procedures. This indicated that ACCT was not working well. Mental health in reach teams also faced serious challenges both inside and outside prison, which affected their work and impeded their CPA. As a result of increased prisoner numbers that did not match up with an increase in resources, the teams' client base expanded to provide care and support for prisoners with a variety of mental health conditions (The Bradley Report 2009: 101–103).

The first national evaluation of mental health in reach teams showed that the majority of their clients (60%) did not suffer from SMI. Of them, 41% had a personality disorder, 34% had minor mental illness, 42% did not have either, and 70% had a drug addiction. The teams complained that they were unable to cope with the increased demand, which diverted them away from their original role. They identified lack of investment in a variety of mental health services and human resources along with resistance from community mental health teams and services to assist in prisoner resettlement as the main issues impacting on the quality of their work (The Bradley Report 2009: 103–104, 110).

Despite the known high prevalence of dual diagnosis, substance misuse and personality disorder in the prison population, bespoke care and support were either non-existent or a hit and miss. Drug detoxification provision varied significantly across the prison estate, many prisons did not have alcohol detoxification courses, and there was no provision for personality disorder cases (The Bradley Report 2009: 107; Bromley Briefings 2010: 47). The Bradley Report also found that prisoners in need of transfer to a secure or acute psychiatric unit continued to experience long delays for a variety of reasons that were both prison and NHS specific. In two-thirds of cases, delays were due to a lack of specialist beds and advance assessments of the availability of resources in the community. Differences in the working approach between prisons and hospitals, which followed from their different institutional orientations (custodial for prisons and therapeutic for hospitals), created problems in their communication and co-operation, contributing further to delays in prisoner transfers (2009: 105).

Last but not least, mental health awareness among frontline staff was poor despite the introduction of relevant training. Its evaluation found again poor implementation. This was attributed to staff pressures, resulting in difficulties in releasing officers from duty to attend such training, lack of clarity regarding the respective contributions of ACCT and mental health awareness training, and the self-directed learning style of the training, which did not allow for the sharing of views and experiences. Based on a 2007 thematic review on mental health by HM Inspectorate of Prisons, only around a quarter of officers had mental health training, delivered over a three-day period, with most officers calling more training (The Bradley Report 2009: 111).

Although the Bradley Report stopped short of calling prisons unsuitable for mentally ill people, which was a greatly missed opportunity, it confirmed that the state was failing in its duty of care to the large numbers of prisoners with mental health conditions. In doing so, it let the state's human rights obligations to protect the non-derogable rights to life and freedom from torture and inhuman or degrading treatment or punishment at the mercy of the Aeolian winds. To remind ourselves, *Edwards* and *Mubarek* had four victims, not two. Their killers were both dangerous and vulnerable whom the state also failed to provide with the required standards of mental healthcare and management. In the mental health sphere, dangerousness does not preclude vulnerability and pain. But this truth is buried deep in an uncritical approach to public protection that at the end it harms rather than protects.

The Bradley Report made a series of recommendations with the aim to improve practices and procedures for better mental healthcare outcomes for prisoners within the constraints of a system where public protection remained the priority (2009: 7). Among its recommendations were the redirection of mental health in reach teams to SMI cases by increasing the variety of mental health services and improving mental health primary care; an evaluation of reception procedures that focused as much on mental health as on learning disabilities; the development of a dedicated personality disorder (PD) service; the adoption of the 14-day target for transfers to severe/acute NHS psychiatric wards that the Department of Health had piloted; a rapid assessment of the security at low- and medium-risk psychiatric units to enable diversionary measures; and the availability of mental health and learning disabilities awareness training for all prison officers that tapped the service user experience (2009: 102, 104, 106, 109, 111). All its recommendations were underscored by the need to build partnerships and links across the range of the different departments and organisations so as to be able to divert early offenders from prison or the criminal justice system, to timely and comprehensively support them while in contact with the criminal justice system, and to assist them in resettling into the community. In this respect, the Report placed particular emphasis on the need to strengthen the presence of liaison and diversionary schemes, which despite their obscure definition and standing had shown great potential in multi-agency co-operation, covering and linking up the different stages in the criminal justice process (ibid.: 81–87, 101, 115–117).

Five years after the Bradley Report, an independent review by the Bradley Commission and the Centre for Mental Health (2014) showed that little progress had been made in prison mental healthcare in the intervening years. On the positive side, the quality of primary healthcare was improved and was linked up with secondary care in some prisons. Psychologically Informed Planned Environments (PIPEs) in some mainstream prisons for people with PD were also created as part of a wider strategy to increase treatment options for this group, albeit not without criticism from experts, such as Genders and Player (2014).

With the future successes HMP Grendon—an exemplar of therapeutic prisons in England and Wales—being already undermined by budget cuts, Genders and Player expressed serious reservations about the prospects of 'realisation of the positive obligations inherent in the prison's duty of care', and more specifically about 'the extent to which prisoners were able to defend their interests by holding prison authorities accountable for the standards of treatment delivered and for any consequential harms caused' (2014: 442, 449–450). Their reservations reflected already publicly expressed concerns over the not-so-successful working relationship between the NHS and the National Offender Management Service (NOMS), the capacity of the mainstream prison estate and the expertise of its staff to care for PD prisoners (ibid.: 442).

The state of other aspects of prison mental healthcare was also disappointing. There was simply no progress made in increasing mental health awareness training opportunities for frontline prison staff. Similarly, the recommended 14-day target for transfers from prisons to psychiatric units was not adopted, with such transfers being 'something of a postcode lottery' (Centre for Mental Health 2011). Drug and alcohol detoxification programmes were still not integrated with mental health services, and resettlement support for prisoners with mental health issues remained unsatisfactory as 'not all mainstream community support and acre services yet considered offenders as being part of 'their business'' (cited in The Bradley Report five years on, 2014: 24–25).

In 2015, another two major Reports were published, carrying loud messages that although they had been expressed before, they remained unheeded. These were the *Harris Review into Self-inflicted Deaths in Custody of 18–24 year olds* and the Inquiry Report of the Equality and Human Rights Commission (EHRC) on *Preventing Deaths in Detention of Adults with Mental Health Conditions*. Covering the period from 2007 onwards, the *Harris Review* examined 'whether appropriate lessons have been learnt from those deaths and if not, what lessons should be learnt/what actions should be taken to prevent further deaths' (2015: 14). The EHRC Inquiry looked into the circumstances of non-natural adult deaths across three institutional settings, police cells, prisons and psychiatric hospitals for the period 2010–2013. Its purpose was to examine the potential contribution of an increased focus on Art 2 to the prevention of such deaths, and the quality of treatment and support for people with mental health conditions.

Both Reports make a depressing reading. They document a delusional belief on the part of the state in imprisonment as the panacea for social ills and individual vulnerabilities, the state's waste of public finances in failed solutions despite its own claim for the need and imposition of public cuts, and its very own incorrigibility in learning lessons from past mistakes. Their findings were in agreement over policy-related, systemic and individual failures in protecting human rights and safeguarding the most fundamental right of all—the right to life. Based on the *Harris Review* and the EHRC Inquiry, 101 young people (children and young adults aged 18–24) committed suicide and 295 adults died prematurely in prisons between 2010 and 2013 (The Harris Review 2015: 23; EHRC 2015: 4).

The *Harris Review* questioned the desirability and usefulness of youth imprisonment in general and was outspoken in its belief in the need for 'a radical shift in the philosophy of detention in this country' (2015: 10, 53). It offered a damning picture of prisons and YOIs as 'grim' places unable to provide a constructive, rehabilitative and caring experience for young people due to (the familiar-by-now themes) reduced structural and human resources, a lack of leadership, as well of adequately trained and professionalised staff (ibid.: 9–11, 76–77). The recurrent finding on disjoint working practices against the official 'joined government' approach to public service delivery measured on the basis of adopted 'cross-government' targets (The Bradley Report 2009: 13) led to a recommendation for a statutory duty of co-operation. In dedicating a separate chapter to the Purpose of the Prison, the Review reminded all that the overarching aim of imprisonment should be rehabilitation, informed by human rights considerations (The Harris Review 2015: 10, 13, 53).

Likewise, the EHRC raised the issue of the impact of the prison budgetary cuts on prisoner safety and was also outspoken in its views. There were prisoner deaths that 'could have been prevented if prisons got the basics right'. The crux of the matter was that for some people their mental health conditions rendered their imprisonment inadvisable on human rights grounds (2015: 6). The EHRC attributed the premature deaths across the three institutional settings to issues that had been identified before and were thus well known to the state. The *Harris Review* also reported the same issues, demonstrating minimal to no progress being made in ameliorating a deeply problematic and dangerously careless situation. More specifically, the EHRC found: '(a) a lack of communication and sharing of information among agencies regarding the mental healthcare needs of people in custody and care; (b) a lack of involvement and consultation with family and friends regarding the mental healthcare plan and tragic death of their loved ones; (c) lapses in risk assessments due to inadequate record keeping, erratic follow-up observations of people's progress, and a lack of mental health awareness training among employees; (d) no common working definition of restraint practices; and (e) a lack of psychiatric beds and treatment options in the community' (Karamalidou 2015).

The EHRC made four main recommendations. These were for a statutory duty to be placed on all three organisations to report publicly on inspectorate bodies' recommendations; for a much greater focus on staff training and partnership work so that recommendations are timely and properly implemented; for consideration to be given to the application of the duty of candour, which had come into force for the hospital sector (also recommended by the Harris Review), to the police and the prison service; and the adoption of the Commission's Human Rights Framework by all three institutions (2015: 4–5). The Human Rights Framework is a practical guide to compliance with Art 2 and 14, which is modelled on the Articles' requirements based on human rights law. Under the Framework, four obligations are laid out: to treat people with respect for their dignity and human rights, to effectively assess their needs and risks, to adequately support them, and to investigate death incidents in an impartial and public way (ibid.: 8).

Like the 2014 Bradley Review Report, the 2016 EHRC progress review was not encouraging. Premature prisoner deaths have increased year on year, 'greater access to specialist mental healthcare' is urgently needed, prison-wide information on the number of prisoners with mental health conditions and on restraint practices is still not available, and mental health awareness training is yet to be made widely available.

Among the recurrent findings of all these reports and their follow-up reviews is that even well-devised policies and recommendations by monitoring bodies are not properly implemented, or are not implemented at all (e.g. The Harris Review 2015: 10). A pertinent example in this respect, which is heavily laden with Art 2 obligations, is the quality of the investigation procedure into deaths in custody.

Investigations into Prisoner Deaths

Since *Keenan v UK* (2001) there have been some positive changes in respect of the investigation procedure into prisoner deaths. Since 2004 the responsibility for investigating such deaths has passed from the Prison Service to the Prisons and Probation Ombudsman (PPO) (Livingstone et al. 2008: 55, 57). This move coupled with additional changes through the years in the all important area of the family's involvement in the investigation has addressed to a great degree the Art 2 procedural requirements. Now an independent body is in charge of such investigations that practises 'full and simultaneous disclosure to all parties in the investigation' (PPO Disclosure Policy 2009: para. 51). Now the family is given the opportunity to access relevant documentation during the investigation and to provide its views on the PPO's draft report like the Prison Service unless advance disclosure to the Prison Service is required to give the opportunity to individual members of staff to respond to 'specific and substantial criticisms against their person' (ibid.: para. 51–53, 55, 57). The PPO report, which also contains recommendations on how to prevent similar events in the future, is made public at the end of the inquest, increasing the transparency and accountability of the investigation. Also, a family liaison officer (FLO) is now assigned to the family whose role is to keep the family informed of the investigation progress and to enable them to address needs that may arise from the fatal incident (PPO, Family Liaison, undated).

In addition, since 2011 legal action against the Prison Service under the 2007 Corporate Manslaughter and Corporate Homicide Act is possible. The extension of the Act to the Prison Service provides bereaved families with an additional avenue of redress. While this is positively received as a re-affirmation of the prison service's positive duty of care, scholars (see, e.g. Genders and Player 2014) have expressed scepticism about its effectiveness in practice. Their scepticism stems from the legislative provisions that set a high threshold for findings of gross breach of duty and do not require organisations to foresee the risks at hand as the common law interpretation of gross negligence manslaughter does (ibid.: 443).

Moreover, the 2009 Coroners and Justice Act has amended the coroner's system to further compliance with the investigative aspects of Art 2 and to assist institutions in preventing future deaths. Admittedly, the changes have not been prompt since they came into force late in the summer of 2013 and did not make any changes in respect of legal aid for victims' families at inquests. This can arguably affect the degree to which the family can effectively participate in such proceedings. Under the new system, when a case can potentially involve Art 2, the 'how' parameter of the investigation involves determination of the circumstances that brought about the death (2009 Coroners and Justice Act, para. 5(2)). A new statutory duty is placed on the coroner to make a report to the relevant organisation regarding the need for action to be taken in order to prevent future deaths, without prescribing though actions. This duty arises when the coroner's investigation shows 'circumstances creating a risk of other deaths will occur, or will continue to exist, in the future' (Sch. 5, para 7(1b&c), 2009 Coroners and Justice Act). The organisation must respond to the coroner's report within 56 days (extension can be granted), identifying actions to be taken and their time framework. Both reports can be made public at the Chief Coroner's direction (Reg. 28&29, Coroners (Investigations) Regulations 2013).

The effectiveness of the changes to the investigation procedure has been limited and/or compromised by a repeated failure on the part of some prisons to implement PPO recommendations despite recently introduced action plans at every prison, and the PPO's lack of power to take action against their non-enforcement. Also, prisons continue to be unsympathetic and inconsiderate in their contact with prisoners' families, with their own version of FLO attracting considerable criticism for their insensitivity and inexperience (The Harris Review 2015: 164–165, 167; EHRC 2015: 59–61). In order to turn recommendations into tangible actions and assist (further) institutions in complying with their human rights obligations, the PPO has taken the step to produce thematic reports. Called *Learning Lessons* reports, they focus on specific areas of concern, such as restraint practices and risk factors in suicides. Lastly, to increase pressure on individual institutions, since 2013 HM Inspectorate of Prisons (HMIP) examines the degree to which PPO recommendations have been implemented at the inspected institution. HMIP communicates its findings to the PPO and includes them in its inspection reports (EHRC 2015: 60–61).

Life and Indeterminate Sentences for Public Protection

As mentioned before, in the last 20 years the category of life and indeterminate sentences for public protection (IPP) has seen unprecedented increases. Not only have England and Wales the highest prison population in Western Europe for some years now but also have the highest number of prisoners on life and indeterminate sentences (Bromley Briefings 2015: 22). Based on the latest CoE Annual Penal Statistics, life sentences represent 10.4% of the prison population and indeterminate sentences 7.2% (Aebi et al. 2015: 96). In 2015 there were 7439 lifers, of whom more than 50 were on whole life tariffs; the numbers on indeterminate sentences were 4614, out of whom 3532 were detained beyond their tariff (Bromley Briefings 2015: 22–23).

With reference to the legalisation of prisoners' human rights, lifers in this country represent a special case. They have been the most active litigants and have successfully put prisoners' human rights on the map, arousing of course controversy. For example, *Hirst* (2002), *Hirst v UK* (2005), and *Dickson v UK* (2007) were all cases on important matters pertaining to imprisonment in general that lifers brought before the courts; the first two, notably, by the same individual. In finding a violation of Art 10 (freedom of expression), *Hirst* (2002) re-affirmed the principle, confirmed first time in *Golder v UK* (1975), that imprisonment does not entail automatic loss of fundamental rights and freedoms except for the obvious deprivation of liberty. Freedom of expression does not only involve the right to hold and express views, but also to access and impart information, as well as the ability to vote (van Zyl Smit and Snacken 2009: 249). In the present case, under Art 10 the prisoner had the right to contact the media (by phone) in order to contribute his views on prison issues of legitimate and public interest, such as prison conditions, prisoner treatment and miscarriages of justice (Easton 2011). *Hirst v UK* (2005) can be regarded as one of the two most significant cases (the other one is *Vinter & Others v UK* (2013)). In the strongest possible terms, it re-affirmed that the Aristotelian notion of human beings as intrinsically political animals applies equally to prisoners, who retain the right to participate in public life behind bars by casting their vote. The Edwardian notion of 'civic death' embodied in the blanket prisoner disenfranchisement was ruled disproportionate (Hirst v. The United Kingdom Judgment 6 October 2005: para. 59–61, 69, 73–85). While *Hirst v UK* reminded us of the social and civic dimensions of prisoners' identity, *Dickson v UK* (2007) reminded us that they are also private individuals who like the rest of us may wish to enter a private relationship and found a family. This forms part of both people's (the prisoner's and their partner's) right to respect for private and family life under Art 8. In certain instances like the present case, the state must facilitate their enjoyment of this right by allowing prisoners (and their partners by association) to access artificial insemination (Easton 2011: 166–168).

As we shall see below, lifers' and IPP prisoners' treatment is paradigmatic of the English and Welsh position of prisoners' human rights, that is, a position which does not really believe that human rights apply to this social group and pays lip service not only to the aim of rehabilitation but also to that of public protection. Ultimately, this is a position that recognises only one goal—incapacitation in its purest form where nothing else matters.

Life Sentences

The legislative and policy framework of life sentences is an exemplar of what has just been said.

The legislator created three types of life sentences with their own subtypes, reflecting the offender's age at the time of the offence. These were: (a) mandatory life sentences for murder under the 1965 Murder (Abolition of the Death Penalty) Act; (b) discretionary life sentences for offences that could attract a life sentence, such as manslaughter, rape and arson, and were committed by individuals assessed as dangerous; and (c) automatic life sentences for a second serious violent or sexual offence. All these life sentences were for adults (Livingstone et al. 2008: 563–564).

Mandatory Life Sentences

The mandatory life sentence has two phases, each reflecting different punishment aims. The first phase, known as tariff, expresses retribution and individual deterrence, which are reflected in its fixed length. The second phase, which commences at the first review of the sentence, aims at public protection and is purely preventive in nature. As long as the mandatory lifer poses a risk, they remain in custody indefinitely. Here risk refers to the danger the lifer poses to the public, the possibility of their committing 'further imprisonable offences', and the likelihood of their failing to comply with licence conditions (Livingstone and Owen 1999; Livingstone et al. 2008: 571–572).

The mandatory life sentence has been controversial for four main reasons. First, from its inception until the mid-2000s, it did not legally differentiate between degrees of murder, compromising the principle of proportionality between the seriousness of the offence and the severity of punishment. Second, the executive in the capacity of the Home Secretary (basically a politician) had the final say until the early 2000s on the length of one's tariff and their release, along with the power to increase an already fixed tariff (Livingstone et al. 2008: 568–69, 571, 574, 590). Third, until the mid-1990s a mandatory lifer was not allowed knowledge of the judges' recommended tariffs, their final fixing by the executive and the reasons on which they were refused parole (Livingstone and Owen 1999: 381). Fourth, from the early 1990s, a mandatory life sentence could effectively mean lifelong imprisonment with the imposition of a whole life tariff that until quite recently (with an interim change from 1997 to 2005) did not envisage the possibility of a lifer's release based on considerations of rehabilitative progress made on their part (Vinter & Others v UK Judgment 9 July 2013).

All these aspects have become the subject of domestic and international litigation that managed gradually to effect changes, leading to the judicialisation of the mandatory life sentence.

For example, *ex p Cox* (1991) ruled that mandatory lifers had the right to know of the executive's reasons for refusing to authorise a Parole Board (PB) recommendation for their release. In such instances, the reasons given had to be transparent (Livingstone and Owen 1999: 381, 397). Three years later, *ex p Doody* (1994) ended the behind-closed-doors practice of tariff-setting, which was found to fall short of the natural justice requirement of procedural justice. On these grounds, mandatory lifers had the rights to know of the judges' recommended tariff and the reasons for them, to make representations against the recommended tariff, and to know whether the Home Secretary had overruled the judicial recommendations (Creighton and King 1996; Livingstone et al. 2008: 573).

The countdown to the end of the executive's involvement in the administration of the mandatory life sentence began at the ECtHR with *Stafford v UK* (2002) and ended in the House of Lords in the same year with *Anderson.*

Stafford v UK (2002) concerned the lawfulness of a recalled mandatory lifer's continued detention who had served two-thirds of his new six-year sentence by which point he was entitled to be released. The applicant argued that his continued detention based on the Home Secretary's view that 'he might on release commit a non-violent crime involving no conceivable physical harm to others [and being] wholly unrelated in nature and seriousness to the original offence of murder' was arbitrary, in violation of Art 5(1) (Stafford v. The United Kingdom Judgment 28 May 2002: para. 10–26, 57–58). Also, the PB did not meet under Art 5(4) the requirement of being a body with judicial powers, such as to order release. The PB could only direct a mandatory lifer's release, which was subject to the Home Secretary's approval (ibid.: para. 85). The case was successful. In respect of Art 5(1), the Court ruled that the continued detention of mandatory lifers based on the likelihood of committing non-violent as opposed to violent offences run contrary to the rule of law and was arbitrary. There was no domestic law authorising one's continued detention on such grounds (ibid.: para. 82–83). There was also a violation of Art 5(4) since not only could not the PB order release but also its reviews lacked important procedural guarantees, such as prisoner access to oral hearings. The fact that PB reviews involved considerations of lawfulness entailed the need for a body with judicial powers and guarantees (ibid.: para. 89–90).

The government responded with interim measures. Since 1 January 2003 mandatory lifers have the rights to an oral hearing before the PB, to legal representation in PB hearings, to full access to the release sections in the PB dossiers, and to call and cross-examine witnesses (von Bulow v. The United Kingdom Judgment 7 January 2004: para. 19).

However, cases continued to reach the ECtHR, alleging violations of mandatory lifers' right to liberty and security (Art 5). In 2004 the ECtHR delivered three more judgments. These were *von Bulow* (2004), *Wynne v UK* (2004), and *Hill v UK* (2004). All were successful. On the same grounds as the previous two cases, *Wynne v UK* and *Hill v UK* claimed that their rights under Art 5(5) had also been violated as they could not seek compensation for their arbitrary detention.

In *Anderson* (2002) The House of Lords brought an end to the executive's involvement in the mandatory life sentence in respect of which they issued a declaration of incompatibility. They ruled that the executive's tariff-setting function violated Art 6(1) that reads 'in determination of … any criminal charge, everyone is entitled to a fair and public hearing by an independent and impartial tribunal established by law.' In setting mandatory life tariffs, the executive exercised in private a sentencing function while they were not a judge, and they could not be considered independent and impartial in view of their original capacity (Livingstone et al. 2008: 575). The interplay between politics and media campaigns for tough law and order measures endangered their independence and impartiality, impacting on the fairness of the sentencing procedure.

The next significant development in the mandatory life sentence policy came more than a decade later, with *Vinter & Others v UK* (2013). The outcome of the case has huge future consequences for the definition and administration of life sentences, as well as our understanding of what imprisonment in the twenty-first century should aim to achieve.

Vinter & Others v UK (2013) concerned three lifers on whole life tariffs. We mentioned earlier that whole life tariffs open the door to lifelong imprisonment. As a result, they are imposed on mandatory lifers whose murder offences are 'sufficiently heinous … [and] so wicked that even if the prisoner is detained until they dies it will not exhaust the requirements of retribution and deterrence' (Ex p Hindley 2001: 417; cited in Vinter and Others v. The United Kingdom 9 July 2013: para. 46). The applicants argued that their whole life tariff status violated their rights under Art 3 and 5(4). They evoked the irreducibility of their whole life tariffs following from a lack of relevant review procedures in the context of a European penal policy that laid particular emphasis on prisoner rehabilitation and reintegration. The ECtHR accepted the applicants' argument in respect of Art 3 and declared inadmissible their Art 5(4) claim (ibid.: para. 97–101, 130–132).

In respect of Art 3, the Court's assessment of the relevant law and policy revealed omissions, lack of clarity in law and a rather limited possibility of release that rendered it unrealistic. Regarding omissions, the current law, the 2003 CJA, did not include in its provisions the introduced (in 1997) review of whole life tariffs, or similar arrangements. The law on lifers' release was also unclear. By virtue of Sect. 30 of the 1997 Crime (Sentences) Act the Home Secretary had the power to release a mandatory (whole tariff) lifer and the 1998 HRA placed a duty on them to do so when the mandatory lifer's continued detention ceased to serve a legitimate penal aim. However, the Prison Service Order 4700, which provided guidance on the circumstances in which the Home Secretary would exercise their power to release, provided very restrictive criteria. The criteria were essentially one—release on compassionate grounds (Vinter and Others v. The United Kingdom Judgment 9 July 2013: para. 42–43, 124–129).

The ECtHR contextualised its finding of a violation of Art 3 with reference to the malleability of penal aims with the passing of time that recognises offenders' ability to change; the central place of rehabilitation and reintegration as penal aims in European and international law, even for those on life sentences; the espousal and application of these aims to their lifer populations by the majority of the ECHR member states; and the inextricable link between rehabilitation and protection of human dignity (Vinter and Others v. The United Kingdom Judgment 9 July 2013: para. 111, 114–115, 117). In relation to the last point, the Court referred especially to the 1997 and 1986 judgments of the German Constitutional Court in which the latter ruled that lifelong imprisonment without the possibility of release on grounds other than compassionate reasons contravened the German constitutional principle of human dignity (ibid.: para. 69–70, 113).

The progressive direction of *Vinter & Others v UK* with its commitment to a living interpretation of the ECHR has been halted (hopefully for the moment) by the British Court of Appeal in *Newell* and *McLoughin* (2014). Like *Vinter & Others*, the domestic case concerned the incompatibility of whole life tariffs with Art 3. In an unprecedented move and language, the domestic court ruled the same provisions, which were under consideration in *Vinter & Others* and were found in violation of Art 3, compatible with the Article's requirements. Its judgment reads, 'We disagree. In our view, the domestic law is clear as to "possible exceptional release of whole life prisoners"…As we understand the Grand Chamber's view, it might have been thought that the fact that policy… has not been revised is of real consequence. However, as a matter of law, it is, in our view, of no consequence…In our judgment the law does provide to an offender "hope" or the "possibility" of release in exceptional circumstances which render the just punishment originally imposed no longer justifiable' (2014, EWCA Crim 188, para. 29–30, 35).

Newell and *McLoughin* have not brought closure; quite the contrary. In 2015 the Chamber of the ECtHR ruled in *Hutchison v UK*, which raised exactly the same issue, that the whole life tariff framework was compatible with Art 3. Drawing on *Newell* and *McLoughin*, it stated that 'the national court has specifically addressed doubts and set out an unequivocal statement of the legal position, the Court must accept the national court's interpretation of domestic law' (Hutchinson v. The United Kingdom 3 February 2015: para. 25). The case has been referred to the ECtHR's Grand Chamber and was heard in October 2015. At the time of writing the jury on whole life tariffs is still out as we wait for the Grand Chamber judgment.

Detention During Her Majesty's Pleasure (DHMP)

Detention during Her Majesty's pleasure is the equivalent of the mandatory life sentence for children and young people aged 10–17 and was treated as such well into the 1990s in relation, for example to tariff-setting, progression through the lifer detention cycle, PB reviews, release on licence, and recall (Livingstone et al. 2008: 583). Among the different lifer groups, HMP detainees have been the least active in terms of litigation activity. The few cases brought before the courts by HMP detainees focused on achieving parity of treatment with discretionary lifers on the grounds of the minor of their age at the time of their offence.

Ex p Prem Singh (1993) was the first HMP case and concerned HMP detainees' access to relevant documentation in preparation for PB reviews. Like mandatory lifers, they did not have the right to access such information, but discretionary lifers did. The domestic court ruled that DHMP was more akin to the discretionary life sentence than mandatory life. Like discretionary lifers, HMP detainees were detained principally on preventive grounds where emphasis was placed on risk reduction and rehabilitation support. As a result, they should have had the same rights of disclosure (Livingstone et al. 2008: 583–584).

The Home Secretary's differing view on HMP detainees' status (they were to remain mandatory lifers) led to *Hussain and Singh v UK* (1996). Evoking the similarities between DHMP and discretionary life, the applicants argued that their continued detention post their tariff and their disadvantaged position in the PB procedure deprived them of the procedural safeguards protected under Art 5(4), which the state already applied to discretionary lifers. In the Court's view, DHMP was similar to discretionary life, especially in its post-tariff phases. As a result, the applicants' rights under Art 5(4) had been violated. Like discretionary lifers, HMP prisoners should have had the rights to legal assistance and representation, to an oral hearing, and to call and cross-examine witnesses. Recognition and protection of these important safeguards had an added urgency for these young lifers whose most vulnerable and crucial for their development years were stigmatised by imprisonment. In the Court's view, regular and careful assessments of HMP detainees' progress, especially post tariff had to accompany these safeguards. Cursory and irregular assessments risked a considerably lengthy detention of already stigmatised and gravely afflicted young people, involving potentially Art 3 concerns. Unlike *ex p Prem Singh, Hussain and Singh* had an impact. Changes introduced via the 1997 Crime (Sentences) Act provided HMP detainees the same rights with discretionary lifers regarding PB reviews and recalls (Livingstone et al. 2008: 584–585).

Four years later, *T and V v UK* successfully challenged the Home Secretary's tariff-setting function. This was a special case in its own right as seven years earlier at the time of their offences, the applicants attracted pure venom from the media, society and politicians alike. They made claims under three ECHR Articles, involving a variety of issues. They argued that: (a) Their criminal prosecution at the low age of 10, their adult-like and public trial, the public outcry they had had to endure during their trial, the publication of their identities after the trial, and the uncertainty of their tariff violated their rights under Art 3. (b) Their adult-like and public trial, as well as the tariff-setting arrangements, violated their right to a fair trial (Art 6). (c) Their sentence and its review procedure violated their right to liberty and security under Art 5(1) and (4) (Livingstone et al. 2008: 587–588).

The ECtHR did not find a violation of Art 3 and 5(1), but it did find a violation of Art 6(1) and 5(4). Despite 10 being a low age of criminal responsibility, there was not a common approach to this aspect of criminal justice policy among Council of Europe (CoE) member states. The impact of the trial circumstances on the applicants did not reach inhuman or degrading levels of suffering, and neither did their sentence. In addition, the three-year period that had elapsed before their tariff was set was not long enough to engage Art 3. In respect of Art 5(1), DHMP was not arbitrary; it was provisioned in legislation and ordered by a competent court. However, Art 6(1) required the defendant's ability to be actively involved in their trial and an independent and impartial tribunal to try and sentence them. In the present case, the trial circumstances were intimidating which coupled with the defendants' very young age did not allow them to actively participate in the proceedings, such as to consult with their lawyers and contribute to their legal defence. Moreover, their tariff was set by the Home Secretary who as a politician and member of the executive was not an independent and impartial judge. Lastly, Art 5(4) required the defendants' ability to challenge the 'lawfulness of their detention speedily by a court and their release ordered if the detention is not lawful'. The applicants were not able to do so since the Home Secretary had the ultimate authority (ibid.).

In the same year with *T and V v UK*, the ECtHR examined two more DHMP cases, *Downing v UK* (2000) and *Curley v UK* (2000), which again concerned the review arrangements of the DHMP sentence. While the Court struck out *Downing v UK* (the applicant had reached a settlement with the Government), *Curley v UK* produced a finding of violation of Art 5(4) and (5). Mr. Curley was not afforded the opportunity of a speedy review of their sentence by a body empowered to order his release and could not seek compensation for the violation of his rights (Curley v. The United Kingdom Jufgment 28 March 2000: para. 28–29, 32–34, 36–38).

Following *T and V v UK* (2000) the Home Secretary relinquished their tariff-setting power which was passed to the Lord Chief Justice in 2000. However, the lessons from *Curley v UK* and *Downing v UK* were completely ignored with the abolition of the DHMP reviews, which was successfully challenged in *Smith* (2006) (Livingstone et al. 2008: 588–589).

Discretionary Life Sentences

The discretionary life sentence is an indeterminate sentence for adults who have committed violent and/or sexual offences serious enough to attract a life sentence. Its indeterminacy is justified on the grounds of the offender's mental instability at the time of the offence, which is seen to increase their risk of re-offending on the same or a greater scale of seriousness. In light of this, it is a type of preventive detention, albeit not a straightforward one, which is indicative of the wide range of problems preventive detention is besieged by, raising fundamental issues of proportionality, fairness and justice. Like the other life sentences, discretionary life has also a retributive phase, a tariff. A discretionary life tariff should not be longer though than the equivalent determinate sentence (including early release entitlements) the offence would have attracted if the offender had not been assessed as mentally unstable. If the offender does not pose a risk at the end of their tariff, they must be released (Livingstone et al. 2008: 563, 576–577).

Moreover, like mandatory lifers (adults and young people), for a long time discretionary lifers had their rights to a fair trial (Art 6) and to liberty and security (Art 5) violated. The Home Secretary would set their tariff and had the power of veto over their release. Their treatment was further worsened by the illogical practice of having their tariff set three to four years into their sentence, with the first PB review after three years or so (ibid.: 577), blurring in effect the limits of the retributive and preventive phases of the sentence. Last but not least, the grounds for the imposition of discretionary life are elusive, raising two questions: To what lengths are we prepared to go to protect ourselves against a risk that may or may not materialise? And, if we accept that we have no other option but to adopt drastic measures, why do we knowingly keep adopting the least effective ones? Prisoner litigation brought all these issues to the foreground. As we shall see in this section and in the next one on IPPs, some issues were addressed, and some were ignored and were carried forward, causing much greater problems for all parties concerned: for offenders, the public, HM Prison Service and the government.

Ex p Hanscomb and Others (1988) kick-started a series of legal cases by discretionary lifers both domestically and internationally. The case concerned the above practice of delaying the fixing of the discretionary life tariff and subsequently the timing of the first PB review of the sentence. The applicants successfully argued that the practice culminated in their being punished more harshly as the length of their detention proved to be disproportionate to the seriousness of their offences. The court ruled that discretionary life tariffs should be fixed immediately after sentencing and not be longer than the equivalent determinate sentence. The ruling was highly significant as it made a clear distinction between mandatory and discretionary life sentences. They were imposed on different grounds and therefore in the interests of justice and fairness their administration ought to reflect this (Livingstone et al. 2008: 577–578).

In the same year, *Weeks v UK* (1988), which concerned a serially recalled to prison lifer, highlighted the inadequacy of the review arrangements that contravened Art 5(4). The PB fell short of being a court that determined speedily the lawfulness of the applicant's continued detention and could order their release. Moreover, the review procedure did not afford the applicant access to relevant documentation so as to be able to prepare his case for release (Livingstone et al. 2008: 580).

The success of *Weeks v UK* in Strasbourg did not reach the UK. It took another case, *Thynne, Wilson and Gunnel* (1991) (it raised the same issues with *Weeks v UK*), for any changes to be made. Notably, the courts took control of the tariff-setting power, which was formerly exercised by the executive, and important procedural safeguards before the PB were at last recognised. For example, discretionary lifers have now the rights to be promptly informed of the timings of PB reviews, to an oral hearing, to appear in the PB review hearing in person and/or to be represented, to access release dossiers and to make representations, and to call and cross-examine witnesses. Additionally, the PB has now the power to order a discretionary lifer's release although PB recommendations pertaining to a lifer's progression through the system (e.g. from closed to open conditions) are subject to the Home Secretary's approval (Creighton and King 1996: 162–165; Livingstone et al. 2008: 618).

Notwithstanding this breaches of Art 5(4) in relation to the speediness and regularity of PB reviews continued. For instance, in *Oldham v UK* (2000) a lapse of two years between a recall hearing and a direction for release was found unreasonable, with similar findings being reached in *Hirst v UK* (2001) and *Blackstock v UK* (2005).

In principle, reviews are to take place biannually once the tariff is served but, as relevant ECtHR case law shows, this does not always happen, and the circumstances of the case also have a bearing on assessments of timeliness. These are of course challenging matters arising out of the preventive character of detention that are of great consequence for the person concerned. Their detention is risk-based, and definitions and assessments of risk are not set on stone (O'Malley 2010: 42), creating all sorts of dilemmas that can lead to human rights violations. For example, in the case of the discretionary life sentence the offender's risk is interpreted as 'risk to life and limb' based on *ex p Benson* (1989), and the degree of this risk needs to be 'substantial; no more than that it is not merely perceptible or minimal based on *ex p Bradley* (1991)' (Livingstone et al. 2008: 578–589). Suffice to note here that qualifications such as the one just mentioned are based on predictive calculations. These do not speak of hard facts and become hugely controversial when no or inadequate investment is made in enabling *risky* individuals to be risk-free, or at least reduce their risk.

By way of conclusion, the repeated human rights violations that the lifer litigation exposed led to the overhaul of the legal and policy framework surrounding life sentences principally via the 2003 CJA. The following notable developments have taken place. In respect of all life sentences, it is the judiciary that determines their tariff within the relevant legislative provisions and sentencing guidelines. Also, the PB is the body responsible for making decisions on lifers' release. Schedule 21 of the 2003 CJA introduces three minimum terms for mandatory life. These terms act as starting points for the determination of the tariff, supported by additional criteria for the categorisation of murder offences under the relevant minimum term, such as mitigating and aggravating circumstances.[4] Moreover, automatic life sentences were abolished, albeit not for good, and two new indeterminate sentences for public protection (one for adults and one for young people) were introduced along with a new determinate extended sentence for public protection (EPP). With direct applicability to these new sentences, Schedule 15 of the 2003 CJA introduces the 'dangerous offender' by listing 153 specified violent and sexual offences that they may commit. As the number of the offences betrays, Schedule 15 is wide ranging, covering a broad spectrum of offences. Lastly, all recalls are now initiated by the courts instead of the PB which remains responsible for recall hearings. While some of these changes were welcoming, others, such as the indeterminate sentences for public protection, have created troubles that are still with us today.

Before we move to the next section, we must mention that since December 2012 we have one more life sentence for adults, the automatic life sentence, (re)introduced by the 2012 Legal Aid, Sentencing and Punishment of Offenders Act (LASPO). Bearing the exact same name with the automatic life sentence (!), which the 2003 CJA abolished, the

---

[4] For example, for offenders 21 years and over, a whole life tariff is the starting point for 'exceptionally high' in seriousness murders, 30 years for the 'particularly high' in seriousness category and 15 years for murders that do not fit in the first two categories.

new life sentence is similarly imposed for a second serious violent or sexual offence; only now there is a list of 'automatic life' offences (more than 40 in number) that can be found in the new Schedule 14b of the 2003 CJA, introduced by the LASPO Act.

Indeterminate prison sentences for public protection (IPPs)

The 2003 CJA introduced the indeterminate sentence for public protection for adults (IPP) and detention for public protection (DPP), its equivalent for young people under 18. Although the 2012 LASPO Act abolished these indeterminate sentences, their reverberations are still felt today, first and foremost by the prisoners serving them, as well as the wider system.

IPPs are another example of what is wrong with our penal policy. They expose a penal policy that can be described in the following three ways. We can say that our penal policy is ideologically incapacitative and thus prepared to go at great lengths to defend its belief in incapacitation, trumping prohibitive costs and expert evidence on the futility of this approach. Or, we can say that our penal policy is inept in matters of effectiveness and efficiency despite its espousal of managerialist practices. Or, we can actually say that both descriptions are valid. The very basic feeling that IPPs leave us with is that we have a penal policy that while it aspires to be effective and efficient, it refuses to modernise itself, starting from the fundamental issue that is none other than its punishment approach. As the *new* automatic life sentence mentioned in the previous section shows, instead of modernisation, we get recycling of measures.

Since they came into force in 2005, IPP and DPP have been imposed on offenders whose offences were among the 153 listed in Schedule 15 of the 2003 CJA and could attract a maximum penalty of ten years or more. Their indeterminacy has been qualified on the grounds of the offenders' 'significant risk to the public of serious harm occasioned by the commission of further offences' (Sect. 224–236, 2003 CJA). While the 2003 CJA is informative of the offences, it fails to be in respect of the constitution of serious harm. Guidance on this is provided in sentencing guidelines, which have defined serious harm as 'death or serious personal injury, whether physical or psychological'. In the case of adult offenders, prior convictions for a specified offence triggered automatically an IPP unless there were exceptional circumstances involved in the commission of the offence. Prior convictions for specified offences were interpreted as evidence of an existing significant risk of serious harm. This presumption of dangerousness did not apply to young offenders. Before imposing a DPP, the courts had to consider whether the determinate EPP could be an equally appropriate measure for the purposes of retribution, deterrence and public protection (HM Chief Inspector of Prisons and HM Chief Inspector of Probation 2008).

Like life sentences, the IPP and DPP have had a tariff period during which prisoners would take part in rehabilitative interventions so as to reduce their risk of dangerousness. If by the end of their tariff the prisoner has not shown sufficient progress and/or has not completed the required rehabilitative programmes to safely re-enter society, they progress to the preventive phase of their detention. As long as risk assessments considered at PB reviews show that the prisoner's risk of dangerousness is high, they remain in custody indefinitely. In the event of release, the IPP and DPP prisoner is on licence for at least ten years before they become eligible to apply to the PB for their licence to be lifted (HM Chief Inspector of Prisons and HM Chief Inspector of Probation 2008: 11).

In the first years of their introduction, IPPs were imposed at a monthly rate of 150, with the average tariff being initially two years or less, increased to 38 months by the end of 2007 (HM Chief Inspector of Prisons and HM Chief Inspector of Probation 2008: 12; Bromley Briefings 2011: 21). These relatively short tariffs reflected of course how wide ranging Schedule 15 has been, covering a broad spectrum of offences that are all deemed serious. The profile of IPP prisoners is predominantly of a young male with a complexity of needs, which render them particularly vulnerable. For example, 1 in 5 has received psychiatric treatment and is on psychiatric medication, 1 in 10 is receiving mental health treatment in prison, and 1 in 20 has spent time in a psychiatric environment. In terms of criminogenic needs, IPP prisoners have an average score of 6.3/10 compared to 4.4/10 for lifers and the mainstream prison population (Sainsbury Centre for Mental Health 2008b). In short, they are an acutely vulnerable prisoner group in need of intensive support and treatment.

Neither the Prison Service nor the PB had the resources, however, to administer the sheer volume of IPPs ordered by the courts effectively and timely. They also saw no investment so as to be able to cope with the increases in prisoner numbers and adequately support IPP prisoners. Moreover, the probation service's involvement with IPPs was limited, with consequences for the quality of licence supervision afforded to IPP prisoners and their prospects of successful reintegration (HM Chief Inspector of Prisons and HM Chief Inspector of Probation 2008: 16–17). The relatively short tariffs exacerbated the Prison Service's resource pressures and exposed an inconsistent and poor implementation of existing procedures, such as risk assessment and sentence planning, as well as an insufficient provision of OBPs. Additionally, lifer management arrangements under which IPP prisoners fall under were under strain that affected IPP prisoners' timely progression through the system. The Lifer Unit had to manage increased numbers of lifers and IPP prisoners with reduced human resources and few lifer prisons that could accommodate the increase in demand for places (HM Chief Inspector of Prisons and HM Chief Inspector of Probation 2008: 15, 26, 41–43; Bromley Briefings 2010: 15).

All this meant that the majority of IPP prisoners continued to be detained well beyond their tariff. As they experienced considerable delays in transfers to lifer prisons, they remained in local establishments, which are typically transit places, and therefore could not access OBPs. As a result, IPP prisoners would reach the end of their tariff without being in a position to demonstrate progress (Sainsbury Centre for Mental Health 2008b: 52–53). Moreover, concerns have been raised about OBPs, their usefulness in relation to resettlement and IPP prisoners' ability to successfully complete them. In its 2008 review of OBPs, the Sainsbury Centre for Mental Health notes the professionals' view that 'offenders with mental health problems should be mentally well prior to attending OBPs' (p. 6). Evidence shows that ill mental health affects one's ability to cope with the programmes and that some OBPs, such as sex offender treatment programmes, can aggravate the prisoner's mental health state (ibid.). It has been found that IPP prisoners are excluded from OBPs precisely for these reasons (Sainsbury Centre for Mental Health 2008b: 44–45; Bromley Briefings 2010: 16), leading to HM Chief Inspectors of Prisons and Probation to describe the situation as 'Kafka-esque' (HM Chief Inspector of Prisons and HM Chief Inspector of Probation 2008: 3). OBPs are also only designed to address thinking patterns and behaviour to the exclusion of resettlement support that is known to greatly impact on the risk of re-offending (Sainsbury Centre for Mental Health 2008a: 9, 11). Lastly, the PB did not have the manpower to additionally handle the substantial increases in IPP numbers, increasing further the time prisoners spent in prison beyond their tariff (HM Chief Inspector of Prisons and HM Chief Inspector of Probation 2008: 17; Bromley Briefings 2012: 21).

Three years into the introduction of IPPs, their choking effects on the prison and parole systems forced the government's hand to introduce legislative changes in order to stem further big IPP flows into the system. Also, the parole system began to see some investment in human resources in order to ease the backlog of case review hearings (Bromley Briefings 2011: 21). The legislative changes brought in by the 2008 Criminal Justice and Immigration Act lifted the presumption of dangerousness applied to adult offenders and stipulated a minimum tariff length, set at two years (Prison Service Instruction 27/2008). These last-minute, plaster-like measures have been unable to undo the mess and damage they have caused. In 2010 there were around 6000 IPP prisoners, out of whom more than 2000 were detained beyond their tariff. In 2012 this increased to nearly 60% of IPPs, with only 502 people being released between 2005 and 2012 (Bromley Briefings 2010: 15, 2012: 20–21).

In the meantime, legal challenges began to emerge. In 2008 *Walker and James* ruled that the Home Secretary had acted unlawfully in failing in their duty to provide sufficient rehabilitation resources so as to enable the claimants to timely demonstrate their eligibility for release at the end of their tariff. In 2009 *Walker and Wells* ruled that the lack of assessment of the resource implications of IPPs and adequate preparations to meet the likely needs was irrational in public law (Easton 2011: 117–118). In 2012 the ECtHR delivered its judgment in *James, Wells and Lee v UK*, which concerned the continued detention of three IPP prisoners beyond their tariff. While individually they claimed additional right violations, all three argued that their rights under Art 5(1&4) had been violated. In respect of Art 5(1), they cited their inability to access timely the required OBPs for a number of reasons (e.g. non-availability of programmes, over-subscribed programmes and delays in their transfers to lifer prisons) and argued that 'there had been no meaningful review of the legality of their post-tariff detention,' as required under Art 5(4) (James, Wells and Lee v.

The United Kingdom 18 September 2012: para. 13–20, 45, 49, 78, 80, 223). The ECtHR found a violation of Art 5(1) but not of its paragraph 4. The applicants' continued detention was arbitrary and thus unlawful as a result of delays rooted in 'seriously defective structures'; however, both the PB and the courts, which they could access, could direct their release (ibid.: para. 103, 221, 229–232).

Last but not least, in *Faulkner* (2013) and *Sturnham* (2013) the Supreme Court ruled that a 'significant' delay in a prisoner's realistic prospect of release caused by lack of resources would entitle the prisoner to compensation under Art 5(5). The cases concerned two IPP prisoners who had experienced long delays in their PB reviews following the end of their tariffs as a result of the PB's aforementioned capacity problems. In circumstances where a prisoner's release is less likely, evidence of distress judged to be sufficiently serious would also give rise to Art 5(5).

There were 4133 IPP prisoners in 2016. 81% of them have served their tariff. Based on Sect. 128 of the 2012 LASPO Act the Lord Chancellor has the power to change the test of release for this category of prisoners. This power has not been used yet (Bromley Briefings 2015: 23, 2016: 2–3).

Conclusion

The above account of developments that have taken place in English penal policy and their impact on prisoners' experiences of incarceration and human rights allow us to make the following uncomfortable observations. The English penal policy itself has been one of the victims of its politicisation. Its politicisation, coupled with the dominance of a risk discourse in the wider public and political life, does not afford easy political solutions to the dead end it has reached, that is, an overcrowded, overstretched and understaffed prison system with increased levels of violence and drug use.

From the 1990s to the present day, review after review and inquiry after inquiry have demonstrated beyond any doubt that we unnecessarily overuse imprisonment as punishment. The prison's failure to reduce re-offending and limited relevance to public safety in the long term, as well as its destructive effects on prisoners and their families, are publicly and widely available. Yet, we keep sending vulnerable and non-serious offenders to prison and on short sentences, in full knowledge that they are more likely to re-offend than to learn a lesson and/or turn their lives around. The latest reform efforts that aspire to revolutionise offender treatment through a renewed focus on offender rehabilitation are evidence of the knee-jerk nature and lack of direction and foresight of the English penal policy that shows no pragmatism. Overcrowded prison conditions and lack of resources are not conducive to a successful *rehabilitation revolution*.

Typically, revolutions aim to overthrow the status quo. So, before any changes are made to the delivery and provision of rehabilitative services, we must first start reducing the prison population. This is where the *rehabilitation revolution* should aim to start from if it aspires to be successful.

4

Dutch Penal Policy and Prisoners' Human Rights

Introduction

As mentioned in Chap. 2, by the time *Contrasts in Tolerance* (Downes 1988) was published, the Dutch prison population had already been rising, indicating a shift in penal policy from a traditional mildness to a more authoritative approach. Although there is now a consensus that Dutch prison figures have been both deflated and inflated to a degree over the years owing to the exclusion and inclusion of different prisoner categories in different statistical sources, it remains a fact that there has been an upward trend from 1985 to 2005, albeit less steep than the statistics showed. From 2005 to the present day, this has been gradually reversed, culminating in a prisoner rate similar to that in the latter part of the 1990s, of about 69 per 100,000 in 2014 (van Dijk 2010; van Swaaningen 2013: 349; Walmsley 2015: 11).

Against these developments, the obvious questions to ask are what has caused these long, sustained increases and recent decreases in Dutch prisoner rates and what impact they have had on the prisoner experience and their human rights.

A. Karamalidou, *Embedding Human Rights in Prison*,
DOI 10.1057/978-1-137-58502-8_4

The Punitive Years

Regarding the increases between 1985 and 2005, relevant literature and Dutch prisoner accounts (see Chap. 6) point the finger to the effects of globalisation on Dutch society, its culture and politics, which coupled with increases in serious crime between 1990 and 2003, such as violent and sexual offences, including drug smuggling, have led to a tougher penal policy (Pakes 2005: 148–158, 2008; Boone and van Swaaningen 2013: 10–12). This tougher penal policy, as the statistics nevertheless show, involved a greater use of imprisonment across the board. More specifically, Boone and Moerings attribute the increase in the prison population in the first decade (1985–1995) to the imposition of more short sentences along with longer prison terms for violent crimes, serious vandalism and drug trafficking. Regarding the second decade (1995–2005), they single out the greater use of pre-trial detention, more entrustment orders for mentally disordered offenders, and more sentences targeting repeat offenders as the main drivers behind the continuing prisoner increases (2007: 59, 72–73).

While the aforementioned increase in serious crime can help us understand one of the contributing factors to the increase in prisoner numbers (i.e. long sentences for such offences), it does not account for the other factors, and explanations must be sought elsewhere.

As early as 1986, van Dijk (2010) pointed out to the depillarisation of Dutch society, a process that had been well under way from the 1960s onwards. Rising living standards and the resultant affordability to widely consume saw the emergence of an individualistic and secular culture in which the informal social control that the pillars had been able to exercise through social settings began to lose its appeal and power. The thinning of social/religious ties, which had until then created a common sense of belonging, identity and purpose (always within the pillars), shifted people's faith in the centralised power of the state and its formal mechanisms of social control and punishment (Downes and van Swaaningen 2007: 37–38). The impact of this social transformation where people would now turn exclusively to the state and expect their government to act so as to protect the quality of their life was evidenced in governmental policy papers (Boone and Moerings 2007: 70–71; Downes and Swaaningen 2007: 47–50).

In the 1985 *Society & Crime* policy paper, scholars, such as Blad (2003), saw the first signs of a risk discourse with its emphasis on managerialist practices. Driven by actuarialism (Blad calls it penal instrumentalism), criminal punishment was to become a medium of social engineering, which for it to be effective had to be applied in a 'consistent, consequent and credible manner' (Society and Crime 1985; cited in Blad 2003: 132). Under actuarialism, not only must offenders be punished but also be prevented from causing public harm all too soon. To this end, public protection was to become the focus of the state's attention that translated in more frequent, longer, indeterminate and specialist sentences, as well as tougher community penalties. In this way, the victims' suffering was recognised, societal rules were re-affirmed, perpetrators were punished and contained, and future offenders were forewarned of the certainty and magnitude of the consequences of being irresponsible (ibid.: 132, 134, 136).

In the 1990s globalisation forces accelerated the governmental 'punitive turn' (ibid.: 132) and the implementation of its adopted risk managerialist discourse. Dutch liberalism in the areas of prostitution, gambling and drugs in combination with the country's geographically strategic trade position for centuries (Andeweg and Irwin 2005) attracted the volatility of international organised crime, which also posed spillage risks for other European nations (Blankenburg and Bruinsma 1994: 56). Faced with its responsibilities as an EU and CoE member to stem the tide of organised crime, the Dutch government tightened the regulation of coffee shops and brothels and increased prison sentence lengths for smuggling stolen goods, drug and human trafficking to align its punishment levels with mainstream European practice (Pakes 2005: 149–154).

In this context, and confronted with a prison institutional crisis as a result of cell shortages and a series of prison escapes in the early 1990s (Resodihardjo 2009), the 1990 and 1994 policy papers *Law in Motion* and *Effective Detention* drew a line with the past. As their names betray, the priorities were twofold: (a) a criminal justice policy that would effectively respond to (rather than address the causes) and punish crime through tough penalties, such as imprisonment in order to restore public confidence in its relevance to the times, and (b) a penal policy that would bolster institutional security and order by toughening prison security and regimes and rationalising the management of the prison system itself (Downes and van Swaaningen 2007: 53–54; Resodihardjo 2009: 72–73).

National and global events by the 2000s became the catalyst for the end of the already-waning Dutch tolerance and humane paternalism that the country once came to be known of. Public opinion became resolutely less forgiving, demanding tough action against senseless violence and anti-social behaviour on the streets (like in England and Wales) in a number of public demonstrations between 1997 and 2000, known as white marches (Boone and Moerings 2007: 71–72). The harshening of the public mood was further amplified by the reverberations of the 9/11 terrorist attacks, which brought into the open public anxiety over immigration and long-held ambivalence towards Dutch ethnic minorities. Media coverage on the disproportionate involvement in crime of Moroccan youths fuelled public and political debate on (the failures of) multiculturalism and the ethnic minorities' (unsuccessful) integration into the Dutch society, which took unprecedented for the country dimensions in the early 2000s (Downes and van Swaaningen 2007: 55–59). In 2002 the populist right-wing politician Pim Fortuyn, who grabbed the headlines for his Islamophobic views, was assassinated by an environmental activist. Two years later, the film maker Theo van Gogh was killed by a Dutch-born Islamic fundamentalist on an Amsterdam street (Buruma 2006).

These last two events in particular shook public and political life from its foundations and brought violently to the fore the limits of Dutch tolerance. Criminal justice developments moved deeper into the punitive path, with Pakes commenting on the establishment of a 'Dutch-style Garlandian crime and security complex' in which crime was transformed from a social issue to a law and order issue (like in England & Wales long time ago), driven by public security considerations and the protection of Dutch moral values and way of life (2004: 285, 292–295). Exemplary of this Dutch version of Garland's crime complex (2001) was the 2002 policy paper *To a Safer Society*. With 105 proposals, it outlined measures for inter alia an increase in penal capacity in general and in immigration detention capacity in particular, an extensive use of electronic tagging and community service orders, and stiffer sentences for recidivists and violent offenders (ibid.: 291–293).

Return to Pragmatism

Fast forward to the present day and we are confronted with a Dutch paradox. As mentioned before, since 2006 there has been a steady decrease in the prison population that has been met with incredulity and scepticism over its causes and sustainability. In offering 'tentative explanations that to a large extent are still hypothetical', van Swaaningen (2013: 350–353) attributes the documented decrease to the following: there has been less use of remand and of imprisonment for property crimes. The seriousness of violent and drug offences has decreased, thus attracting lesser penalties. Until 2010 prisoners on entrustment orders were transferred earlier to a forensic psychiatric institution after serving one-third of their sentence. The 2008 and 2011 economic crises have re-ordered public and political priorities and have led to more serious media reporting, with concerns about the economy and healthcare dominating over crime.

What complicates matters further are: this new phase of penal reductionism has taken place on the back of a Dutch public opinion that remains disillusioned and pessimistic about the future, seeking relief from its angst in its unwaning support of a law and order approach (ibid.: 355). To which, the government has responded with a penal reductionist policy that now dares to exchange emotiveness and moralism with cool-headedness. This is astonishing considering the relatively short time within which this change in the direction of the penal policy has taken place and, more importantly, the intensity (public and political) of emotions that have driven up incarceration rates. Given the name *Masterplan*, the rationality of the latest policy direction is predicated on a complex predictive statistical model that foresees a reduced need for prison in the future (Pakes and Holt 2015).

Equally remarkable (perhaps even more so) are the emerging Dutch rental prisons, referred to in Chap. 2, with two Dutch prisons already being rented out to Belgium and Norway (Pakes and Holt 2015; Dutch Ministry of Security and Justice 2015). We may be heading down the path of a sort of penal tourism; only that here the operator has the exclusive right to decide the destination. Worse even, the very concept itself connotes an underlying attitude towards prisoners that is evocative of slave practices. Rental prisons are by definition the deal struck following a financial transaction between two parties. Like slaves, in this kind of deal between states prisoners become commodities to be transported where it suits most their custodians financially. This nascent development has human rights implications, with the most obvious being prisoners' right to private and family life, and resettlement support, and raises important questions about the ethical context of the execution of imprisonment.

Impact on the Prisoner Experience and Human Rights

The toughened-up approach to punishment in those 20 years was followed up with actions that saw a toughened-up approach to the treatment of prisoners. This toughened-up approach to the treatment of prisoners is still with us today.

To begin with, the 1999 PPA has effectively changed the prison experience. Having its own contrasting features, on the one hand, it recognises the authorities' positive duty of care to prisoners, the importance of a promptly executed sentence and the principle of as few restrictions on prisoners as necessary (Art 2). On the other hand, it places restrictions on prisoners' human rights, albeit with safeguards, and waters down the principle of reintegration. For example, the constitutional right to the inviolability of one's person may be restricted for the maintenance of safety and control as much for the prisoner's own interests as for the interests of others (Art 27). This restriction can take a number of forms, such as frisking and strip-searching upon entry and leave from the institution and before/after visits and internal physical examination (Art 29–31). Also, Art 37(2–4) allows interferences with prisoner mail other than privileged correspondence, and Art 38(2–4, 6) and 39 (2–4) provide for restrictions and supervision of prisoners' visits and calls.

Regarding the principle of reintegration, the 1999 Act states that the sentence 'shall be aimed at preparing the person as much as possible for reintegration in the community' (Art 2(2)). In contrast, the 1953 PPA stated that 'the implementation of the sentence will also serve to prepare the return of the prisoner to society' (cited in Boone 2007: 231); and the 1999 Act goes a step further. Through the introduction of penitentiary programmes and a standard regime,[1] it places firmly the onus of responsibility for a successful reintegration on prisoners (Kelk 2001: 480). Based on this new way of thinking brought in by the Act, prisoners' responsibilisation, to borrow Garland's term (2001), is the newly cut key that grants access both to an enhanced regime and resettlement opportunities. An inverse relationship between the two is thus established along with a new prison aim, that is, selective rehabilitation as opposed to (the former aim of) rehabilitation for all.

Another development ushered in by the Act, which is indicative of the reshaped priorities of the Dutch prison system, is the re-ordering of the selection criteria for prisoner allocation to establishments, wings and regimes. Under the 1953 Act, the main selection criteria were gender, age and sentence length. Under the new Act, these are supplemented with security and special committal with particular emphasis placed on security, enabling a much greater differentiation in and specialisation of prison regimes (Boone 2002: 6; Tak 2008: 143–148).

Differentiation in itself is very important as it directly relates to accountability. It involves making decisions regarding a variety of issues (e.g. allocation to a specific prison, placement in a specific regime or unit, transfers, disciplinary punishments and participation in/withdrawal from penitentiary programmes). Boone distinguishes between external and internal differentiation, with external differentiation referring to the Ministry of Security and Justice and judicial authorities, and internal differentiation to prison service administration (2002: 6–7). She notes that since the end of the 1990s the practice of internal differentiation has been growing apace. Old practice had it that staff from DJI Headquarters would go on a fact-finding exercise and hold meetings with the prisoner and the prison's management. Based on the findings of the exercise, a selection committee would then make a decision on the prisoner's allocation. Nowadays, this extra layer of accountability has given way to an exclusive

[1] The standard regime involves 26 hours' work per week, 6 hours' recreation, at least an hour for visits and 1 hour in the fresh air (Kelk 2001: 479).

reliance on prison management reports. The Prosecution Service's statutory responsibility to oversee all kinds of penalties, as well as the judges' discretionary power to proffer advice are reduced to an empty formality (ibid.: 6).

Penitentiary Programmes

Based on DJI (2000), penitentiary programmes aim 'to facilitate a gradual transition from detention to society, a phase by phase return to it'. In addition to their stated rehabilitative and reintegrative purpose, they have also had a practical and financial value. Especially at the time of their introduction, they were seen as a way to relieve the constant pressure on penal capacity by decreasing the length of long-term stay in prison and reducing related expenditure (Junger-Tas 1998).

As the plural form denotes, there are different kinds of penitentiary programmes focusing on three broad areas: education, employment and mental health. Each programme consists of a weekly minimum of 26 community hours that are tailored to the prisoner's needs, and prisoners are electronically tagged (DJI 2000: 3, 5–6). As a conduit for selective rehabilitation, penitentiary programmes are not accessible to all prisoners. Prisoners have to apply to the governor who decides whether to recommend them to the Selections Department of DJI that has veto powers (Art 7(1&4), 1999 Penitentiary Order). Participation to the programmes is governed by a selection procedure that shortlists candidates against predetermined criteria (Tak 2008: 142). Eligible participants must be (a) adults or have been tried as such; (b) be sentenced to a minimum of one year unconditional sentence; (c) have already served half of their sentence, excluding early release calculations; (d) still have to serve between six weeks and one year before their release date; and (e) have acceptable housing arrangements (Art 4(2), 1999 PPA; Art 7(3e), 1999 Penitentiary Order). Further selection criteria are the prisoner's seriousness of the offence, risk of recidivism, adaptability to the prison regime and rules, and capacity to take on wider responsibilities and to cope with the challenges of free life (Art 7(3a–d), 1999 Penitentiary Order).

The programmes have been unpopular among prisoners due to the strict conditions attached to them (Boone 2002: 6) and have attracted scholarly criticism over legality, fairness and human rights issues. Regarding prisoners' views, as we will see in Chap. 6, particularly my male participants were critical of the programmes' selection process, locus and quality. To them, the promotion of the programmes as a resettlement opportunity for those who convincingly demonstrated commitment to change was empty rhetoric. In their view, the shortlisting criteria were inflexible and highly selective, achieving the opposite of what it was intended, namely, to identify the ones who had the determination to change. The criterion of one's adaptability to the prison regime and rules discriminated especially against those that needed such an opportunity the most—the young prisoners who were impulsive and temperamental, and thus frequently in trouble. Moreover, the community character of the programmes induced deceitfulness in order to experience freedom sooner than later. Lastly, the programme activities were seen as useless and patronising. Work placements lacked employability value and cognitive/social skills training was infantilising.

Relating to the note made earlier about differentiation, the selection process for penitentiary programmes, prisoners' daily schedule, modifications to it and disciplinary action for breaking the conditions attached to the programmes are all aspects of internal differentiation. It is DJI that has the final word on them. According to Boone there are three big question marks over this arrangement that are interrelated and can give rise to human rights issues. The first issue is whether the programmes are a component of the prison sentence ordered by the courts. The second issue is that if they are, should not the courts have a role to play in their administration, especially when things go wrong (e.g. conditions are broken and prisoners are recalled to prison)? The third issue concerns the implications of the absence of judicial intervention in the administration of the programmes if the first two points are valid (ibid.: 10–12).

Boone argues that the programmes are constitutive of the prison sentence, engaging Art 5 because when a prisoner is withdrawn from them, it is to 'secure incarceration after a conviction by a competent court' as opposed to 'the fulfilment of any obligation described by law'. This in effect means that the available disciplinary measures and recall to prison are sanctioned under the authority of the original prison sentence. So, the execution of the programmes should be governed by a judicial organ (ibid.: 11). In this context, similar to the executive's involvement in the administration of life sentences in England and Wales, the division of powers between the executive and the judicial branches of government become obscure, undermining prisoners' procedural and substantive rights (ibid.: 12). As judicial intervention in prison life weakens, prison accountability also weakens in the absence of an external and independent means of oversight. To make a decision on a prisoner's suitability for and withdrawal from the programmes is not a matter of no consequence; it has a great impact on the prisoner's access to rehabilitation and prospects of release and reintegration. To let the prison administration decide upon all these important matters runs the risk of solidifying a culture of dependency and favouritism (Chauvenet 1996; cited in Faugeron 1998), further widening divisions between staff and prisoners, and among prisoners themselves. Under the new aim of selective rehabilitation, this is an even greater risk.

To conclude on penitentiary programmes, based on their underpinning philosophy and practice, they can be described as a mix and match of rehabilitation and actuarial control, with the balance tilting more towards the latter. Prisoners' actuarial management commences effectively at the selection stage where great selectivity applies, and continues well into the execution stage with their monitoring by electronic tagging. The fact that a minority of those eligible for the programmes succeeds in securing a place on them (Tak 2003: 95; Boone and van Swaaningen 2013: 23), as well as completing them, is further evidence of this.

While selective rehabilitation is at the service of actuarialism, the majority of prisoners, among whom we find those on short sentences who typically have the highest re-offending rates, is excluded from rehabilitation. For example, based on the latest CoE Annual Penal Statistics (Aebi et al. 2015: 91, 96) in 2014 there were 2420 prisoners on sentences from less than a month to less than a year, representing 44.3% of the prison population. Due to their sentence lengths, they are automatically excluded from penitentiary programmes and are unconditionally released. Based on the above the innovation of penitentiary programmes (Kelk 2001: 479) is that they are quite uninnovative, succeeding at excluding most of their target group, as well as those most at risk of re-offending. Perhaps, the innovation lies precisely here considering the break from tradition that the Dutch penal policy has taken over the years.

The EBI Regime in Vught

It can be argued that the aforementioned break from tradition is best exemplified in the one and only supermax facility in Vught. It opened in 1993 following a spate of highly publicised and violent escapes from the four dispersed extra-security units (EBIs), as well as mainstream establishments, in the early 1990s (Resodihardjo 2009: 53–54, 59–68). The supermax houses prisoners who pose a risk of escape and/or whose escape poses a threat to public safety (King and Resodihardjo 2010: 73), and since 2006 people 'charged with, or sentenced for, a terrorist offence, or of spreading a message of extremism among fellow inmates' in a separate terrorist department (CPT 2008). Although it has been a proven success in the sense that no escapes have taken place, it has been controversial. It has attracted severe criticism from the CPT through the years (CPT 1998a, 2002b, 2008) and has led to successful cases before the ECtHR where its regime was found in violation of Art 3.

Being a supermax, the facility is a fortified place. It is manned by a selection of experienced staff and is highly regimented. Its daily activities do not follow a set timetable lest preparations for escapes be made (Boin 2001). EBI prisoners have the same rights with mainstream prisoners under the 1999 PPA and Penitentiary Order, but, evidently, due to their high-security status their prison life is structured in a way so as to meet the overarching security needs of the institution. This unavoidably impacts on their prison experience, rendering it far more restrictive and controlled. EBI has its own rules, the 1998 EBI House Rules, and placement procedure (Lorse & Others v The Netherlands 2003).

For example, based on the 1998 EBI House Rules:

Contact with the outside world of non-privileged nature is recorded (e.g. correspondence, calls and visits). Visitors are searched before an open visit, and physical contact between them and prisoners is limited to a handshake on arrival and departure (ibid.: para. 37). In terms of the regime in place, prisoners are handcuffed both inside and outside the institution. Inside, the practice is usually applied when the prisoner may access dangerous objects, for example, on their way to open visits and to the health clinic. Frisking and strip-searching are customary when arriving in and leaving the institution, before and after open visits, after visits to the clinic, the dentist and the hairdresser. For the maintenance of security or the protection of the prisoner's own health, an internal physical search may also take place, which a doctor or a nurse performs (ibid.).

The EBI regime in Vught is a stark deviation from the once firmly held belief in and practice of humane containment that was deemed suitable even for escape-prone prisoners. In the past, such a security fortress was not seen as a pragmatic, viable and productive solution to security issues. It was generally agreed that ubiquitous restrictions on space, time, association and activities, coupled with round-the-clock surveillance, would foment, gradually but surely, widespread discontent and unrest that could, instead of preventing escapes, lead to them. Heavy-handed methods of control and order were thought to be a ticking time bomb. In erecting intractable communication barriers between officers and prisoners and isolating them from each other, intelligence information and tacit co-operation would be lost, compromising the institution's ability to pre-empt control and security problems. Based on this way of thinking, relational security as opposed to physical security was the safest and most effective approach because 'content prisoners would not try to escape' (Boin 2001: 336, 338).

As mentioned earlier, the supermax has disproved this belief. Discontented prisoners would not try to escape provided that security is high, and control and order are uniformly exercised and applied. While self-evidently no escapes are an indicator of a reformed system (Resodihardjo 2009: 153–176), they do not tell us much about the quality of the reform and its sustainability or even its desirability in the long term. CPT inspection reports and relevant ECtHR case law clearly demonstrate this, highlighting that a reformed system is not always a good system worthy of emulation.

To date, the CPT has inspected the supermax facility three times, in 1997, 2002 and 2007. While the focus of the first two inspections was the now-centralised EBI unit, the last inspection focused on the recently created terrorist department. In the first two inspections, the CPT assessed the EBI regime to be very impoverished and sounded the alarm regarding prisoners' continued deprivation of wider, regular and constructive human contact (CPT 1998a: para. 67, 2002b: para. 37–39). Its 1997 inspection findings were so disconcerting that led the Committee to the conclusion that 'the regime…could be considered to amount to inhuman treatment. To subject prisoners classified as dangerous to such a regime could well render them more dangerous still' (CPT 1998a: para. 69). Central to the CPT's conclusion was prisoners' development of emotional, mental and psychological afflictions, which were manifested in feelings of helplessness and powerlessness, rage against others and own self, and poor verbal skills. The gravely damaging effects on prisoners continued long after leaving the institution, with former EBI prisoners also complaining of insomnia and anxiety (CPT 1998a: para. 68, 2000b: para. 38). It was not long before the CPT warnings that the regime itself was dangerous and unsafe became a reality. In 1999 a prisoner's death during a fight with a fellow prisoner in the exercise yard exposed the limitations and limits of security. As a result of the officers' physical separation from the exercise yard by armoured glass panels and the prohibition of direct contact with more than one prisoner at a time, the fight that broke out very quickly could not be stopped (CPT 2002b: para. 35).

In addition, the CPT has expressed concerns over the lack of medical confidentiality and the fairness of EBI placements. It has criticised officers' presence and the handcuffing of prisoners in medical examinations, as well as the physical separation of prisoners from medical staff by a glass screen in consultation sessions (CPT 1998a : para. 76–77, 2002b : para. 43). It also found that once a decision was made to place a prisoner in EBI, their placement was hardly likely to be terminated. First time EBI allocations and their renewals were based on the same criteria (e.g. the seriousness of the offence, the offender's risk of danger and escape, and public reactions to it), without taking into account positive behavioural and attitudinal changes. This resulted in prisoners being detained in maximum-security conditions till their release (CPT 2002b: para. 41).

The CPT expressed the same concerns over the lack of medical confidentiality and clarity in the placement procedure in its 2007 visit to the terrorist department, calling for the introduction of comprehensive individualised risk assessments and regular reviews of such placements. Moreover, it highlighted the implications of the restricted association in place, which due to the small size of the terrorist department risked being akin to isolation when prisoner tensions arose and prisoners had to be separated (CPT 2008: para. 41–42, 47, 52–53).

Interestingly, a preliminary study on the EBI regime by Nijmegen University[2] in 2001 showed that staff was discontented. Many considered that their physical separation from prisoners complicated further an already highly demanding job and viewed the regime as monolithic. They believed that there was scope for more flexibility and diversification, which would enable them to establish a close rapport with some of the more receptive prisoners—an essential prerequisite for combatting stress, insecurity and mistrust on both sides. The study revealed that informally a more diversified approach was gradually followed, and there was a general consensus among officers about the value of sharing knowledge, experience and feelings. Arbitrary and aggressive behaviour on their part was seen as injurious to their role and was widely condemned (Boin 2001: 342).

The Nijmegen evaluation was followed up with research by the Free University of Amsterdam into the psychological effects of the regime on current and former EBI prisoners. Published in 2003, it partially supported the CPT findings. It concurred with the CPT that the dearth of intellectual stimulation contributed to the atrophy of prisoners' cognitive functioning. EBI detainees were also more likely to suffer from depression than those held in a restricted but community regime, the onset of which was accelerated by the unanimously regarded as humiliating strip-searches. Their daily life, however, had a routine that provided a sense of security while there was no supporting evidence of persistent psychosomatic symptoms afflicting prisoners (Salah v The Netherlands 2006).

[2] The Nijmegen and Free University of Amsterdam evaluations were the government's response to the CPT's recommendation for an independent examination of the regime's impact on current and former EBI detainees' psychological well-being.

Before long though, within three years these research findings were supplemented with five ECtHR judgments on EBI prisoners' treatment, which all concluded that aspects of the regime violated Art 3. The five EBI cases, which are actually clone cases, are *Van der Ven v The Netherlands* (2003), *Lorse & Others v The Netherlands* (2003), *Baybasin v The Netherlands* (2006), *Sylla v The Netherlands* (2006), and *Salah v The Netherlands* (2006).

Central to the ECtHR finding of an Art 3 violation in *Van der Ven v The Netherlands* and *Lorse & Others v The Netherlands* were (a) the unnecessary and unjustified regularity (more than once a week) of and circumstances within which the practices of cell-searching and anal examinations, known euphemistically as visitations, took place (irrespective of whether prisoners had left their cells or had a visit), and (b) their cumulative detrimental impact on the prisoners' mental, psychological and physical well-being. When the practices were examined vis-à-vis the nature of the regime, which was by far the most oppressive nationally, the known to the authorities frailty of the applicants and their atypically lengthy detention in EBI (3 years and 5 months, and 6 years and 4 months, respectively), they were found humiliating and degrading (Van der Ven v The Netherlands 2003: para. 52–63; Lorse & Others v The Netherlands 2003: para. 64–74).

The government responded quickly to the above findings and amended the EBI House Rule 6(4) on strip-searches within a month of the delivery of the judgments. Since March 2003 strip-searches have stopped being a standard aspect of the weekly cell inspections and take place instead randomly in the course of or after cell searches (Baybasin v The Netherlands 2006: para. 21). This, however, did not bring 'closure'. In the space of four months, the troublesome Rule had to be modified twice on judges' orders. In June 2003, 13 EBI detainees were granted an interim injunction against the March amendment that resulted in another one. Since July 2003 the practice is individualised on the basis of monthly risk assessments and its combined application with cell searches is abandoned (ibid.: para. 22). Meanwhile, three similar to *Van der Ven* and *Lorse & Others* cases reached the ECtHR, and a violation of Art 3 was again found in respect of the prisoners' subjection to weekly strip-searching between 1998 and 2003 (Baybasin v The

Netherlands 2006: para. 49, 57–61; Sylla v The Netherlands 2006: para. 58–62; Salah v The Netherlands 2006: para. 55–59).

To conclude on the Dutch supermax prison, in the wake of the escapes the Dutch Prison Service and the government were undoubtedly confronted with formidable challenges. The escapes did represent not only a security crisis, revealing structural and operational deficiencies in urgent need of reform, but also a legitimacy crisis, exposing the failure of the state to run efficiently one of its institutions and to protect its citizens and employees. In situations like this one, drastic measures may seem befitting, but, as the CPT and the ECtHR have shown, they do not fix security issues for good and do not solve the legitimacy crisis; actually, they augment it. The tragic prisoner death in 1999 was further proof of the relevance and instrumentality relational security has in fostering and sustaining a safe and secure custody environment, as well as in enabling the state to fulfil its positive duty of care to those in its custody and care. At the end, difficult situations entail taking difficult decisions. In the present case, the difficult decision is to recognise and protect as much prisoners' human rights as those of the public.

TBS Combined Sentences

The entrustment order for mentally disordered offenders (TBS), which involves hospitalisation in a forensic psychiatric setting, is among the oldest criminal law sanctions, introduced in 1928 (Downes and van Swaaningen 2007: 63). Based on the Dutch dualistic system of criminal sanctions, it is a measure as opposed to being a penalty. As a penal measure, it does not require conclusive proof of criminal liability and is forward looking; that is, it does not aim at retribution and general prevention but at individual deterrence and public protection (Tak 2008: 111).

The TBS measure is reserved for violent and/or sex offenders, who have diminished/strongly diminished responsibility, or a total absence of responsibility due to suffering from a mental disorder, and whose offences attract a prison sentence of four years or more. TBS aims to decrease the offender's risk of recidivism by treating the underlying mental disorder that is assessed to be an associative cause of their criminal behaviour (de Ruiter and Trestman 2007; Koeraadt and Mooij 2007). TBS offenders have usually a personality disorder (PD), with some suffering from psychotic disorders following from a dual diagnosis (Koeraadt and Mooij 2007: 173, 180).

TBS is directly relevant to the carceral context because in cases of diminished and strongly diminished responsibility it can be combined with a prison sentence (ibid.: 173). The prison sentence precedes TBS, with the latter following within six months of the completion of the former (Art 76(1), 1999 PPA).[3] When the statutory six-month limit cannot be met (e.g. due to shortage of beds), the transfer to the psychiatric clinic can be postponed for three months (Art 76(2), 1999 PPA). The legislation does not set a maximum number of delays that can be allowed. Moreover, TBS patients can be detained in a prison remand centre as an interim measure when there is no availability of forensic beds (Art 9(2f), 1999 PPA).

Once TBS commences, it is reviewed biannually by the courts and can be extended for one or two years each time. For treatment purposes, six years is the maximum length of a TBS order. However, if at the six-year mark, the patient's risk remains high, they are transferred to a long-stay ward. There, their case is reviewed every two years. In long-stay wards, the focus shifts from treatment, aiming at the patient's return to society, to the provision of 'the necessary security and psychiatric and medical care' (DJI 2007a: 2). From this stage onwards, the patient's secure hospitalisation can effectively be lifelong if the outcome of their reviews shows no acceptable reductions in the risk they pose. In such cases, they can only apply for supervised leave on humanitarian grounds (Santegoeds 2013). Following a review of the forensic psychiatric sector in 2006, the government has extended the supervision of TBS released patients in the community to nine years. The rationale behind this was that the effectiveness of psychiatric treatment could only be judged with the passage of time, and nine years provided ample time for informed evaluations and assessments of changes in care plans (DJI 2007a : 2–3, 2007b : 28). Suffice to note here that in the case of other prisoner groups,

[3]To ease pressure on the penal capacity, in 2000s the Fokkens regulation enabled prisoner transfers to clinics after serving one-third of the prison sentence. This came to an end in 2010 (van Swaaningen 2013: 352).

we would call this a licence period. While this move can be interpreted in the vein of the old saying that 'one way of abolishing prisons is to turn society into a prison', which van Swaaningen brings to our attention (2013: 354), this is not the most controversial aspect of TBS as we shall see below.

Based on its submission of evidence on mental healthcare in the Netherlands to the UN Committee Against Torture, Stichting Mind Rights reported that there were between 2100 and 2200 TBS patients in 2010. Ninety-five percent were male between the ages of 30 and 40, with 60–70% of them being Dutch nationals, with research showing a higher incidence of psychotic disorders in ethnic minority defendants (Santegoeds 2013 : 46–47; Vinkers et al. 2013 : 1401–1403). In 2011, less than 50% of those who had started treatment in 2002 were back into the community (Santegoeds 2013 : 46–47). The figures reflect big increases in the number of TBS patients and in their length of their orders, a trend that started in 1986 and continued through the 1990s and 2000s (Brand v The Netherlands 2004; Koeraadt and Mooij 2007: 179–181). The increase in the number of people with mental disorders has been attributed to addictions, the increased complexity of mental health conditions and wider societal issues, such as marginalisation (Koeraadt and Mooij 2007: 168; Vinkers et al. 2013). This has put the TBS sector under immense capacity pressure that became the focus of CPT reports, raising concerns over the quality of TBS care and the treatment of such patients (CPT 1993 : para. 130, 1998a : para. 110–134), and the subject of successful litigation.

It must be said that TBS combined sentences are intrinsically controversial. The controversy arises from the very fact that the TBS measure and the penalty of imprisonment can be actually combined, and that the prison sentence takes place before TBS hospitalisation. From a therapeutic and a human rights perspective, this combination and arrangement raises issues over prisoners' right to equivalence in healthcare and the state's duty to protect not only those in its custody/care but also its employees. To start with, as things stand, the aim of TBS, which is to provide mental health treatment to the prisoner, is defeated. While in prison, the prisoner cannot access the specialised care that the very imposition of TBS shows that they need. No matter how well organised and resourced in prison mental health services are, a mainstream prison is not a therapeutic environment. It is always custody driven, with mental healthcare playing a secondary role to control, order and security. The waiting period in prison, which can be substantially prolonged, can in combination with the lack of treatment lead to deterioration in the prisoner's condition.

Apropos of all this, it would have been in the prisoner's and the public's best interests if TBS had preceded the prison sentence or if the latter was not imposed at all. The provision of timely treatment surely stands a greater chance of success. Successful treatment means improved health and quality of life for the patient whose reduced risk enhances public safety.

The chronic capacity shortages in the TBS sector exemplify these concerns while *Morsink v The Netherlands* (2004) and *Brand v The Netherlands* (2004) show that delays in patients' transfers from the prison to the clinic can compromise their right to liberty and security (Art 5). In *Morsink* and *Brand*, which are clone cases, the applicants argued that the continuation of their detention in a remand centre beyond the end of their prison sentence due to a lack of available TBS places was unlawful. Based on their argument, (a) their continued detention bore no correspondence to the purpose of TBS, which was to receive specialised treatment they had been unable to access, and (b) it was unacceptable practice to detain TBS offenders in prison remand conditions. The ECtHR found that a delay of more than 15 months in *Morsink* and more than 6 months in *Brand* were unacceptable, giving rise to a violation of Art 5(1). It is worth noting the Court's view that 'A significant delay in admission to a custodial clinic and thus the beginning of the treatment … will obviously affect the prospects of the treatment's success within the statutory two year timeframe for the initial validity of a TBS order' (Morsink v The Netherlands 2004: para. 4, 50, 60, 68–69; Brand v The Netherlands 2004: para. 4, 11, 46, 56–57, 65–66).

In addition to delays in the commencement of TBS, legal procedural failings in TBS renewals have also featured in ECtHR case law. In *Erkalo v The Netherlands* (1998) the ECtHR found a violation of Art 5(1) after the state had failed to ensure its legal procedures were respected. The Prosecution Service had failed to meet the deadline provisions stipulated in the Code of Criminal Procedure (CCP) for requesting a TBS extension order. As a result, the applicant was in custody for 82 days without knowing whether he would be released and fundamentally with no judicial authorisation of his detention. Moreover, the reviewing court had failed to 'ensure the applicant's release from detention would not be unreasonably delayed' since it was the applicant who brought the authorities' attention to it (para. 51–60). In *Rutten v the Netherlands* (2001), the ECtHR found a violation of Art 5(4). The judicial decisions authorising the applicant's TBS renewal had been delivered far beyond of what could be regarded as reasonably late and acceptable for the purposes of Art 5(4). The statutory two-month limit the Regional Court had to decide on the prosecutor's request for an extension of the applicant's TBS detention had been exceeded for more than a month, while the Court of Appeal had taken more than three months to deliver its judgment (para. 39, 52–55).

In 2005 and 2006, the clone cases of *Nakach v the Netherlands* and *Schenkel v the Netherlands* brought to light another procedural failing. Pursuant to Art 25 of the CCP, a court judgment must be accompanied inter alia by an official record of its hearing. This official record should document 'the statements made and of any further events that have occurred at the hearing' (Nakach v the Netherlands 2005: para. 25). Both applicants argued that the absence of such a record in their appeal judgments against the prolongation of their TBS treatment violated their rights under Art 5(1) since 'a procedure prescribed by law' had not been adhered to. Noting in its judgment three separate Supreme Court rulings, which had invalidated judicial decisions on the above grounds, the ECtHR concluded that the procedural requirement of Art 5(1) had not been satisfied (Nakach v the Netherlands 2005: 39–44; Schenkel v the Netherlands 2006: 32–33).

Lastly, in *van der Velden v the Netherlands* (2012) the ECtHR similarly found a violation of Art 5(1). The applicant's extension of his TBS detention beyond the four-year period did not abide by the relevant CCP requirements since the offences he had been convicted of were not 'directed against, or endangered, the bodily inviolability of one or more persons' (para. 18, 25, 34–36).

Based on the above, the potentially indeterminate nature of TBS and the possibility of recall to the clinic in the course of the nine-year community supervision render the measure fearsome (Koeraadt and Mooij 2007: 177). We can arguably say that it is more akin to a penalty than a measure, resembling either an indeterminate prison sentence or a life sentence. As such, TBS is not unique but part of a wider trend towards a greater use of penal preventive detention of offenders who have particularly complex and challenging mental health needs. Like other similar Dutch and non-Dutch interventions (see Chap. 3, and the ISD measure in the next section), it selectively incapacitates those it identifies as risky for as long as necessary. In short, it is another measure in the arsenal of actuarial justice.

The ISD Penal Measure

Further evidence of the degree to which twenty-first-century Dutch criminal justice policy has been driven by an actuarial discourse is found in the ISD penal measure. The ISD measure, which means 'institution for repeat offenders', was introduced in 2004, replacing the SOV penal measure that had been introduced three years earlier (Struijk 2015).

In some respects, ISD is the same with SOV. It too targets persistent offenders in an attempt to 'tackle a societal nuisance' (Downes and van Swaaningen 2007: 63), involves automatic pre-trial detention and can last for a maximum period of two years. However, its target group is not limited to addicts but extends to persistent offenders of all kinds of backgrounds, including illegal immigrants since 2009. Also, it can be ordered as many times the courts judge that it is required but not in combination with a penalty (e.g. imprisonment) like in the cases of SOV and TBS. Crucially, whereas SOV aimed at public safety and rehabilitation, which was reflected in its regime, ISD focuses solely on public safety by the means of pure and simple incapacitation that is evidenced in its adoption of the standard regime (Struijk 2015: 158, 162).

In an examination of the ISD measure, Struijk (2015: 164) concludes that the jury is still out regarding the use and future of the measure. For example, in 2012 ISD was ordered 280 times compared to 420 in 2005. While judges have supported the measure and its aims, they have not done so uncritically, striving to balance the competing interests of public safety and offenders' rights. This shows that judicial considerations of rehabilitation have not altogether disappeared (ibid: 161). However, we cannot but notice the following developments.

Penal measures, such as TBS, SOV, and ISD are being in actuality employed as penalties, aiming at preventive detention and incapacitation, all in the name of public safety. Moreover, SOV and ISD go a step further and become textbook examples of actuarial justice. In targeting specific groups of people, who have been identified as persistent recidivists, they selectively incapacitate them in a 'consistent, consequent and credible manner', as envisaged in the policy paper *Society and Crime* (1985; cited in Blad 2003: 132) more than 20 years ago.

This approach to punishment and treatment of offenders, which has no nationality, promotes a deeply cynical view of human nature and potential. In doing so, it individualises, pathologises and essentialises human weaknesses, and rebrands social ills and the state's inability to protect its citizenry everywhere and from everything as personal failures. In choosing whom to condemn to perpetual failure (selective incapacitation and preventive detention) and whom to give a second chance (selective rehabilitation), risk assessments and their statistical calculations acquire a messianic quality that plays God with people's lives.

Life Sentences

Based on the latest CoE Annual Penal Statistics, in 2014 there were 32 lifers in the Netherlands. Although this is not a high number in absolute terms, with lifers representing 0.6% of the Dutch prison population (Aebi et al. 2015: 96), when we examine it in relation to earlier periods and practice, we are confronted with a situation that is at odds with ECHR.

Bearing in mind that the Dutch Criminal Code does not provide for a mandatory life sentence like the English Murder (Abolition of Death Penalty) Act 1965 (Tak 2008: 112), in the 1970s no such sentence was ordered by the courts, and in the 1980s, only three were imposed in 1982, 1983 and 1987, respectively (Noorduyn 2008). While in theory life has meant lifelong imprisonment, up until 1998 lifers could petition the Crown for pardon through the Pardons Act, which, if granted, commuted their lifelong imprisonment to a fixed-term sentence. Moreover, there was a general acceptance in official policy circles that the principles of rehabilitation and resocialisation applied equally to lifers. Like fixed-term prisoners, they too were expected to be released. Evidence of this is found in a 1978 ministerial directive entitled 'For the selection and detention support of long term inmates and of persons sentenced to imprisonment and placed at the disposal of the government'. Despite the omission of life sentences from the title, its procedural guidelines on issues, such as sentence planning, risk assessment and progress evaluation, were inclusive of the lifer group; and it allowed of pardon (Noorduyn 2008: 12–13).

Confirming Pakes' s observation of the advent of a 'Garlandian crime complex' (2004: 285), the above directive was abandoned in 1998, and in 2004 a ministerial announcement on life sentences clarified that pardon was no longer an option; Dutch lifers had no prospect of release. This position was endorsed in 2006 by the Supreme Court and the Council for the Administration of Criminal Justice and Protection of Juveniles (Noorduyn 2008 : 13).

This has been another unprecedented development for Dutch standards, a cause for grave discontent among lifers (see Chap. 6) and a seriously alarming step from a human rights perspective. More specifically, human rights soft law, such as CoE Recommendations (2003) (23) and (22), and relevant CPT standards are ignored. All three sources treat a life sentence as a determinate sentence, albeit a long one, and consequently see rehabilitation and reintegration as integral to the execution of such sentence. For example, Recommendation (2003)23 *on the management by prison administrations of life sentence and other long term prisoners* lists among the objectives of life sentences to 'increase and improve the possibilities for these prisoners to be successfully resettled in society and to lead a law abiding life…' It therefore makes explicit the expectation that a lifer will be eventually released on the grounds of which their access to rehabilitation and resettlement initiatives is as relevant as that of 'security and safety considerations'. Recommendation (2003)22 *on conditional release* provides a strong re-affirmation of the expectation of release and calls for a review mechanism for 'real life sentences…to establish whether a life sentence prisoner can serve the remainder of the sentence in the community and under what conditions and supervision measures'. In a similar vein, CPT standards on *Life sentenced and other long term prisoners* call for 'individualised custody plans and appropriate psycho-social support…in assisting such prisoners to come to terms with their period of incarceration and, when the time comes, to prepare for release' (CPT 2015: 28).

Moreover, the implications from relevant ECtHR case law on life sentences have not been duly considered yet (Claessen 2014: 2–3). For example, *Kafkaris v Cyprus* (2008), *Iorgov (no.2) v Bulgaria* (2010), *Vinter & Others v UK* (2013), *Laszlo Magyar v Hungary* (2014), *Ocalan (no.2) v Turkey* (2014), *Harakchiev and Tolumov v Bulgaria* (2014), and *Murray v The Netherlands* (2016) have all established the following: while states enjoy a wide margin of appreciation as to the length of life sentences, and lifelong imprisonment per se is not at odds with the ECHR, such sentences must nevertheless be de jure and de facto reducible to be compatible with the ECHR; otherwise, they amount to inhuman or degrading treatment or punishment (Art 3). This entails that (a) the lifer must be offered opportunities for rehabilitation and an assessment of their needs based on which a rehabilitation plan can be drawn; (b) they must be in a position to know from the start of their sentence what actions they need to take to prepare themselves for release, the time framework within which a review of their sentence would take place and/or how to avail themselves of this opportunity; (c) there must be an established review procedure in place so as to adequately assess the lifer's progress for the purposes of release; and (d) the power to release must be clear and real (ECtHR 2016c).

All the above conditions are absent from the Dutch legislative and policy framework for life sentences. The current practice highlights an approach that is unrecognisable. To exchange humane containment, even if paternalistic, for strong retributivism may not be so difficult to understand in the context of the changes and events that have taken place. But, to also abandon pragmatism considering the risk of human rights violations is difficult to understand.

Conclusion

In the space of 20 years, Dutch penal policy has undergone major transformations. From being a beacon of humanity and the envy of other Western European countries, it took a punitive turn towards incapacitation and harsher punishment before it returned to more pragmatic penal politics.

Penal policy developments during the punitive years 1985–2005, their context and effects on the prisoner experience and rights share many similarities with the English experience. During that period both countries' penal policies became harsher under the influence of a risk discourse and a penal populist rhetoric in public and political life that seized upon late modern concerns about crime and anti-social behaviour, as well as about immigration and the social integration of ethnic minorities against the backdrop of international terrorism. Moreover, in order to restore/increase public confidence in government and its criminal justice system, as well as to rationalise it, both countries' systems adopted actuarial and managerialist practices that have resulted, among other things, in increases in preventive detention and life sentences. These practices led to violations of the rights of prisoners falling into these categories and in the case of the Netherlands negatively impacted on the quality of its mainstream prison regimes (see also Chap. 6). In this context, the once worthy of envy Dutch prison aims of rehabilitation and resocialisation for all became aims for those few who showed willingness to and potential for change, supported by the newly found aim of public protection through selective incapacitation.

While it can be argued that the Dutch turn towards punitivity was an expected eventuality (it would have happened sooner or later) as a result of the Netherlands being part of the global world and thus susceptible to its forces and pressures, its return to decarceration has not been expected and offers some early valuable insights.

It tentatively shows that a decarcerative penal policy is possible without the public's backing provided that there is political willingness and no major national/international events that can spark public fears over security and safety. More importantly, it shows that in contrast to progressive developments, regressive ones are particularly aggressive and establish themselves very quickly. Quantitatively, Dutch prisoner numbers have gone down for the moment, which creates dignified living conditions and provides for a greater sense of safety and security for both prisoners and staff. While these are of course positive, re-affirming the importance of maintaining sustainable prisoner numbers, a return to the formerly practised rehabilitation and resocialisation *for all* prisoners has not taken place. Selective rehabilitation and selective incapacitation have survived the punitive phase along with maximum security facility. For those who find themselves in prison, material conditions may indeed be good, but whether, based on the rehabilitation provision they can access, their chances of reintegration are equally good is another matter.

5

Human Rights in English Prisons: Prisoners' Views

Introduction

The chapter presents English prisoners' views on human rights in prison based on semi-structured interviews. Between 2004 and 2007, I interviewed 34 adults, both men and women, while they were serving their sentences or being on licence. Out of the 34, 13 were women. Ten were interviewed in prison and three in a probation office. Similarly, 12 males were interviewed in prison who fell in the lifer/CAT category,[1] and nine in the community. All participants were British citizens of different ethnicity, with the majority being white. In the male category, for six out of the nine on licence, it was their first time in prison. Three had already been sentenced to imprisonment twice before, and one had been both in a YOI and an adult prison. In terms of their age, the majority was in their thirties, with 29 being the average age. The average time spent in custody for those on licence was 20 months. In the female category, the majority was in their twenties, with the youngest being 18 and the oldest 41. The

[1] Information on lifers/CAT A prisoners is not available as a result of restrictions in place at the time of the fieldwork.

A. Karamalidou, *Embedding Human Rights in Prison*,
DOI 10.1057/978-1-137-58502-8_5

average age was 28. For eight women, this was their first prison sentence. Out of the remaining five, two had two previous prison sentences, 1 three, and 1 had one previous sentence. Two women were serving life sentences. The average time spent in custody for the female participants was three years.

In the interviews the dominant themes were prisoners' humanity and personhood. They were human beings with their own individuality, characteristics and needs like any other human being. Their prisoner status did not define or negate who they were and what they could be, aspire to and achieve. Irrespective of their prisoner status and the label of the prison, they were still, for example, social and sexual beings who had experienced parental, family and work responsibilities like any other normal person. While not all shared the same experiences and responsibilities, they were all individuals and social beings on account of their humanity, and it was on this basis that they explored human rights issues in prisons.

The chapter is divided into three main sections. The first section documents prisoners' awareness of their human rights, their understanding of the term as such and views on the idea of prisoners having human rights. The second section documents the contribution human rights can make to prisoners' lives and details ways for its realisation. The third section shifts the focus of attention from human rights to human responsibilities and presents prisoners' views on the idea of human responsibilities against the backdrop of their views on human rights.

Human Rights Awareness and Understanding

Human Rights Awareness

Interview responses on prisoners' human rights awareness and understanding revealed a mixed picture. With a few exceptions, while participants identified a good number of civil, political, social, economic and subsistence (human) rights either by name or through examples, they were generally uncertain about whether they were legally entitled to some of them. Asked about if they knew of or thought that there was an English human rights law, their replies ranged from *I do not know* to

I would imagine so. Only one participant named the 1998 HRA, and the lifer group pointed out that they were only aware of the ECHR. In the first case, the prison library was the source of the prisoner's knowledge, while in the second one it was the media and fellow prisoners. Moreover, while the majority treated *human rights* as more important than *rights*, they had difficulties in distinguishing one concept from the other one. They attributed their uncertainty and lack of knowledge to the inconsistent and differing application of rules in and between institutions and to the lack of official information on their human rights, given either by prison staff or their legal representatives. The quotations below capture this widely shared view.

> Each prison is so different so I do not actually know what I am entitled to. You hear a lot of people say, 'this is against our human rights', but no one really knows what your rights are in prison.
>
> When you are coming to prison, you are not told about your human rights. They should tell people because they do not know what they are entitled to and what not; what they should and should not be doing. If you are not told, and it is not explained to you, you do not know at the end of the day.

In dissenting from the above view, for the lifer group and one of the participants the underlying reason for prisoners' lack of knowledge of their human rights was not to be found within the prison walls but in the outside world.

> In this country we do not have a written constitution. No constitution means that we are not taught what it means to be a citizen, what makes a good and a bad citizen. No constitution-no protection of human rights; and not knowing what our duties and responsibilities as citizens are.

It is worth noting that this was not the only instance where participants linked human rights in prison with human rights in society in general. As we will see, in spite of their disagreement over the origins of human rights, they were conscious of the great influence both the state in its political and legal constitution and culture have on societal attitudes towards human rights, the scope of their recognition and the degree of their protection. Also, their reflections on whether prisoners are deserving of human rights protection compared to the ones offered by the Dutch (see Chap. 6) can be seen to be indicative, to some extent, of sensitivities specific to the wider culture they were part of. This was further evidenced in their conceptualisations of human rights in prison, with the comparative exercise bringing to the foreground the lasting impact of their differing legal cultures and political economies.

In this context, the most common understanding of human rights was in terms of equality within the scope of the non-discrimination principle and freedom from ill-treatment (physical, psychological and mental). The next most common reference was to *the basic entitlements and needs as a human*, being described as the rights to eat, to drink (water) and to maintain one's personal hygiene through regular access to washing facilities. These were followed by the rights to communicate with the outside world through visits, correspondence and phone calls; to respect for private and family life; to work and education; the freedom of thought, conscience and religion, with the ability to complain without the fear of penalisation; the rights to a professional and easily accessible medical care; to legal assistance and representation; to vote; and, lastly to autonomy in the sense of being able to choose whom they could socialise with and would confide about their problems.

English Prisoners' Understanding and Reflections on Their Human Rights

Despite their struggle to pinpoint the difference between human rights and rights, the majority recognised the privileged status of the former. Based on their views, they formed into three groups: *the humanists, the positivists,* and *the pragmatists*. In an argument strongly redolent of theorists such as Rousseau (1762), Paine (1791), Midgley (1978), Gewirth (1983) and Brugger (1996), *the humanists*, representing the majority, saw in human rights axiomatic principles and natural entitlements, which symbolised and facilitated the expression of their humanity. Their argument was that our advanced mental faculties, the gamut of our emotions and the wide range of our psychological needs render being human unique. Human rights protected the very essence of being human, cast in terms of our abilities to act, to exercise our intellect, to have and communicate our feelings and emotions.

> The ability to think rationally, to listen, to comprehend, and to engage in a dialogue. It is a rational thing as opposed to an animalistic activity.
>
> We are individuals, breath, cannot be separated and be placed in boxes. Each individual decides what is good for them to do; what they want to do in their life; what they think is good and right for them to do.

In contrast, *the positivists*, representing the minority view, opined that human rights are legal entitlements whose content and provision are decreed by and are wholly dependent on the will of the state. Their purpose is to ensure that people are *treated properly* and thus to maintain *normality*, and their legalisation is put into place to effect this. When positivists talk about *proper* treatment, they refer to *equal* and *considerate* treatment, captured in the dictum 'Do as you want to be done onto.' Normality refers to an organised and reciprocal system of living where people can pursue their interests without being impeded by and impeding others, with a Hobbesian state of affairs being envisaged as the opposite. For positivists, unless human rights are legally enshrined, they are stripped off legitimacy. To quote Bentham (1843), they are 'nonsense upon stilts' whose intended objects and subjects of protection change at whim.

> I believe that human rights are things, which have been set out by the government, by law. They are about how prisoners are to be held properly in prisons. Once you are in prison, anything can happen to you. From the time you commit a crime, go to court, and the judge sentences you to prison, that's it. They look at us as prisoners. Once you come here, all the little things that you could take on board when outside are not happening. The government can change it. Unless the government says this is the way things will start running in prisons, obviously those running the prisons will run them differently.
>
> Human rights is like law, is written in black and white. You have the human right to be treated fairly and although you feel you deserve the right to be spoken with respect, it is not actually a human right, is it?

Pragmatists, who represented the next most dominant view, shared with humanists the view of human rights as natural rights on account of the commonly observable and experienced attributes of human nature. They saw, however, the state and its officials as the catalyst for human rights recognition and enforcement, with a few raising the thorny issue of human rights relativism whose scope and provision was seen to be affected by society's culture and the form of political government. This element of precariousness made some pessimistic and fatalistic about the human rights cause in general and its prospects in prison in particular.

> I come originally from China. I would not like to be in prison there. If you compare England and China, prisoners in England have human rights. They are respected. You hear about human rights abuses in China. Back at home the individual is not important; where they belong to is. So, it depends on the perspective you want to see it from. I am happy I am in England.
>
> Everyone is born with human rights, but I suppose it depends where you are. In other parts of the world, people got locked up 20 to a cell. That's not proper treatment. They do not have human rights. They cannot treat us like that here because of the government. They will get done. Here, we are free. We have the House of Lords, Democrats, and all that. They make decisions and if they do not agree, they can say this and do not have to go forward. Whereas, I do not know if I am right, in other countries they just have one government and are not free. So, when decisions are made, they are made.
>
> In prison, human rights count nothing.

As discussed, while the participants recognised the primacy of human rights, they treated different things as human rights, some identified more than others, and their opinions diverged on the foundations of the human rights idea. As soon as consideration of whether prisoners are deserving of human rights recognition and protection was under way, these divisions disappeared quickly, but not entirely. Responses yielded a unanimous but qualified yes. As long as the discussion remained general, the question had a unifying effect. Once it went into specific prisoner groups, divisions re-emerged.

Typically, the participants' immediate response was a strong reminder that irrespective of their offences they were still human. To them, this was self-evident. Since they embodied typical qualities of human nature, consequently they had and deserved human rights. At this point, they were all humanists.

In their experience, imprisonment did not erase their instinctual needs for personal and social development, and their sociability. Confinement, whatever its length, was incapable of negating their humanity and suppressing it. From a human rights perspective, their self-portrayal as human beings qua 'reasoned and purposive agents', if they are allowed to be, re-affirms Gewirth's (1983: 2, 12) proposition of action and, more specifically, of the ability to act as the core of human experience and human rights. Like Gewirth (1983: 14–15), they singled out volition and intentionality as the 'generic features of action', and identified the abilities to reason and to make decisions, and the right to protect their dignity and self-esteem as 'its proximate necessary conditions'. Furthermore, their references to their abilities for self-determination and taking personal responsibility for their actions, as well as their need for meaningfulness in life by making, inter alia, lifestyle choices, coincide with Brugger's (1996) 'image of the person'[2] that his human rights formula of personhood is built upon. Ultimately, their self-portrayal is the embodiment of Kantian dignity, defined in the Metaphysics of Morals (1897) as the human capacity for autonomy and self-discipline.

> Living and hoping. The prison does not get to know you as a person.
>
> We are able to decide for ourselves, to understand right from wrong although not abiding by it. We are capable of adapting if they allow us to.
>
> We are all individuals. We got rights to things and have opinions. So, we should not be shouted at. It does not matter if you are white, purple, pink.
>
> Yes, because we are human, alive and got souls. We are real, aren't we? We are people. Our mind makes us unique. We all think differently.

---

[2] Brugger's (1996) human rights formula of personhood aims at enabling a 'self-determinate, meaningful and responsible way of leading one's life' (p. 4). To be able to lead such a life we need: (a) self-determination; (b) meaningfulness—the ability to exercise and enjoy autonomy in a manner and in an environment that foster a sense of belonging; (c) the exercise (of personal and social) responsibility; (d) protection of life, and (e) lifestyle—to be able to choose and follow one's preferred way of living even when it is not socially, culturally or spiritually supported.

Their human status and the necessary conditions to protect it were not the only premises upon which the participants qualified their right to human rights recognition and protection. In their view, any dividing line between themselves and law-abiding people ceased to exist by the mere fact of serving their sentence. They gave three reasons for this. First, their prison sentence was passed by an officially recognised and competent court. In passing a sentence, the court publicly upbraided and punished them for their prohibited deeds. The authority that the court carries in itself and lends to its decisions signals that justice was served. By virtue of the court's legitimate authority, in the wake of its judgment no one had any legitimate role and purpose in aggravating their punishment. Second, and related to the first reason, their prison sentence communicated not only the type of sanction and its length but also its nature. Their imprisonment was their punishment, and not for punishment. Crucially, it was the most severe punishment they could receive for it deprived them of and limited a number of fundamental freedoms and rights, starting with the second most fundamental right in life after the right to life itself, that is, the right to be free.

It is worth noting that the participants' reference to the right to free went beyond the right to liberty and security. The deprivation of their liberty had a domino effect. It did not only affect them, but it reached out to those close to them. Although its impact was vicarious and differed, it did not negate the fact that their friends and families were also constrained by their imprisonment. In more detail, their own lack of physical freedom entailed limited freedom to move spatially within the confines of the institution, to socialise, to work, to support their family, to express themselves, to make choices, to be in contact with people of their choice and to invest on relationships with them, with the last two equally applicable to their friends and relatives.

The third ground upon which they argued for the rightful recognition and protection of their human rights was the prison's legitimacy as punishment. The prison's legitimacy rested on its effectiveness. For the prison to be effective, its aims and administration ought to reflect the character and needs of the people in its custody. In this respect, emphasis was placed on fallibility and the ability to learn from one's mistakes and improve as characteristically human characteristics. Their humanity required that punishment in general and prison in particular should aim principally at enabling them to appreciate the error of their ways with a view to assist them in leading a responsible life. Recognition of and respect for their human rights were instrumental to this end.

> Your rights should not be taken away because everything else has been taken away from you, especially if you are married, or have kids, a girlfriend on the outside. You still have your mother, father, brother and sisters. All your family is suffering, as well as you. There is always someone out there, who has not been in prison and has made a mistake; maybe a serious mistake and they got away with it. There is the police out there committing crimes and get away with it. Because of this everybody should have rights really. Everybody does something wrong in their life. That is how we learn. You just got to learn from your mistakes. If you do not learn from them and keep going back in, then you have a serious problem.
>
> Our freedom is taken away. That is where punishment stops. We paid our debt to society. It is not even that we have to pay our debt to society. We did something wrong; that is, why we are here.
>
> They think we do not deserve anything because we are criminals. At the end of the day everyone is human. No one is perfect. They need to be careful carrying on with that because they have families and children. They could end up in the same situation. How would they feel if they were treated that way? It is discrimination and laziness. They do not care and always want to go as if they are so perfect because they have a home to go to, have the keys. It is hard as it is, and they do not have to rub it in.
>
> If you want to rehabilitate people back into society, you should give them some sense of belonging rather than always create distance and suppress them.

The last quotation above is an exemplar of the English view on the overall aim of imprisonment within a context of a human rights-informed penal policy. It identified prisoners' rehabilitation and social reintegration as the aims of imprisonment, and human rights as the means to achieve them through their normalising influence on prison life. More specifically, by drawing attention to the human rights potential to individually empower and socially emancipate prisoners so as to be able to productively contribute to society upon their release, it starkly highlighted the inextricable connection between human rights recognition in prison and in society at large.

Equally important is also its unequivocal re-affirmation of prisoners as members of society despite their imprisonment. As said in the introduction, the participants' acceptance of their prisoner status did not equate with their identification with it. They did not regard their prisoner identity as defining who they were. Across interviews, they reiterated the point of their being as normal as the next person on the outside. As one participant put it, *it could be me sitting there, and you sitting here.* Their criminal record did not make them abnormal, at least not all of them as we shall soon see. Their commonly shared humanity with others, including their having close relationships with *normal others,* was a testament to this. In addition, their views on certain prisoner groups were a further powerful testimony to their still being members of society.

As mentioned before, divisions amongst the participants re-surfaced when the interview turned to the issue of whether *all* prisoners, in their view, were entitled to human rights recognition and protection. As a prompt, an example of a property offender, a sex offender and a murderer was given. Just about half of the participants answered unreservedly yes, invoking their common humanity and membership of society, individual and societal causes of offending, the social construction of crime, the principle of non-discrimination, and rehabilitation purposes. Their responses remind us that prisoners' existence is not amoebic and that their imprisonment is not meant to be indeterminate; their return to society was taken for granted. It was taken for granted because their roots were found nowhere else but in society where their existence acquired meaning and purpose through the myriad interactions and experiences society generated. Again, the fact that all prisoners developed and maintained reciprocal relationships at some stage in their lives signifies their sociability and its concomitants of having feelings and longing for human contact just like the *normal other.*

The social dimension of their personhood is reinforced when crime causation is taken into account. Prisoners (and all of us by virtue of our common humanity) are not only architects of our destinies but also products of our social environment. Without romanticising or absolving prisoners from their responsibility for their crimes, participants' references to experiences of child sexual abuse and individual pathology as plausible causes of sex offences, as well as to the acceptance of paedophilia in some quarters against fierce social censure, speak of criminality as a socially constructed and produced phenomenon. While criminal behaviour may not be the norm, it is nevertheless created by and takes place within the very fabric of society.

Dissenting from the above view and reflecting society's strongly negative sentiments towards sex offenders in particular, for the other half of the participant group, the starting point was that the seriousness of one's crimes should be reflected either in the nature of their human rights entitlements or in the scope of their provision, or both. Three categorically rejected the idea of human rights recognition specifically for paedophiles. The majority favoured the separation of sex offenders from the mainstream prison population on grounds of retribution and for their own protection from other prisoners. In this context, participants' identification of autonomy as a human right in prison, cast in terms of their ability to choose whom to socialise with, turned into a call for a prisoner allocation policy based on the nature of the offence and the degree of risk of dangerousness posed by serious offenders.

Overall, participants' reflections on themselves and fellow prisoners reaffirm that the prison is not a micro-cosmos of society. It is society itself in the diversity of its beliefs and attitudes, and a carrier of its prejudices, fears and hopes, thus debunking the idea of their *otherness.*

A representative sample of prisoners' reflections on their fellow prisoners is given below.

> Yes. At one point I never used to think like that, but I changed when I started believing in God. I am not here to judge and criticise paedophiles. Yes, they did something wrong, but they are still human. There must be a problem there. The same thing could have happened to me. I could have turned into a paedophile and would still want human rights. You have to put sometimes your foot into their shoes. I mean, I do not agree with what they do, but the fact is that they are human beings.

That is difficult. It is very hard really. Deep down, I will say no. But then again to be fair, I will say yes because everybody deserves human rights, no matter what you have done. Maybe some of the paedophiles were abused by a male member of their family and that is why they turned up how they are. Before they did their crimes, there were normal human beings. They have sometimes a mental problem; sometimes it is down to society. They do not assess them properly, do not realise that something is wrong with them till late. That paedophile is probably a father to a child out there, a husband to a woman or a son to their parents. Somebody's child anyway, no matter what they have done.

If the idea is punitive, no. If it is rehabilitation, you have to give them back a sense of self-identity. Because maybe they did not think what they did was wrong. There were maybe factors to why they committed these crimes. I mean some people think it is quite natural to have sex with children. Society says no, but some people are doing this for years. There are basic human rights in society. They are members of society. So, when they are in prison, they should have access to human rights. Why deny them in prison?

No! I know that by saying this I discriminate and contradict what I said before, but everyone is entitled to their opinion; maybe because I have a child. A lot of women in there were very upset with them. You do not even want to see them. People like that should be separated not only for our own benefit but also for their protection.

Give them rights, but separate them from the rest. Why should my kids be next to them? If you put them with us, they will be killed.

The Contribution of Human Rights to Prison Life and Prisoner Treatment

Human Rights and Self-Identity

One of the highlighted themes in participants' contributions so far has been the unequivocal connection, they made, between human rights and self-identity, crediting them as the means to its development or its re-discovery in prison. The connection between human rights and self-identity formed the backbone of participants' interpretations of human rights. We came across a powerful expression of this connection earlier when rehabilitation was explicitly identified as the vehicle for giving back to prisoners a sense of self-identity. The immediate inference drawn from this connection is that imprisonment threatens inescapably one's self-identity, which turned into a blanket and condemning observation in participants' accounts.

Coalesced into one body, the participants were effusive in their vituperation of their being continually undermined by prison staff and were exasperated with the multiplicity of means employed to this end. While they recognised the institutional needs of security and control, they were at pains to understand the logic in the institution's insistence to denigrate them. Especially when even the 'caretakers of [their] punishment' (Scott 2006) could find themselves in a similar position with them on account of human fallibility, it seemed imprudent to continue such a practice. The crux of the matter was that from the very start their biggest loss—freedom—and its accompanying deprivations that were seen earlier had tilted the scales of power in the institution's favour. They were the very foundations of the authority the prison had and exercised over them. Since these deprivations were unshaken for the duration of their sentence, so too the institution's power and control over them. Built on confoundedly strong foundations, the prison did not need, therefore, extra aid to administer their imprisonment.

Thematically, the meaning that prisoners attributed to the concept of self-identity involved a melange of different elements and drew similarly on a variety of human rights for its protection. These were derived inductively through participants' descriptions of the ways their sense of self-identity was endangered in prison, identifying in this respect their depersonalisation and a seeping confusion about their sexuality and gender identity.

Depersonalisation

Staff attitudes towards prisoners were a perennial subject in the interviews. This was not surprising given the inherently antagonistic relationships between custodians and the confined that total institutions, such as prisons engender (Goffman 1961; Crewe 2009; Drake 2012).

The participants were furious at what they felt was a judgmental, dismissive and patronising staff attitude, which showed no commitment to their job role and lacked active engagement in their duties. They experienced the said staff attitudes as emotionally and mentally abusive, and as an additional pointless burden that eroded their ability to cope with their sentence and to prepare for release. To them, active listening, basic courtesy and sympathy, face-to-face communication, and the provision of feedback were essential characteristics of a civilised qua normal behaviour, which a lot of officers and healthcare personnel were in want for. Commenting deprecatingly on staff behaviour, they attributed it to ignorance and pathology.

It has to be said that their fury was not directed blindly against all. Equally, they witnessed professionalism and dedication in a lot of officers, who were willing to and *did that extra mile* for them. Three participants also touched upon the perennial issues of overcrowding, staff shortages and overtime. They recognised their negative impact on staff morale and the resultant constraints placed on them in effecting a seamless daily schedule without undue delays and last-minute cancellations. However, the issue remained that there was a good number of staff whose unsuitability for the job cast a blight on their colleagues' good efforts and intensified the consequences of the operational pressures, which were felt by prisoners and staff alike.

A representative sample of prisoners' contributions on the impact of staff and the administration of imprisonment on their self-identity is found below.

> Some people come to do just their job, but some come here to be God. Maybe they had a bad life or have been bullied. Some will treat you like a human being, some like animals, like they can just lock you in and out when they want to; like they have certain rights over you. I think it is fundamental not to take that self-awareness, self-respect, dignity away from you. *What's your number?* Ask me my name! Do not ask me about my number! Don't just look in my file and think it's me! Talk to me!
>
> There is a lot you can sit and have a conversation with, and there are a lot who do not have respect for anybody really. I think there should be some sort of tests because you can tell some screws could not find a normal

job anywhere else. Some have a grudge against society. They seem to hate their job. It is a probably a wage, and they do not know anything else. They should have been trained more towards other religions, cultures, colours. As I say, you will always have a racist element in the prison service.

Screws always like to talk down on you. They just dictate to you. But, the psychologists are the big problem. They think they can read you. You get called in to see them, and especially when it is for a parole hearing, they are just sitting on that chair, distant, no contact. They just fire questions, take notes and make us do these stupid psychometric tests. They think they can measure our risk. Can you tell us how are we supposed to trust, really talk to and ask for their help when they play with our freedom? It's like Russian roulette with them. They are supposed to help people with their problems. Where's the confidentiality between doctor and patient? Then, you get a knock-back and cannot even see what they have put down. Why not? It concerns us! No accountability!

You get a 21 year old officer, *What are you coming on the wing for? Should have you been on the wing? Are you sure now?* They are young enough to be my child. They are just patronising. Do not talk to me like that! You do not want young staff talking to you like crap and putting all of you on the same boat. *You are all doing drugs.* This is what gets me most, to be treated like an idiot, like you never worked. I would like to say to them that I have worked and done more than them. I have been on better salaries than them. But, you are not allowed to say this.

I felt that somebody was lying to me. I felt I was stupid. One said one thing, and someone else said another. They should have listened to what I had to say. The officers were ignoring me. I think officers should be trained to be sympathetic to mothers. As a mother, I felt we should have been allowed more privacy. Every time I used to wash my baby, they always used to come and interfere, saying *does not like it, stop doing it.* I felt a lot of mothers were like that; like they were not our babies. I felt I was the nanny! I am the mother!

You cannot talk freely because it gets against your parole. You cannot express your feelings! You just want to scream out loud. If you scream out loud, you go on report like a child. You just feel like throwing things in your room. You cannot do that because you are wrecking the place. You feel like a rapport with someone. If you talk about things you would not tell anyone else about and they go and tell someone, that's it. The trust is gone. That officer that came in I really trust her. I think she is really a lovely person. But, you do not know what they put on the sheet about you. If you could express yourself freely, you would take a lot off your chest. I would not have to put everything up. Everything is bottled up. You just cannot be on your own, be your own person. You cannot have a normal life.

Say I am sort of down, not suicidal, but I am down. They take all the meds off you and you cannot get in possession of them. So, you cannot say that. I am talking to my mum and get a day where I feel angry with the bloke I was with before. I cannot say that on the phone because it goes back to probation. *Oh no, you did hate him.* No, I did not hate him. I cannot say how I feel about his family. I have got to shut up. If I want to swear on the phone, this could be threatening to the person. That's why I should have the right to speak what I want to speak about... Please stop-searching me. It's dignity. It's degrading showing your body parts to people you are not close to. Just any officer can strip-search you. You cannot say *I do not want that officer. Can I have another officer?* I would not like that officer I get on well with to strip-search me. It is something with myself and stems from the partner I was with. He used to say very horrible things about my body. I feel paranoid. I think, *what is she thinking?* It's sort of like child abuse, I suppose. If you have been abused as a child and are standing there naked, that's what is like.

I know they have to watch us and do these checks. But, it would be nice if we could pull a curtain across. There are a lot of girls who just want to be on their own, but we cannot and have nowhere to go apart from our rooms. You are screwed if you are in a double, especially if you and your partner do not get on. You have no privacy. You have to hide in the toilet. I mean once they lock us in, where are we going to go? So, why they cannot let us have this curtain? It would be nice if they would not push our door open once it is shut. It's sort of, *Hold on. We are having a private conversation.* But, they have to be there. They have to know exactly what is going on. There are women who actually won't cry in here because they have nowhere private they can go to.

I am a self-harmer, and I cannot talk to an officer about it. I can talk to my roommate about it. She's also a self-harmer. Now the officers think that I want to go and talk to the psychologists. I do not want to talk to the psychologist! I want to be able to choose who I talk to about it. It is easier to open up to somebody who won't turn around and say, *why did you do it?* I won't tell you. You have no idea why I have done it. You feel a lot more comfortable talking to people who actually are in the same situation with

> you, not just coming here to work. It's easier to talk to one of your friends because with Listeners you have to go over the reasons again and again. They have them on a rota system so the girls can actually get some sleep. You cannot be trained to be a good listener, to know where to draw the line. It's something that you are born with.

As the above contributions show, the participants pointed to infantilisation as one way to belittle them. Claimed to be exercised by prison officers and medical staff, infantilisation is manifested directly and indirectly, is both deliberate and inadvertent, and takes on a variety of expressions. These range from patronising, stereotyping and stigmatising prisoners to being indifferent to their needs or showing favouritism. In the prison environment that is typically devoid of equality and balanced relations of power between staff and prisoners (Liebling 2011), not only does infantilisation accentuate prisoners' feelings of insecurity, helplessness, loneliness, dependence and abandonment, which imprisonment so naturally gives rise to, but also attacks with force the core of their being, that is, their individuality.

First of all, to treat adults who are conscious of and have had responsibilities characteristic of adulthood (e.g. family and employment) as children doubts their agency and diminishes their hitherto achievements. Regular exposure to such treatment, compounded by the structural limitation on their ability to make choices, generates self-doubts about their capacity to meet their own and others' expectations, and envelops them in feelings of personal inadequacy and guilt.

As prisoners have to restrain themselves to survive their dependency on staff and to cope with their expressions of authority, their self-assertiveness is being endangered, plunging them into an emotional deterioration and isolation, which alienates them from themselves. As their names fall into disuse and numbers substitute for them, recognising and identifying who they are is the next hurdle. The impersonal mode of address corrupts the integrity of their self and eats away at its individuality. The enforced dissociation from their names breaks down and separates their external image—what they see in the mirror—from their inner self, its experiences, traits and feelings, rendering it foreign to their eyes and thus alienating them from themselves. Their ensuing depersonalisation reduces them from active participants to passive observers of their interpersonal relationships since they are unable to situate themselves in them.

Their depersonalisation has a deadening effect on the emotional drive necessary for self-determination and contaminates other dimensions of their identity except for the strictly personal one. As their self-awareness is dwindling away, it saps them of confidence and assertiveness. The weakening of their emotional strength forces them to concede defeat and seek respite in fatalism. Only that fatalism breeds procrastination, which affects their ability to appraise and act upon their appraisals. This impacts negatively not only on their autonomy (what is left to exercise in the confines of the prison), but also on the interpersonal sphere of their lives, for example, on their capacity as parents and, generally, their perceptions of the outside world.

This state of numbness is not brought about by infantilisation alone. It is also caused by the character of the prison and its dominant preoccupation with risk identification and management. The principally diagnostic and managerialist purpose of mental health provision in prison does not tend to prisoners' need for emotional release. It leaves prisoners no room (figuratively and literally) for admission to and reconciliation with their inner feelings and emotions and provides them with no outlet to deal with the underlying causes of these feelings and emotions. As a result, they become fixated on their emotional and mental plight and continuously regress.

Sexual and Gender Identities

Aside from depersonalisation, the participants talked about the conflicting feelings they experienced about their sexuality and gender identity, and the corrosive impact of these feelings on their self-identity. Their accounts were heavily gendered, highlighting like previous prison studies (see, e.g. Owen 1998; Crewe 2006) as much the masculine culture of the prison as the importation of hegemonic gender discourses into prison life. In doing so, they remind us about the important role gender relations play in colouring experiences of imprisonment.

In more detail, both men and women were worried about the effect of their 'involuntary celibacy' (Sykes 1958: 70) on their sexuality and made a direct connection between its vulnerability and the lack of conjugal visits. Conjugal visits enjoyed a rather wide base of ardent support,[3] with the majority taking the view that they should be recognised as a human right. The very first question male lifers and one of the female lifers asked me was whether there were any positive developments on the issue of conjugal visits,[4] and what the authorities' argument against their introduction was. Prisoners' call for the provision of conjugal visits was based on pragmatic and substantive grounds.

On pragmatic grounds, conjugal visits could have a pacifying effect on prison life, creating a more emollient atmosphere amongst prisoners and between prisoners and staff. Their tightly regulated living conditions, which effectively kept the lid on their emotional expression and spiritual freedom, aggravated even more their natural sexual frustration that resulted from the painful carceral deprivation of sexual relationships. Without lawful means to release this frustration, it transformed into aggression and violence, and could potentially lead to sexually abusive relationships among prisoners. On substantive grounds, sexual intimacy was a compelling biological need, which for humans had an added significance beyond carnal gratification. It enabled them to feel

[3] Four participants dissented from the majority of view for three reasons. Sex deprivation was seen as an intrinsic characteristic of prison as punishment, and in the overall scheme of things the prospect of conjugal visits barely contributed to prisoners' quality of life, posing at the same time the risk of pregnancy for female prisoners. However, two participants made an exception in the case of long and life sentences, acknowledging that they did not know if they would have been able to cope for a prolonged period of time, with one of them repeating the observation about the risk of confusion about and change in their sexuality.

[4] It is interesting to note that although Dutch prisoners took immense pride in the provision of conjugal visits in their prison system, only one person took advantage of them among those eligible (one of the three lifers). Dutch prisoners explicitly referred to conjugal visits as evidence of Dutch pragmatism and progressiveness, which they treated as quintessentially Dutch socio-cultural characteristics despite the harshening of public attitudes through the years. To be pragmatic and progressive were seen part of the national psyche. They agreed with English prisoners on the added benefit of conjugal visits in reducing prisoner stress and violent outbursts and thus increasing safety and security. Only one participant (a female serving a long sentence, who did not use such visits) discussed the contribution of conjugal visits in terms of its protection of the prisoner's sexuality and gender identity. Amongst those eligible, their main reason for not using the provision of conjugal visits related to issues of privacy. They disliked that officers and fellow prisoners knew of these private moments and also did not want their partners to be subjected to more security checks.

complete by fulfilling the human need for belonging and a sense of self-worth, and to experience their sexuality and gender identity, as well as the latter to be accepted and appreciated by others. Both men and women bemoaned the weakening of their social bond with their partners and the eventual loss, in some cases, of these personal relationships as a result of their deprivation of sexual intimacy and the strain of their imprisonment.

Although like the male lifers the (heterosexual) female prisoners were prejudiced against homosexuality, labelling heterosexuality as *more right and normal*, they openly described a change in their sexual orientation as unavoidable. Both heterosexual and lesbian women rebuked a part of the female prison estate for disallowing and penalising the forming of lesbian relationships (see, e.g. Owen 1998; Commission on Sex in Prison 2014). With two exceptions, unlike the females, the males were silent on the impact of imprisonment on their sexual orientation and the prevalence of homosexuality in prison. Only one participant talked about the issue with reference to his own personal intimate experience with a married fellow prisoner.

Reflecting the intrinsic maleness of the prison, which is augmented, on the one hand, by the deprivation of heterosexual relationships and, on the other hand, by the over-representation of male prison staff and their own masculine work culture, the males (especially lifers) were particularly concerned about the slow erosion of their masculinity (see, e.g. Crewe 2006) and its standing vis-à-vis their partners' femininity. In this regard, the same participant, who revealed his personal intimate encounter, noted the significance of having female prison officers who were credited inter alia as a civilising force again on the basis of gender stereotypes.

"They should be our human right. A woman has got needs. That's why you have a lot of lesbians in here. I am not a lesbian, but if I was doing a long time, I would turn a lesbian. I would feel more like a woman, that I still got sex drive. I have been in prison before and finished with my partner because I know he is out there with other girls. But if he could have had sex with me in a visit, maybe the relationship would have been better with him, and I would not end up finishing it with him. If you are doing life, that's a long time. If you are not a lesbian, you have to turn into one because you cannot get a man".

A lot of girls are sexually frustrated and are ending up with another female to relieve their frustration. But if you are not that way, you have to go without. It will relieve a lot of frustration. There would not be so many marriage break-ups. It breaks up the whole family when you come into prison. I think I could get on with my sentence a bit easier. You go so long without it. It is natural for someone to want to do this. It is a need. I think it would lift depression a bit.

Having sex is natural. We need it. It takes the stress out. In X, where I was, we could associate more freely and go into each other's cells. The officers knew what was happening behind closed doors, but they allowed it. Here such behaviour is not approved. I got nicked for doing it with my girlfriend.

I suppose for the most of the world the prison population is male dominated. So, a man mixing just with men is not particularly healthy. Women are part of our world. Obviously, it is a subjective thought, but women are by large loyal, faithful and emotionally stable. Only in prison it seems the worst male traits are exacerbated or exaggerated. It is quite interesting how in prison a lot of the guys are quite childlike in their reactions. If they do not get what they want, they either stomp their feet like a child or punch somebody. Basically, the first reaction is always violent…Having sex is part of human existence; the simple thing of touching people, simple physical contact. It might discourage-I have never witnessed it though-some prisoners from sexually abusing other prisoners. Some are vulnerable, bullied or have not been looked after. Prisoners who are sexually frustrated reign and abuse them. It is just an animalistic act for them devoid of any sort of emotional feeling. I give you an example. I am gay. I have been caught kissing a prisoner. He got called up in front of an officer. Basically, the officer was homophobic. He told him that he did not like him because he was a drug-addict and a thief, but most of all, because he was gay. The irony is he was not gay. He was married, had problems with his wife, and it was just an interaction. If he had access to his wife, maybe he would not have had homosexual instincts.

Do you know that when we enter the prison, the screws give us condoms? Giving men condoms? What is this about? Is it like telling us that they want us all to be homosexuals? Why can't we have conjugal visits? We are doing a long time. Do you know what it does to you? You end up not feeling, having no emotions. A lot of guys here become cynical. They only see the dark side. This is what happens when you cannot express your feelings to your girlfriend or wife. You forget how to do it and what it felt like. It is very important to be able to keep the relationship going. The woman makes you remember who you are. Otherwise, you lose your male identity, the image of being a man. You do not know what you are at the end of the day, what your role, duties and others' expectations of you are.

Human Rights and Social Identity

As said in the introduction, the participants identified themselves in more ways than one. Their reflections on their being worthy of human rights recognition and protection held vital clues to what these different identities may be. As seen, they began unravelling a mixture of human traits, which were uniformly manifested in their physical, emotional and mental constitution, but they were variously patterned. All commonly referred to their individuality and personhood, but not all of them identified themselves as parents, spouses, heterosexuals or previously employed. Moreover, on occasions, references to their individuality and autonomy blended with the *reciprocal* and *the social*. It was just in the previous section where their individuality, as expressed through their sexuality and gender identity, was seeking other people's recognition and appreciation so as to acquire meaning, to be practised, and to be enjoyed. The *reciprocal* and the *social* are not the tail of the *personal* but its progression into the more advanced stage of human existence. Both are apposite to their personhood and have to be nurtured for their being to be complete.

In prison, as their sense of self was challenged and eroded, and their self-worth was doubted, the social dimension tried to save their selfhood from oblivion and to restore their worth. Despite the engendering depersonalisation and confusion about their sexuality and gender role, their social drive was not only strong but also on the increase. It is sociability as an instinct, memory and future idea that helped them survive the adversity of their situation. No matter how distant their memories of the outside world and their release were, to all their eventual return to society was an anticipated fact. It was in society where they were born, used to live and would go back to after serving their sentence. Their anticipated return to society was envisaged at two levels. At micro level, they would return to and join their families, and at macro level society at large. The participants discussed their release and return to society in the context of their successful social reintegration. They equated (their) rehabilitation with (their) reintegration, treating them as the only legitimate aims of imprisonment.

Return to Family

For the participants, their return to family was emotionally and mentally challenging and a source of great anxiety for the women in particular, revealing again hegemonic gender divisions in terms of roles and expectations. They stood a chance of overcoming the challenges if the state treated them and their families equally with others in the community and enabled them to maintain quality family contact during their sentence. Being in a position to maintain quality contact with family and friends, and the fragility of such relationships were on top of all participants' concerns, identifying more frequently scheduled child visits along with greater privacy, intimacy and autonomy as instrumental in fostering quality contact.

Compared to men, the women—who 9 out of the 13 were mothers—were predominantly preoccupied with their children. They were pained by their likely loss of the maternal bond with their children as a result of their absence from their upbringing and the lack of intimacy between them in visits. They were also worried about the potentially negative impact of their imprisonment on their children's psychosocial development, as well as on their parenting abilities. Although the majority of the mothers (7 out of the 9) was against the idea of raising their kids in prison, and one had opted out of child visits, all argued strongly for the opportunity to decide whether to keep their children with them and praised the existence of Mother and Baby Units. Alluding to the principle of equality and equal treatment, they strongly opined that their children should not be discriminated against and vicariously punished for their parents' deeds. Their prisoner status could not nullify motherhood. If not for their own good, the mother and child relationship should not be undermined for the child's welfare. They have human rights too; the rights to know and be cared for by their parents, to privacy and family life, and to adequate state support when in the guardianship of others.

> You go all these searches. So, why do we have to be so far away? You have your boyfriend. With the officer there is impossible to relax. They can put the cameras under the table. At least you can feel you are together, and they can bloody watch it, but not in your face like that.
>
> Child visits should be more than once every 2 weeks and more private, not in an open room next to a mass murderer. You should be able to spend quality time with them in a room on your own, to have little playtime with them and to see what they have learnt. Your child has to sit. When you have kids up to 7 years old, they do not want to sit on their chair looking at you. Kids cannot stay still. No matter what, they are still kids and are yours. They are still part of our lives. They cannot block it out.
>
> There should be more help for families for their benefit and for children who are looked after by guardians. They should organise coaches for them once a week because it is not easy to visit. Especially if you are not driving, it is hard to find some prisons. It is also a lot of money. I have missed a big part of his life. But I would not feel good about it at all for him to be locked up in a place like that for my crime. It would have been different if I had given birth here. Keeping your child with you has its advantages but more disadvantages. I wonder if they will think it is all right to commit crime when they grow up. Plus it would be a long-term psychological impact for them. If it is a choice, that is good.
>
> I have forbidden my children to visit me. This is my third time inside and I do now want them to think that is something good. I would not have them with me here. It's like putting your child in the prisoner category. I would not be giving them the choice. But you should have the right to have them if you want. I think here they are doing well because there are not many female prisons offering that. Visits are fine for me. If they were anything better, it would not bother me that I see my family in this environment. It does bother me to see the officers and the bars on the windows. But I also want my family to see this. If they feel bad about it, I will feel bad about it.
>
> They made me separate from my baby at 6 months. I should have been given the chance to go to the other prison. He's better off with his mum.

> I am the one who gave birth to him. If I get my parole pass, I will be able to go to the open prison. There is nothing like this. I will have more freedom. He will know I love him and I am there for him. In May, I can apply for town visits. I will be able to spend time with my family. They are not the only victim here. I am a victim as well because I am away from my family so long. I know people are scared of me and will judge me, but I will be looking at my son.

As we can see, for the participants maintenance of family contact performs a triple function. It serves as a coping mechanism against their depersonalisation and infantilisation, eases their transition from the prison to the community and increases their reintegration prospects. Fundamentally, family support provides emotional stability that is essential for strengthening prisoners' resolve to initiate change in their lives. Their family's faith in the existence of some goodness in them and trust in their abilities are empowering as they help them in starting to appreciate themselves. Additionally, the family seems to have some sort of shaming and guilt inducing effect that can be reintegrative (see Braithwaite 1989) on account of its source, namely, the prisoners' nearest and dearest. Moreover, as also seen in the section on depersonalisation, to be allowed and encouraged to invest on their family relationships can have an educative potential in terms of developing a sense of personal responsibility. A connection is made between mothering with agency and a prudent lifestyle post release from prison. Specifically, to provide the imprisoned mother with the opportunity to be involved in mothering not only enables her to forge a bond with her child and contributes to the latter's psychosocial development but also it can sensitise the mother to her parental responsibilities.

Return to Society

The participants spoke trenchantly about their mixed feelings of elation and great anxiety for the moment of their release. The appeal the idea of freedom held to them never waned, but they were perturbed at their readiness to experience it. In prison, life lost momentum and was in want of a powerful spur. According to the participants such a powerful spur could and should be found in regular and direct contact with the outside world; effective sentence planning and resettlement preparation; work opportunities and a fair remuneration for prison work; and in a better communication and co-ordination of different services.

A representative sample of prisoners' contributions on the challenges of release is given below:

> Because I have been in prison for 5 years, I need to get back to the community and to get normal things again. If I just go straight out on my own, I will be lost. If they give us the right direction, guidance [and] a home leave, it might help us; it might not. I do not know because I have never been outside. I will just go and offend again. I have got nobody. They do not even show you your personal officer. I asked who mine was, but they should, shouldn't they? If you can befriend somebody, then you got someone speaking and listening to you. I will feel human. I will feel I worth my feelings.
>
> Nobody came to ask me, *how are you doing?* I got off my own back to do my courses. There was no encouragement. Maybe if there was a forum with your personal officer and the governor where you can talk and express your concerns, or just on one-to-one basis every so often to check and see if you feel your needs have been met.
>
> A lot of prisoners are very detached, isolated and more prone to re-offend when they are released because they have not really been in touch with what is going on outside. All they have been doing is thinking and, maybe, having bitter and negative thoughts. Maybe if they have contact with charities and local groups, this would change.
>
> They need to help us re-engage with the outside. The contact needs to be on a regular basis, not just an odd town visit. Preparation is important. You need time to know how you go about your needs.
>
> In prison everything about you is decided by someone else. You forget what it is like to make a decision on your own. *Do I want this or that, now or after?* You need to start getting used to do all this again by yourself before you go out because nobody will help you. You need to pace yourself in there.
>
> We should equally have the right to work like everyone else. Wages are an exploitation of our labour. How are we supposed to want to work when they pay peanuts? Where is the incentive? We are not getting educated

> about the value of work. They should streamline the services. They should have a common structure and professional conduct, and to liaise with each other. Every time you enquire about something, they give different reasons. So, when you go out, what? We need to get to know how to deal with the institutions outside. Another thing is education. They put restrictions on what you can do. They say, *why do you want to do law? You have a criminal record, cannot practise anyway*. There are guys who did journalism or law and are now working for papers and voluntary organisations. Education is not about the job. It's about self-development.

So far participants' accounts of the challenges their prison life and release held for them and their thoughts on how these challenges could be overcome bring powerfully to the foreground how inextricably linked the personal and social dimensions of their identity are and the primacy of a constructive social interaction. Constructive social interaction normalises the prison experience and is instrumental in restoring prisoners' self-esteem, empowering them and enabling them to develop a sense of purpose in life through contact with family and the real world, education and work.

It is important to note that the participants invoked both negative and positive rights in relation to the development and protection of their self and social identity whose protection was cast both in terms of limited and proactive interference. For example, for the protection of their self-identity, they invoked passionately the freedoms of speech and from discrimination and laid particular emphasis on the rights to privacy and self-determination/autonomy in decision-making. For the recognition and protection of their social identity, the right to private and family life was given a prominent place and prisoners' call for equality in treatment was applied to the rights to work, fair remuneration, healthcare, education, and to participation in the wider cultural life. Access to education and healthcare, to be able to exercise autonomy, and participation in cultural life through socialisation with members of the community as part of resettlement initiatives were credited with facilitating both personal and social emancipation.

All these rights raise prisoners' confidence and self-respect that can, in turn, encourage respect for others, thus enabling them to enjoy the benefits of social inclusion and honour their social responsibilities. Their social integration prospects are specifically boosted by the educative potential the rights to work and a fair pay have. A policy that promotes in practice prisoners' financial independence during their sentence by securing enough jobs and a fair pay is seen as instrumental to their appreciation of legal work.

To sum up, the interdependence of the *personal* and the *social*, their reliance on both negative and positive human rights, and the dual protection they require highlight the authorities' social responsibility in protecting prisoners' human rights; a social responsibility, which is derived from the prison aims of rehabilitation and reintegration whose primacy and legitimacy are founded on fundamental human rights principles.

Human Rights and Civic Identity

The normalisation of prison life, which protection of prisoners' human rights engenders and the participants were longing for, has a symbolic significance beyond the (obvious) implementation of practical measures to improve prisoner treatment. In treating the prisoner like any other citizen, bar the restrictions expressly associated with imprisonment, it strongly re-affirms the citizen status of prisoners (Favard 1994; cited in Faugeron 1998). Interestingly, this strong affirmation was not prevalent in the participants' accounts. While there were pockets of strong sentiments indicative of a civic ethos and relevant practices, invoking principles, such as democratic accountability and participation in the running of the daily prison life, freedom of expression and the right to vote, a strong civic identity was missing. This was further evidenced in a general lack of appreciation of their own social and civic responsibilities despite their otherwise intelligible and critical conceptualisations of human rights protection in prison. When combined with prisoners' uncertainty about their human rights and lack of knowledge of their legal status, the need of raising prisoner awareness as much of their human rights as of their *human responsibilities* becomes evident, with implications for prisoner education.

Prisoner Committees

As mentioned above, the participants highlighted the need for democratic accountability on the part of the institution and for their participation in the daily running of prison life through a kind of a prisoner committee with some executive powers. Both these needs, their proposed implementation and effect on prisoners resembled closely those of a therapeutic community practice as identified by Rapoport (1960) and further developed by Shine and Morris (2000).

Based on Rapoport (1960; cited in Shuker 2010: 465–466) a therapeutic community operates on four foundational principles. These are:

Democratisation: prisoner involvement in all aspects of decision-making
Permissiveness: tolerance and understanding of pathological behaviour
Communalism: shared involvement and participation in everyday living, and
Reality confrontation: interpersonal processes as the vehicle for learning and change

Shine and Morris (2000: cited in Shuker 2010: 467) developed this model further pointing to the need for an approach that included a multiplicity of factors (e.g. attachments, criminal behaviour, prison behaviour) for the purposes of a successful therapeutic intervention. Under their model behavioural changes are encouraged and facilitated through regime changes that create spaces for prisoners to exercise personal and social responsibility. In such a therapeutic environment, the focus is on both social learning and interpersonal processes. Prisoners are both confronted when engaging in anti-social behaviour and entrusted to learn and practise new skills conducive to a pro-social behaviour.

The participants' proposed prisoner committees aimed to create a similar living environment. While the organisation of these committees was up for debate, their objective was commonly shared. Having the space to give their views an airing without fear of repercussions and to actively participate in executive decisions on wing matters was seen as a great learning and empowering experience. It would provide them with a pro-social behavioural model that they could apply to the private and social spheres of their lives post release. Starting with the basics, they would learn how to prioritise, manage their finances, negotiate with social institutions, and be accountable for their actions. Should they be allowed to exercise agency, autonomy and initiative than continue to be condemned to dependence and infantilisation, they would feel less insecure and powerless against the reality awaiting them on the outside. Infantilisation and dependence ultimately hindered their reintegration because they left fundamental cognitive and practical skills undernourished.

Additionally, such committees would provide a platform for socialising and thus interacting more closely with prisoners and staff. This could foster across-the-board personal enlightenment through one's sensitisation to society's heterogeneity and the vicissitudes of human life. Only when differences are discussed and confronted, a willingness to be more understanding, without excusing or letting differences and divisions reign free, is possible. Such an interactive environment would provide both prisoners and staff with a stimulus to begin to see in each other the individual person behind the mutually derogatory labels and to be more appreciative of the impact prison has on both groups. This would propel prisoners to confront their own absolutism and tendency to deflect criticism by blaming others. As some participants put it,

> As an individual, you hope for respect from other people and, in turn, you should respect them. Human rights are a two-way process. It is basically just respecting other people's human rights as well as your own, understanding your own and demanding your own. I mean a lot of prisoners say, *I want this and that*, and in a sense it is a reflection of society…An opportunity should be given to prisoners and staff to mingle with other races and to deliberate. Deliberation would be helpful for both. This could breed more compassion and thoughtfulness.

A representative sample of prisoners' thoughts on prisoner committees is given below.

> I was a wing rep. When it comes down to things like more activities for the girls that are going to take officers' time, they do not want to do it for you. They can get you hairdryers all right. Once a month we used to have a

wing rep meeting with a principal and a senior officer. We were putting ideas to them, but when they would send the minutes, they would say, *unable to deal with it at this time.* They did not tell us why they were unable! I think there should be a group of prisoners instead of a wing rep who are given a budget. It should be like 5–6 people in this wing rep team. If anything goes wrong, you got the budget to deal with that. At least, we know it is getting done. We are told it's getting done, and a year later the thing is still wrecked.

They should let us organise ourselves into small committees and talk directly to the management. The screws say they cannot do anything because of the management. They either forget or do not want to do anything. You get to see your personal officer once or twice in 3–4 months. This is not real communication. What kind of behaviour model is this? We live in a democracy. Where are transparency and accountability? What will happen when we go out? We would not know how to ask for and get things done. Where exactly is rehabilitation in all this?

When prisoners are stuffed in their cells for 24 hours a day, they get angry. That anger would make them involved in violent acts. At least if there is a committee where they can air their anger in a verbal way, that's less likely to happen. Routine is very important in prison so it should be happening once a week. The committee needs to be small, 5–10 people. You have a representative and he can talk to the management. It is an empowerment thing.

Contact with the Media and the Outside World

The participants identified the right to contact the media and the outside world as a fundamental aspect of their right to freedom of expression in a democratic society. As they regarded themselves part of society, it was their fundamental right to speak up when state agents misused their powers and to demand that they be held accountable for their actions. Society and the state had the right to know about such incidents so that they could intervene. In their view, the ability to communicate with the media would force the prison to open up its world to public scrutiny, and consequently to become more transparent in its practices. This would have the added benefit of raising public awareness of the reality of prison life and its pains, dispelling myths about its luxuries.

When I was in the maximum security jail, 6 people killed themselves. They did not want the publicity. We tried to get to the outside what had happened but officers were always checking us. We were on the top end of the street and could not tell those at the bottom. It affected us all then. I knew some of them. We should have been able to talk.

We should be listened to and be able to put opinions across. We are not shit bags. We are people.

Freedom of speech is our democratic right. We are doing time in England, not under a totalitarian regime. We understand there are security considerations, but they should find a way around it. What if something really serious takes place? Who can we tell? What about that local jail some years back where officers were abusing inmates? Nobody knew it was actually happening. What about suicides? How many are taking their lives because of overcrowding and late detection?

Human Rights and Human Responsibilities

In other European countries you can still vote. It is our democratic right to take part in the political decisions affecting our lives. We are the ones who know what prison is like. Politicians are coming out with their tough policies. It is like a competition among them. They never ask our opinions. It will work for us and will make their job less stressful. Where else have you seen a politician deciding when a lifer will be released? He is not a judge! Why do we have judges for? How are we going to be educated about our rights and responsibilities? We need to feel and act as citizens of this country. It gives you a sense of belonging.

While the lifers' contribution above is a stark reminder of ongoing and past human rights violations in prisons in England and Wales (see Chap. 3), it also captures very well the general attitude among the participants towards the idea of citizenship and their own role as citizens.

The right to vote, itself an emblem of formal and substantive citizenship, was not among the participants' human rights concerns. Only four people brought up the issue of enfranchisement on their own initiative, treating it as an invaluable means to effect change in society and its institutions like prisons. When the others were asked about whether they could vote in prison and whether voting should be a prisoner's human right, the answers revealed a general indifference. The majority thought that as prisoners they were stripped of their right to vote, and all said that they had never voted either because of a lack of interest in or mistrust of politics. Only one stated that in spite of their personal views, prisoners should have the right to vote since *they will return back to society at some point.*

It can be argued that the participants' indifference to enfranchisement is not at all surprising. This is so when we consider that typically prisoners come from socio-economically marginalised communities whose environment and conditions of everyday existence presents them with no opportunities and tools to build social capital. The resultant absence of interest in a wider civic and political engagement leads to a lack of a sense of ownership when it comes to common affairs and thus to a lack of social responsibility, which was confirmed in the interviews.

When the participants were asked whether they had human responsibilities like they had human rights, and whether committing a crime could be considered a violation of another's person human rights, neither of the two concepts was readily and widely recognisable or openly accepted. The first and, in most instances, only response was that human rights were absolute and thus non-negotiable. As for crime being a human rights violation, this did not draw any comment at all, not even from the lifers amongst whom a couple acknowledged that that they bore personal and social responsibilities (e.g. respect for the country's laws, tax contribution, and being accountable for one's actions).

Overall, the participants had difficulty in appreciating how human rights could dovetail with human responsibilities, understanding what these could involve, and accounting for their purpose. For those very few who accepted that they also had responsibilities, they saw them as a necessary evil in an organised system of living. Such a system, be it the prison or society, has laws and rules that they ought to abide by. Responsibilities are determined by what the state and its authorities prescribe and proscribe, and their duty is to obey them. Otherwise, punishment will ensue that once again will separate them from their families and deprive them of normality.

> We have duties because of the way prisons run. We might not like it. We have responsibilities to ourselves and other prisoners. If you are out, to your family, to the public, to work. Everybody does really. It's like a system. You cannot go breaking the law. You are going to end up back in prison.
>
> Maybe in a way we have responsibilities. I have a child. That is my responsibility. Nobody else is to look after and care for him. Being a good mother is a big responsibility. To ensure that I am in the best of health and do not do something bad when I am out is my responsibility.
>
> If I prove good, I get rewarded something. I do not always have to prove myself, but I think most of the time. People might want a chance to change and when they do, nobody is noticing. If no one is going to notice, what is the point of changing? I never used to blame me when I was out. At the end of the day if I do something wrong, it is my own fault. I do have a mind of my own. I am a mum and have responsibilities to my son. If I do get town visits, my responsibility is to come back on time. If I do not, I lose my allowance, probably lose my parole and go back to square one.

The Hobbesian undertones in the above conceptualisations of human responsibilities are alarming. History itself as well as criminological knowledge on the deterrent value of the prison has demonstrated countless times that obedience to state authority based solely on fear of punishment is rather shaky, to say the least, with ill consequences for society's and the individual's welfare. Even more alarming is the widespread lack of recognition and acceptance of crime as a human rights violation. In light of all this and of the educative potential of human rights for fostering a sense of personal and social responsibility, the implementation of strategies, such as human rights and citizenship studies into prisoner education, is long overdue.

Conclusion

In the participants' view, prisoners deserved human rights recognition and protection on account of their humanity and its commonly held attributes. They were still human beings with feelings and emotions and could equally experience pain. As human beings, they had also the capacity to learn from their mistakes and take action to address them. They too were individuals with personal aspirations and plans and were inherently social, longing for human contact. It was only through interacting and building relationships with others that they could acquire a sense of purpose in life, experience and enjoy their individuality.

Human rights enabled them (and others) to live, breath and feel their humanity, which in prison translated into a normalised living environment that was geared towards prisoner rehabilitation and reintegration. On account of the human rights contribution to the quality of human existence and experience, rehabilitation and reintegration ought to be the prison's aims; otherwise, it had no legitimacy as it negated the very essence of the nature of the punished. In light of this, drawing on both negative and positive rights, as well as on negative and positive state interference, the participants envisaged prison as a place that could foster personal empowerment, independence and autonomy in preparation for prisoners' release into society where they belonged to.

For comparative purposes, it is worth noting that the English placed particular emphasis on the aspects of personal empowerment and individual autonomy in contrast to the Dutch, whose accent was on their social and civic emancipation. This could be culturally explained and be interpreted as a lasting influence of the Diceyan interpretation of human rights (see Chap. 2) which duly emphasises the overarching importance of individual autonomy, independence, and freedom to act and do anything unless it is legally prohibited. Moreover, it can also be interpreted as a sign of the more individualistic culture of the neoliberal political economy of England and Wales in which a high social value is placed on individual (economic) success.

This difference aside, like their Dutch counterparts (see Chap. 6), English participants had difficulties in reflecting about their human responsibilities while they had no such difficulty in offering rich and intelligible accounts of human rights protection. This finding, along with the general prisoner uncertainty (across the two national groups) over the legal status of their human rights, highlights the need for a more diverse prison education that is inclusive of human rights and citizenship education. Implicit in this finding is the need to include the wider civil society in such educative/awareness initiatives. Joint efforts (by the state and civil society) to foster a public (inclusive of prisoners) consciousness about human rights, citizenship, and their contributions to our lives will stand better chances of success. In this way, Girling's (2006) *community of penal sentiment* (see Chap. 1) is more likely to be widely supported and stand the pressure of new social and political risks upon which human rights violations are legitimated and groups of people are harshly targeted and selectively incapacitated (e.g. immigrants, mentally disordered and repeat offenders).

While English participants' views on human rights in prison date back to 2004–2007, as already seen in Chap. 3 they remain very much relevant in many respects. More specifically, based on HM Inspectorate of Prisons (HMIP) Annual Reports covering the last two years relationships between staff and prisoners have improved through the years, but English prisons remain overcrowded and have become understaffed violent places with increased levels of drug use and numbers of prisoners dying of unnatural causes (HMIP 2015: 8, 10–12, 33–34, 37, 2016: 8–9, 41–42). Purposeful activities and resettlement support present a bleak picture, recording the worst outcomes since measurements began. Overcrowding and staff shortages have contributed to this poor state of affairs. There are simply not enough places available on OBPs and other rehabilitation initiatives, when and where these exist, are again not enough and varied, and there is not enough staff to escort prisoners to attend such programmes and/or to supervise them. This means that prisoners spend most of their day in their cells (HMIP 2015: 11, 13–14, 50–55; HMIP 2016: 38–45). Moreover, staff need training in mental health awareness training and safeguarding, and there is a lack of transparency and accountability in the handling of prisoner complaints, the use of force and restraint, as well as segregation. While force and restraint practices as well as segregation have increased, their monitoring has decreased, and there is no advice service on how to access legal assistance (HMIP 2015: 37, 2016: 24–26, 30, 34).

6

Human Rights in Dutch Prisons: Prisoners' Views

Introduction

The chapter presents Dutch prisoners' views on human rights in prison based on semi-structured interviews. In 2008 I interviewed 29 adult men and women in seven closed prisons (2 female establishments and 5 male ones). 13 out of the 29 participants were women. Among the 29 there were four (male) foreign nationals and the majority was white. In the male group, the average age was 49, with the youngest being 34 and the oldest 60. Ten of the men had been in prison before both as adults and youths, having two previous prison sentences. Three of them were prolific drug-addicted offenders sentenced to ISD. The average time spent in custody was 21 months. Among the 16 men, there were 3 lifers who had together spent more than 20 years in prison. At the time of the fieldwork, there were no female lifers (personal communication with a prison governor). In the female group, for 11 women, this was their first time in prison, with average time spent in custody being 14 months. One had been in prison five times before, serving each time longer sentences (3½ months, 9 months, 1 year and 4½ years). The second female with

A. Karamalidou, *Embedding Human Rights in Prison*,
DOI 10.1057/978-1-137-58502-8_6

previous prison experience had been in prison once before, with no further information offered on the sentence.

Like the English, the Dutch explored the issue of human rights in prison with reference to their humanity and sociability. Their prisoner status did not negate their humanity and sociability or render them less deserving of a humane treatment. Like others, they were in possession of characteristically human attributes, such as fallibility, painism and emotional intelligence, and equally longed for the company of others. They were essentially members of society, first and above all. Their membership of the prison community could not negate their being members of society. They were in prison with the expectation (at official and societal level) that they would return some day to society, hopefully as *better people*, as they put it. Their return to society was not only expected but was also seen as natural and given considering their humanity and sociability. Society was the only natural place for a human being to live their lives, in the company of others; and it was this view that heavily informed Dutch prisoners' views on human rights in prison.

The chapter is divided into three main sections. The first section documents prisoners' awareness of their human rights, their understanding of the term and views on the idea of prisoners having human rights. The second section documents the contribution human rights can make to prisoners' lives and details ways for its realisation. The third section shifts the focus of attention from human rights to human responsibilities and presents prisoners' views on the idea of human responsibilities against the backdrop of their views on human rights.

Human Rights Awareness and Understanding

Dutch interview responses on prisoners' human rights awareness and understanding were very similar in some ways to the English ones. Like the English, the Dutch were uncertain about the legal status of their human rights and had received no relevant information by the prison authorities. Similarly, despite their recognition of the greater importance of human rights vis-à-vis rights, they too had difficulties in highlighting distinctive differences between the two concepts. However, compared to the English, more Dutch participants offered elaborate conceptualisations of human rights in general and in prison in particular.

More specifically, only 8 out of the 29 said that they knew that they had legally recognised human rights, citing their lawyers, family, the media, fellow prisoners and previous prison experience as their sources of knowledge; and only three of them pointed to the ECHR, identifying it as part of domestic law. The majority responded elusively, evoking their long-entrenched right to complain (see Chap. 2) via the prison complaints mechanism, prisoner committees and the courts. Although they were broadly confident in the *system's* professionalism, humanity and accountability, for some, as we shall see, the system was failing in its own expectations. On the dissemination of human rights information by the prison authorities, custom had it to be told *what their rights and duties as prisoners were… [and] human rights were not subject of discussion*. For many participants, this absence of human rights talk was seen positively as they regarded its opposite as a sign of prisoner mistreatment and hostile prisoner staff relations.

In this context, the most common understanding of human rights was in terms of basic necessities for everyday life, which comprised the rights to eat, to drink (water), to maintain one's personal hygiene (through regular access to washing facilities and products, and having clothes sent in) and to heating. The right to basic necessities was followed by contact with the outside world, humane and dignified treatment and medical care. All three were mentioned by an equal number of people. Like in the English case, in the Dutch setting visits with and calls to their family were the main aspects of the right to outside contact, dominating over communication with outside organisations and engagement with the community in general. The right to medical care had substantive and procedural elements and was predicated on equality in treatment that entailed the provision of health checks, access to medication and hospital treatment, and respect for prisoners' privacy when hospitalised.

Drawing heavily on the constitution of human nature and resultant expectations about interpersonal human conduct, the right to *humane and dignified treatment* proved to be wide ranging. It was raised in relation to structural, operational and relational aspects of imprisonment. Suffice to mention at this stage that participants identified as defining elements of a humane and dignified treatment: due consideration for others' feelings and needs, fairness, equality, and protection from torture and inhuman/degrading treatment. For them to be *humane* was to be fair; not to discriminate, for example on grounds of ethnicity but to judge one's actions and behaviour on its (de)merits. In prison, fairness translates into accountability with regard to the way the institution operates and manages its affairs, measured inter alia by its adherence to the rules in force and their consistent application. In an accountable prison, prisoners are able to express themselves freely, to be actively listened to, and have recourse to a remedy, such as a hierarchical grievance procedure.

On the other hand, *dignified treatment* in prison means recognition and respect for prisoners' individuality and their need for autonomy, and protection of their well-being (physical, mental and psychological). In this respect, like the English, the Dutch stressed the reintegrative value of a normalised prison life, which they saw conducive to giving prisoners greater autonomy in their lives and thus enabling them to become independent, ready for normal life. In this respect, like the English, the Dutch identified the provision of rehabilitation and resettlement support as integral to their readiness for life on the outside.

In addition, and reflecting to an extent specific Dutch concerns following the punitive turn of the Dutch penal policy (see Chap. 4), participants identified as human rights: the freedom of thought, conscience and religion; to spend one hour in the fresh air every day; to recreation, involving activities such as sports and socialisation with fellow prisoners and staff; to liberty and security and, more specifically, to have one's status speedily determined; to be alone in the cell; to legal advice and representation; to complain; to access the library and education; to privacy; to work; to life; and to access one's prison file and give permission for others to do so.

Dutch Prisoners' Reflections on Their Human Rights

As mentioned earlier, in spite of recognising the primacy of human rights over rights, the Dutch had also difficulty in elucidating the difference between the two concepts. They did comparatively better though, with more than half of the sample group explaining the differing status of the two concepts more lucidly. Moreover, regarding the origins of the privileged status of human rights, Dutch views followed a similar pattern to the English views, falling into the three respective groups of *humanists*, *positivists* and *pragmatists*. The Dutch leaned though much more strongly towards the idea of human rights as innate, with *humanists* forming a strong majority. Like their English counterparts, the Dutch *pragmatists* remarked on the dependence of human rights recognition and protection on the form of political government in place, and the legal and religious culture of the given country. Positivists were in the minority of one.

The Dutch humanist view of human rights drew heavily on the eighteenth-century (secular) natural law and theory of rights and social contract theory. For the Dutch *humanists*, human rights were distinctive in one major respect. They were inherent in human nature and thus inalienable and universal. Their immanence, which established them on the top of the rights hierarchy, emanated from their embodiment of human nature and experience, of what essentially means and feels to be human, which were encapsulated in the rational and emotional aspects of being human, and the respective needs these aspects created. This symbolic value of human rights gave birth to an instrumental one as they prescribed minimum requirements *for walking as a human [being] in life*, which the participants identified as fairness, equality and equal treatment, and ultimately freedom. Freedom assumed, as we shall see later in more detail, an array of dimensions, from spatial, social and cultural to mental and emotional. In all its facets, it was seen as instrumental in promoting autonomy meaningfulness and lifestyle choices, coinciding with three of Brugger's (1996) five elements of his human rights formula of personhood (see note 2 in Chap. 5).

Equally important was the identification of both negative and positive interference with the exercise of one's freedom for its optimum protection, which in the carceral context translated into opportunities for vocational training, recreation, education, and more regular and private family contact. In light of the symbolic and instrumental value of human rights, the general argument was that people have willingly contracted the protection of their inalienable rights out to a political government whose purpose is to represent, promote and safeguard people's common interests and welfare. To this end, national and international human rights laws have been enacted, with human rights being seen as part of the rule of law.

A representative sample of the Dutch humanist view of human rights is given below:

> Human rights are more important than rights because your whole being is human, all your feelings and thinking…If my human rights were stepped upon here, I would do more than if they close you in before the time is up or do not give the food you ask for. Human rights are universal. Rights have to do with politics; they change.
>
> If I am not good to go outside like a human being, if I am an animal, why then do you not kill me? For what, man, only to punish me? To kill me is cheaper.
>
> You have to give people the chance to build themselves up, to speak for themselves, to create their own identity. Human rights for me are to give them the space to develop themselves. That is one of the problems here. You cannot develop or explore yourself. Give more fresh air; let them do more fitness because these guys need something to relax. Give them school. Let them get their degrees here. Give them opportunity. Give them more freedom especially on the weekends because some units only have recreation in the morning. In the afternoon, they have to go to work. It is mostly in the afternoon that you have [some] sun. Some of the prisoners' families do not live far from here. It is fine for them to travel 15 minutes and visit them. From the day you transfer a prisoner to the south of the country, you have to travel 2–3 hours. They do not bother. They transfer you.
>
> That you are treated like a human, and the last 10 years it is getting worse in Dutch prisons. It has no use putting somebody in jail in Holland. When you come out, you have nothing. If you do not have work, you have to wait for social security. This can take 1–2 months. The way they help you to get back to normal life is not enough.
>
> Human rights are recognised by the rule of law. My understanding of the rule of law is that it must be obeyed. The rule of law is decided by law-makers, the members of the national as well as of the European Parliament, which is called the ECHR and is accepted by the country members. They cannot go around human rights. You have different human rights as a minority in a country from those when you are in prison. So, you have rights in general, human, animal, gay rights. They have to be obeyed. If you can see them or not in practice, it is open to question.

The humanist view of human rights permeated participants' reflections on the rightfulness of their human rights entitlements. More specifically, the question on whether prisoners have and should have human rights was met with disbelief and incomprehension. For the Dutch the mere thought of posing such an issue was not only inconceivable but also out of touch with reality. The reality they painted was the same in many aspects to the one the English portrayed; only that the Dutch were much more assertive and passionate in their claims regarding their humanity and sociability and were very vocal in their being members of society.

The reality was, they argued, that they were still human and rational agents. They manifested throughout their lives the human traits of fallibility, painism and emotional intelligence, as well as the human capacities for introspection and remorse. For example, acceptance of their punishment, evidenced in their observance to the prison rules, signified at least realisation of the error of their ways and its consequences although, as they readily admitted, not everyone was willing to acknowledge errors of judgment and try to redress them all too soon. These contrasts demonstrated that to be and do wrong, as well as to reflect upon and take responsibility for one's actions, are the staple of human experience.

Moreover, they were still social beings and members of society; to argue the opposite was nonsensical. They were born into, raised in and were influenced by society. Their existence became meaningful in the openness of society where they were afforded the space to go about their business, interact and form relationships with other people, hence the inherent strangeness of a life in confinement that foreclosed the exercise of autonomy and interpersonal contact of one's choice, leading to alienation. Also, their lawbreaking was not only an obvious example of human fallibility but also an occurrence that was socially constructed and caused. Moreover, their membership of society entailed that like other members of society they were still equal legal subjects and a country's citizens. On these grounds, they were entitled to equality before the law, legal procedural safeguards, and to a humane and proportionate treatment and punishment in order to be equally protected from potential abuses of state power. In short, they were as *normal* as others were. What rendered them normal, or rather why society ought to treat them as such, *when one person did it [and] the other did not do it*, was to be found in the gamut of emotions and the human capacity for reflection and change that were commonly shared by lawbreakers and law-abiding people.

It was on these grounds that commitment to and investment in prisoners' resocialisation were staring the authorities in the face. To dismiss resocialisation as a prison aim defeated two of the often-stated aims of imprisonment, individual deterrence and public protection, and it begged the question as to its rationality. While imprisonment could be seen as the straw that broke the camel's back due to its severity as social censure and punishment, reflected in the deprivation of liberty, it did not ipso facto signal hopelessness. The belief in the human capacity for positive change could help increasing awareness and understanding of the vicissitudes of human life. Cultivation of and institutional emphasis on such awareness and understanding were imperative in prison. In the words of one of the participants, it was imperative to *try to find out, to look for the causation; this is how we can understand.*

For the Dutch the adoption of such an approach was neither charitable nor libertarian; it was pragmatic. Taking a realistic view of the social contract and human nature, they acknowledged that prescriptive standards of behaviour, their inculcation, and punishment for recusancy ought not to be treated haphazardly. Respect for state laws brought order and safety to human life. At the same time the existence and impact of wider inequalities and individual disadvantages on people's lives ought not to be ignored either. Becoming ensnared in them was not a distant possibility. Against this background prisoner rehabilitation was integral to their successful resocialisation and, subsequently, to a reduction in (their) re-offending, and public protection. As such, the provision of rehabilitation in prison fell within the scope of the state's positive duty of care to prisoners and society alike.

Like in the English case, Dutch opinion was divided on human rights recognition and protection for prisoners whose offending history (homicide, sexual offences) was seen to pose a serious risk to the public. There was also a convergence across segments of both national samples. For example, some of the Dutch participants also supported the separation of serious offenders, such as murderers and sex offenders, from the mainstream prison population for their own protection from reprisals, and as an expression of prisoners' right to autonomy in terms of their ability to choose with whom to socialise. These similarities aside, participants' reflections on human rights in respect of different prisoner groups offered further evidence of the Dutch pragmatic outlook on life, revealing at the same time lasting influences and ruptures as a result of penal policy, political and social changes.

Almost half of the participants expressed unreservedly the position that the particularities of one's criminal history should not encroach on their human rights on the basis of their humanity and de facto membership of society, as well as in observance to the rule of law, which in a democracy had no room for brutality, arbitrariness and vigilantism. There was no legitimate substitute for the courts in whose process and judgments the state's authority to inflict punishment laid. Prisoners' eventual release into society did not allow for complacency or unbounded expressions of retributivism. It brought forcefully to the fore that for both prisoners' resocialisation prospects and society's welfare retribution and tackling the underlying causes of criminality should not be treated as mutually exclusive. State intervention in the form of a dedicated rehabilitation provision whose delivery was in the hands of prison employees with a professional and caring ethos was crucially important for prisoners and society alike.

With the exception of two people who categorically opposed the idea of human rights recognition for child sex offenders in particular on grounds of retribution, the other half of the group argued for the need for a balancing act between human rights considerations and public protection, exemplified in their favouring of TBS orders especially for child sex offenders. While they attributed a victim status to this group of offenders, highlighting exposure to abuse and psychological disorders as causes of such offending, they drew attention to the long-lasting multiple suffering of these offenders' victims. Driven by the latter the dispensation of justice and prevention of future victimisation were seen as the state's first priority. In this context, a TBS order met the victims' seeking for justice as its carceral element was *an extra sentence by way of punishment*, added to the time to be spent in a forensic psychiatric setting. In recognition of those offenders' right to resocialisation, their placement in a forensic psychiatric environment allowed for specialised treatment and assessment of its effectiveness so as to reduce their risk of re-offending and enable them to return to society. When treatment proved ineffective, one-third of the participant group favoured indefinite hospitalisation or lifelong imprisonment.

Participants' reflections on their fellow prisoners' human rights exposed a particular mood that was not evident in the English setting. It bespoke mistrust and intolerance of Dutch ethnic minorities and Muslims in particular, which the abolition of the one to a cell rule inflamed. Although this mood was not widely shared, it was brought up and was highlighted as reflective of wider societal anxieties that were partially fuelled by a previously unknown politicisation and racialisation of crime, which contributed to tougher sentencing and increases in prisoner numbers (see Chap. 4).

> The media scare people. This is what they do, for example, when a crime is done by a Moroccan. Then, the public asks for more punishment. Is it only Moroccan teenagers? Even if they are more criminal than the Dutch, this cannot be without reasons. They say the government does not do enough and that they should send more people to prison and for longer. But they do. Prisons are full. Now you can be in a double cell.

Those prisoners who expressed mistrust of ethnic minorities (four males; two with extensive prison experience) admitted that the effects of fear, suspicion and anger that 9/11 left in its wake did not pass Dutch society and its institutions by. This was not, however, the only reason for the creeping intolerance, or sufficient in itself to give rise to it. The Netherlands always had anxieties over immigration from the former colonies and the integration of its immigrant population. Just because these issues were not openly discussed in the past, it did not mean that people were not concerned. What further enabled admissions and expressions of xenophobia and intolerance was witnessing a gradual decline in public order and safety especially in big cities. Senseless violence was not uncommon on Dutch streets back then, and its ethnic minority male perpetrators were a new breed of criminal, who was hedonistic, dangerously impulsive, and with no apparent loyalties. In a penal environment that had become ideologically punitive and restrictive in its regimes, the presence of this new type of criminal brought further instability to an already volatile atmosphere.

I sit here with junkies, killers, Surinamese, and all other nationalities. Who has the right to put me with a Moroccan? I do not know the Moroccan ways! I do not trust him! Your privacy and identity are taken away. They put them all together because of the money. They do not have enough buildings. I do not like these people so much anymore. Dutch society is not as liberal as before. There is hate not only here, everywhere.

Antilleans, Moroccans, Turkish-fighting. *I am Bruce Lee, the big guy.* Respect is finished. The last 10 years there are only carjackers, people who will hit only for your telephone. People outside do not take it anymore. Turkish people outside are speaking only Turkish. If you leave in Holland, no! I think it is a big problem.

The Contribution of Human Rights to Prison Life and Prisoner Treatment

Human Rights and Self Identity

One of the differences between the English and the Dutch accounts of imprisonment was that the Dutch were not exposed to depersonalisation and infantilisation to the degree experienced by the English. Prison officers addressed them by their names, and only four people complained about a dismissive and judgmental attitude among officers.

Based on their experiences of imprisonment and reflections on its purpose, they found the practice of number calling in some English quarters perverse. To some it was a sign of laziness while it reminded others of the military and its driving emphasis on unquestioned obedience to authority. It was seen befitting an authoritarian prison culture that consolidated the institution's power through prisoners' depersonalisation. It enfeebled prisoners and emotionally dissociated the staff from them, thus enabling the latter to tighten the grip on the former. This did not characterise their own prison culture, which rendered the few who complained about officers' attitudes angry rather than diffident. They were angry because their view of the officer's role was to *be social with prisoners* so as to motivate and assist them in their rehabilitation and resettlement efforts. As we shall see later in more detail, the idea of the officer as simply a turnkey was treated as an anathema to a prison system geared towards prisoners' successful resocialisation; a fundamental prison aim, as we have already seen, according to Dutch prisoners the undermining of which stripped the prison off its legitimacy.

The absence of number calling and the very low prevalence of infantilisation did not entail that Dutch prisons were a champion of prisoner empowerment. Dutch prisoners' sense of self was not left intact either, being acutely affected by the prison deprivations of security and autonomy (see Sykes 1958) that became sharper following the introduction of cell sharing and lifelong imprisonment.

Double Cells

Unlike English prisoners who have been customarily doubled up, Dutch prisoners were fortunate to have been spared from the inconveniences of cell sharing for a long time. The one prisoner to a cell rule, which was introduced in 1947 and was religiously observed till 1993, was officially abolished in 2004 (Tak 2003: 99). Against this background, it was not surprising that the real (now) prospect of cell sharing as a result of the abolition of the one to a cell rule was hugely unpopular with almost all participants. Out of the 12 who had had *the experience*, only one talked about it in a positive light; the rest loathed it, and none of the remainder was in favour of it.

Setting aside the typical impracticalities[1] of cell sharing, the Dutch were predominantly concerned about their security. In their view, sharing a cell most often than not with a stranger placed their physical and mental well-being at risk. Although fights among cellmates were not numerous, the men in particular had witnessed or had been involved in one, while both men and women raised safeguarding issues. They were especially worried about the risk of being unexpectedly assaulted by a cellmate as a result of a mental health condition or side effects from medication, as well as of the transmission of infectious diseases

[1] Dutch prisoners referred to issues, such as (un)dressing, eating while their cellmate uses the toilet, sleeping while their cellmate is watching TV/listening to the radio or smoking, and arguing over what TV programmes to watch.

following from a history of intravenous drug use or a risky lifestyle in general. Moreover, they were apprehensive about the impact of relational insecurity on their mental health, which sharing a cell with a complete stranger created. They feared that this relational insecurity could turn outwards and inwards, leading to incidents of violence against their cell-mate or self-harming and suicidal ideation brought about by depression and a mimicking behaviour.

> I said to the psychologist, *I cannot handle it.* They changed me because they worried that I would do something to myself. They have to ask people if they want to be placed together. Two in a cell is dangerous because you do not know who the other is, what they have done to be inside.
>
> I had a cell mate but they transferred her because she was troubled. They really need to think who to put where and with whom. If someone is psychotic, they should be placed with the mentally ill where they can get better healthcare. They keep giving them drugs to shut them up. Some are allergic to them; they become worse. They do not take people seriously.
>
> What if you wake up in the morning and he has taken his life or is holding a knife over you? You will not be able to sleep or you will start feeling like them.

Lack of familiarity with their cellmate was not the only undermining source of prisoners' mental and psychological stability. The loss of space and privacy was another front that they had to battle against.

The general claim was that the cells were materially unfit for shared accommodation. Additionally, there was the opinion that constant intimate exposure was unnatural for humans who, much as they longed for interaction, needed privacy too. To have one's own space where one could withdraw from the companion of others to pursue their personal interests was therefore fundamental. Having space and privacy were also essential for self-reflection and the first building blocks of their rehabilitation as they enhanced their mental well-being that, in turn, provided them with the determination to rebuild their lives.

This seeking for spaciousness and privacy was typically intensified in the controlled environment of the prison that among other deprivations restricted one's right to privacy. Like the English, the Dutch felt that their total lack of control over aspects of their social interaction stripped them off normality. The untoward nature of this existence compounded the gradual erosion of their sense of belonging, and as a defence mechanism they began to withdraw and cling on to their possessions. In the socially isolated and constantly under surveillance prison conditions, possessions were treated like treasure, a treasure that had a sentimental and a symbolic value more than a material one. Personal items connected prisoners both to their selfhood and social identity whose vulnerability in prison rendered the former out of bounds.

Participants acknowledged, however, that these benefits of being alone in the cell could be lost. Not everyone could cope with prison reality on their own or in the same way. Those among them who were less confident and independent sought and found security in a cellmate. Being locked up in a cell daily from 5 p.m. to 8 a.m., without someone to talk to, could trigger pessimistic thoughts and negative reactions, which the mere presence of a cellmate could perhaps forestall. In such cases, one could derive much needed emotional support and strength from a cellmate to withstand personal and prison-related adversities.

On these grounds, all participants called for cell sharing to take place on a voluntary basis. The risks associated with double cells were too great to bear. The only possible safeguards against them, which were not a silver bullet, were a properly developed screening and selection procedure, regular monitoring of joint placements, and vigilance on the part of officers. For example, assessments of such placements should carefully examine the fundamental issue of the two people's compatibility based on their offence type, needs, prison adjustment and age. Importantly, regarding staff vigilance, the officers' working strategy on the ground must be interactive and interventionist. Officers should actively engage with prisoners so that they could be in a position to detect promptly early signs of discontent and intervene. Their role should be akin to a mediator's, endeavouring to negotiate differences among prisoners and creating a trustful atmosphere on the wings. Notably, officers were central to the only positive experience of cell sharing recounted where they were praised for their consistently active involvement with prisoners and their commitment to providing a secure living environment for them.

> I was in a double for 2½ weeks in X. In X, it was better because piwis (the officers) were talking to women, trying to find out if there were problems and what they could do about them. They were trying to ease things not only with women but also between them. Here I find that prisoners are too explosive. It is only on Mondays that piwis are like this.

Lifelong Imprisonment

As mentioned in Chap. 4 since 2004 lifelong imprisonment has been an official practice. The three male lifers, I interviewed, strongly condemned the practice as a blatant and multiple human rights violation, questioning its legitimacy based on fundamental legal precepts, penological aims and humanistic values.

For Simon, who had been ten years into his life sentence, it was chiefly a matter of the nature and role of punishment in a democracy. As a firm believer in the social contract idea, he recognised as necessary the state's power to punish its lawbreakers and the public's expectation of it as legitimate. State laws provided a regulatory framework that enabled the state to function and its citizens to pursue their interests. Both parties carried responsibility for observing the law the disregard of which affected both. A state, which (criminally) victimised its people, was bound to lose their loyalty, while widespread criminality undermined societal cohesion and public confidence in its government. In either case, they harmed each other by harming themselves.

In such circumstances, recourse to punishment was needed and justified on retributive and utilitarian grounds. The act of punishing was intrinsically an act of communicating. First, it expressed reproach for a behaviour considered by the majority as harmful, for its actor's disobedience to state laws, and their indifference to society's welfare. Second, it endeavoured to educate the perpetrator about their personal and social responsibilities as members of society and citizens in order to dissuade them from engaging in similar acts in the future. Failure to account for the infliction of punishment and to actively involve the punished in this process compromised its purpose.

More crucially, deliberate failure to do so dishonoured the social contract and run contrary to its democratic values. It hindered social and political emancipation, thereby permanently excluding offenders from being active participants in their own lives. The state did not have the right to hold them forever responsible for past actions and behaviour. Such an approach was delusionary, unfair and discriminatory. According to Simon what all—governments, the public and offenders—failed to see was that their existence was tightly interdependent. 'In a Durkheimian vein, it was in nobody's long-term interests to incapacitate an increasingly growing number of people socially and politically, and for the latter to accept it. From experience, lest society and state crumbled away, they needed full time citizens and in full numbers' (Karamalidou 2012: 160).

Moreover, and related to its second function, punishment ought to correspond to the offence and reflect the nature of its bearer. In a Beccarian vein, among the fundamentals of a democracy was the pursuit of legal justice a by-product of which was the humane treatment of its people. Proportionality between the severity of the sanction and the gravity of the crime was a basic manifestation of humanity and justice, and the administration of punishment ought to be guided by the potential and needs of its sufferers.

Lifelong imprisonment as practised in the Netherlands failed to meet all of the above except for the expression of retribution. Being in some away analogous to the blanket application of the English mandatory life sentence to all degrees of murder prior to the 2003 CJA, it was indiscriminate, imposed on different serious offenders without allowing for their individual circumstances. This meant that all lifers were to serve the same life term irrespective of differences in their crimes. To make matters worse, it permanently excluded lifers from any rehabilitation programmes, thus denying them the potential of and the possibility to reform and be released.

Doing life without parole was lambasted by the other two lifers. For Paul, who had spent half of his adult life in prison and was by then three years into his life sentence, the death penalty was preferable to a life without the possibility of release. Death was an eventuality that the human mind and psyche could fathom and endure because painful as it were to experience or witness, it was the natural outcome of being alive.

The same could not be said for lifelong imprisonment because freedom was constitutive of a life worthy of a human being. Leading a free life was tautological with *feeling human*. The mere thought that one would be able to lead a free life even after many years in detention was sufficient to give them hope from which they could derive the strength to build a positive outlook for their future.

Peter who had been inside for five years and for the first time explicitly referred to this hope of release as the protective shield against a lifer's dehumanisation. He was adamant that lifelong imprisonment damaged a human being physically, emotionally and mentally. The knowledge that he would never be released entailed two things that set in motion the beginning of an end foretold at the court. First, and linked to the value of hope as a belief and feeling, he had nothing to anticipate, not even a knock back on his parole. Second, he was left with nothing that would give him a sense of purpose since rehabilitation schemes were closed off. Apart from remaining manageable for security reasons, he did not have any meaningful responsibilities. In his opinion, to take away even one's hope against hope that they would be someday free was gravely irresponsible, certainly perilous, and unquestionably inhumane. For the prison system, lifelong imprisonment was a Trojan horse and for the legislature a travesty of justice. A state of complete hopelessness was a volatile state seething with loneliness, desperation, envy, bitterness and revenge that became unbearable with the passing of time and had to find an outlet. Their simultaneous presence increased their toxicity and made the force and consequences of their release difficult to predict.

> In a certain way, it sets you crazy. Somebody gives me a hard time, stab, punch him, whatever. But you try to stay calm. The problem with staying calm is that you have to do it on your own. You cannot talk to anybody. There is no programme. Hope keeps you away from doing very stupid things. It does not allow the system to create the monster, to make me a monster. To have a date to look for keeps you human.

Regression and violent behaviour as a cry for help, survival mechanism and an effect of lifelong imprisonment were also familiar to Paul who additionally showed signs of fixation.

> Sometimes I get fucked up things in my head, but I think twice. But I am going to tell you something. When I will be out, it is fucked up. I will be waiting for them outside. They know.

According to the three lifers if the authorities had any modicum of humanity, they would create a special lifer unit equipped to deal with the complex sensitivities of people with no prospect of release. The dispersal practice in operation as a result of which they were moved from one institution to another created an agonising experience that increased the already great strain they were under. Prison transfers fuelled their despair as they reminded them of their powerlessness to initiate any meaningful change in their lives. People like them whose agency gradually atrophied through a lack of use needed above all stability. Stability created a sense of security and provided people with a sense of control over their lives, a feeling that they were eager to relive even if it was artificial.

Moreover, by being dispersed, they found themselves mixed with mainstream prisoner categories whose presence was destabilising and psychologically taxing. The sight of and interaction with prisoners with determinate sentences deepened their depressive mood by constantly reminding them of a normal life that had long gone. Through no fault of their own, fixed-term prisoners made the lifers wallow in self-pity on a good day, while on bad day the latter wished they could kill themselves. However, there were occasions where fixed-term prisoners selfishly stirred trouble, having consequences for the lifers as well. The most inconsiderable and arrogant were usually those on short sentences who put a show of braggadocio in the safety of their prospective release.

> In another prison, I was with one with 6 years and TBS. They know that after 6 years they have to go to TBS, and it can go up to 12 years. It was very quiet. There was a sort of respect for each other. You know that you have to do a long time so you take it easy. The guy with 6 months says, *Fuck you, in 6 months I am gone*. When the problems are that big that they change activities or other things, I am stuck with that. Then, you have people who are allowed to go every 6 weeks home for the weekend. That gives a certain psychological pressure on the people who have to do a lot more time.

When dispersed and mixed with mainstream prisoner categories, the bravado of some of the other prisoners was not the only challenge a lifer faced. Feelings of exasperations and envy went hand in hand with that of loneliness. Paul and Peter talked at length about the lifer's stigma and its adverse impact on fellow prisoners' and staff attitudes towards them, their self-identity and the quality of their life. The die-hard stereotype of a lifer was someone who was amoral, hence savage. That they had taken a human life—the ultimate crime—was incontrovertible evidence that they knew no moral barriers, which made their behaviour highly unpredictable. So, they could not be trusted. Paranoia and fear set in in their company.

While Paul and Peter sympathised with the uneasiness and insecurity that they provoked in others, they pondered on the injustice that was created and enveloped them by the indiscriminate encouragement of such stereotypes. It was a common secret that human nature was as much fallible as able to reform itself, but their nature was not seen in this light. From the point of sentencing and beyond, they represented depravity and dangerousness that swept away any other dimensions of their identity. Most around them kept their distance to an extent that at times it was difficult to find someone to hold a simple conversation with. This extended to officers who were out of their depth due to a lack of specialised training and understanding of the effects of lifelong imprisonment. The severity of life without parole and its connotations for the lifer's character augmented the unfairness of the perpetuation of their monstrous image, and their resultant social isolation plunged further into the dark recesses of their mind. In short, all the necessary preconditions for the realisation of their alleged monstrosity were in place.

> In this prison now, nobody speaks to me because they are afraid of me. *Yeah, this guy is dangerous. He can kill.* How is it for me? It is like better to kill myself because I do not want to live. But, when you have communication with people, it is different…The people who will work there will know that these guys are on life. Now there are two lifers there, two here, and the guards are not specialised. They do not know how to treat you.
>
> They judge you based only on that moment, and it does not matter what you are doing in the future or did in the past. One wrong decision in a

moment makes him not human? To take away everything from the person for that single moment seems harsh to me. I think people with long sentences think three times before they do something wrong again. They know what they had, they lost it, and after 20–25 years they get back what they want. So, they make sure that there is a difference. These are the normal guys. A really crazy guy does not have the urge to sit at home with his girlfriend or whatever. But, you can pick them out in a few days...Supervision, control...that's why there are certain problems you have to get off your chest, but there is no one to speak to because they do not know how to cope with that. In the 4 months I am here I had only two conversations with one guard. He wants to know what is happening. The rest, no interest.

Human Rights and Social Identity

As mentioned in the introduction to this chapter, prisoners' social identity dominated their conceptualisations of human rights in prison. Despite their deep feelings of unease about cell sharing, they were seeking the company of others to filter the negativity of the carceral experience. We have already seen this in: the lifers' battle against the indelible stigma of their crimes and call for specially trained staff in want of socialisation and constructive interaction; and in the prisoners' emphasis on the importance of relational security in general, sprung from changes in the makeup of the prison population, social attitudes to ethnic minorities and prison regimes. By placing the social dimension of their lives centre stage, not only did they make a case for who and what prisoners were like but also identified the aims of imprisonment and the methodology for their realisation in a human rights context.

For the Dutch, the success of the prison and subsequently its legitimacy rested fundamentally on its recognition and support of their sociability and membership of society. Following from the inalienable social dimension of their existence and its categorical importance for the quality of their life, the purpose of imprisonment was, self-evidently, prisoners' reintegration into society by the means of rehabilitation and resocialisation. Rehabilitation focused on the treatment of individual pathology and the harnessing of cognitive skills. Resocialisation aimed at resiliency and social emancipation through an emphasis on education and wider learning opportunities. Lastly, like in the English case, reintegration concerned prisoner adjustment to society at large and family life in particular, with the rights to privacy and family life, to work, to a fair remuneration, and to social assistance being identified as important enablers. In order to effect the three Rs, prison life had to be normalised as much as possible. This entailed (a) continuity and parity in the provision of care and services between the prison and society; (b) a gradual and structured re-connection with the outside world through systematic sentence planning, weekend leave and community work; (c) freedom to exercise responsibility; and (d) the availability of opportunities to make valued contributions.

Resocialisation

According to the Dutch while resocialisation was still talked about as an imprisonment aim, in practice it did not mean much. They complained about the reduced availability of education provision and its quality. Prison education was basic and did not provide access to advanced learning opportunities for those who were interested in and had the academic ability to engage in more advanced learning. The quality of vocational training posed similar issues since the skills being taught did not reflect the needs of the job market. Lack of quality prison education and vocational training, as well as difficulties in accessing existing provision due to increases in prisoner numbers and staff reductions, compromised prisoners' progress and development. What made the situation worse was a selection procedure that excluded those who needed such opportunities the most, namely, young people.

The penitentiary programmes (see Chap. 4) were a good example in this respect. They aimed to empower prisoners and assist them in resettling back into the community. However, their selection criteria and community-based character compromised these aims. To get a place on these programmes, prisoners had to show interest in changing their lifestyles and the ability to adjust to and abide by the programmes' requirements.

'So, dangling the reward of freedom before prisoners quickly created a long queue where everyone professed to be ready to change their ways. As a result of the selection criteria the age group that was more prone to recidivism-mostly prisoners in their 20s-was unfairly disadvantaged. Older prisoners had witnessed many talented and intelligent young people missing out on opportunities because of their tempestuous youthfulness. Instead, it was them (the older ones) who were offered a place in a programme that most of the time was unsuitable to their station in life. Neither younger nor older prisoners gained in the long term' (Karamalidou 2012: 159).

For more than half of the participants, the remains of the resocialisation agenda were compromised by the politicisation of criminal justice policy in general and prison budget cuts in particular. Strongly reminiscent of New Labour's offender responsibilisation offensive (see Chap. 3), penitentiary programmes and measures, such as SOV and ISD (see Chap. 4), communicated to offenders and the public that there was no room for 'more excuses'. Those who broke the law had to be robustly confronted, imprinting on their minds the certainty and discomforts of punishment.

Punishment could turn from an unpleasant and painful experience into a celebrated transformation, but they—the offenders—held the key to it. Access to resocialisation schemes was no longer an automatic right; it had to be earned. In the prisoners' opinion, the adopted slogan of offender responsibilisation was catching. It satisfied the victims' need for justice and re-assured the public that their government was addressing their concerns. But unless there was financial investment in the offender responsibilisation agenda, the security it offered was temporary and artificial. It failed to address the underlying problem of economic, social and political exclusion that continued post release. As they admitted, they could not wake up to their responsibilities by proxy, but they needed help from the state and society's understanding in order to do this by themselves.

All participants named education as an effective vehicle for their resocialisation, which they treated both as a good in itself and as a means of desistance from crime. Education was powerful because of the richness of its sources and tools, and the skills and outlook on life one acquired as a result.

> Education is going down. You need to give people social skills, to know a trade they can use outside to earn money and live like normal people. Education gives you a push, and you need to be pushed. It makes your mind wide. You are not afraid of things which are new to you.
>
> On behalf of the prison committee I asked if it was possible for prisoners to learn how to resuscitate people. The answer is, *I do not think this is necessary because all the guards have to learn it.* You think that the thief will not resuscitate somebody if he can help? He is human and his first reaction will be how he can help. Teach people valuable things. The more you value somebody, the more you let him see that he can make a difference. If you want to resocialise somebody, the most important thing is to give him trust.
>
> If they want to make what they say true, they should provide better work and education. Even a blind horse can do the work that we do right now. There is a school for computer courses, but it is not easy to get into, and there are not enough teachers. It is not working, and they are not taking it seriously themselves. Probably they have seen that a lot people in whom they put some effort did not make it. So they are probably demoralised themselves. If you do not believe in your job anymore, find another job. Even if it is 1 out of 10, they should put 100% effort. In reality, they put 20% for everybody.

Following from the above, what commands attention is the lens through which prisoners assessed the role of education in their personal and social development. In an Aristotelian vein, they highlight the teacher's decisive role in the student's learning journey and their duties to them. Learning is an interactive process predicated on a mutual engagement between students (prisoners) and teachers (staff), which should strive inter alia to instil an ethos of personal and social responsibility in students. Implicit in this teacher's duty is the need to encourage the student on their learning journey, which is a recognition of the student's ability to learn and do well. Showing confidence here in prisoners' learning potential has the same significance with and shares a similar function to lifers' hope of release. It saves them from defeatism and desperation by strengthening them mentally and emotionally. It also provides them with a network of support that can guide and empower them in their steps to independence.

What underscores prisoners' approach to education in the context of resocialisation is the crucial importance they attributed to social interaction, which they drew attention to twice before—first, in the image of the cellmate as a mentor and, second, in lifers' seeking for an interlocutor. For the Dutch, the educative qua resocialising potential of social interaction was not restricted to the classroom and the workshop. It already existed beyond these spaces, in everyday communication (see, e.g. Warr 2016). On this basis, they argued that the authorities had a narrow-minded idea of the forms that resocialisation initiatives could take and referred to one particular instance that was left unexplored, or rather was abandoned.

They extensively referred to the missed learning opportunities following from the drastic downsizing in officer numbers between 5 p.m. and 8 a.m. and the resultant abolition of evening socialisation. Both changes were lamentable for the following reasons some of which were unexpected.

Self-evidently, more time out of the cell facilitated by evening socialisation was very important on its own considering the distinct possibility of cell sharing. In an environment that deprived them of their liberty, restricted their freedoms of movement and choice, and limited their right to privacy even when banged up, evening socialisation would give them a sense of normality; for a few hours they could be their own masters and decide what to do and in which order. Soothing as this could be, it paled next to the other benefits.

Evening socialisation created immensely valuable learning opportunities. (Re)socialisation required the exercise of volition and interaction with others. Through interaction with other people, they would be presented with learning opportunities on how to approach, communicate and engage in a dialogue with others. This would give them a sense of accomplishment that, in turn, would boost their self-respect and worth, thus increasing their determination to be resocialised. For the Dutch, it was the lack of such opportunities which they felt they were being infantilised by. In this respect, the provision of a dedicated space to interact with one another and with officers was seen as empowering and educational. Adopting a pragmatic approach, they acknowledged that as prisoners they would always entertain suspicions about officers, and the same was true about the latter. The facts were that there were troublesome and dangerous individuals in the prisoner population, and the officers were the people who were tasked with managing them. At the same time, however, the officer was the most immediate contact for the prisoner and as a result in a position to get to know prisoners well. The officer's strategic position could be actively and positively employed to empower, guide and assist prisoners in their resocialising efforts. Those with previous experience of imprisonment lamented the reduced numbers of officers and their reduced availability. Prisoner engagement with officers during evening socialisation was seen as very important. It enabled both sides to get to know each other and become more appreciative of their respective challenges, as well as to learn and practise important social skills.

> The days are from 8am to 5pm now.[2] What everybody is missing is a little bit of social contact with each other. It gives you a kind of feeling that you are here with a big family. It is a missed opportunity to rehabilitate people by giving education at night or watching a movie with other prisoners or doing activities. They think that they can stop crime with harsher punishment.
>
> We need to learn to talk in prison, prisoners and staff. If you do not talk about things, you get nothing from being in prison. I am living again the same things and do not like it. You need more than one person to talk to. You get different ways of seeing things. This is how you learn to handle things better.
>
> The guard[3] is among the first people. You see and talk to him every day. He can give a better opinion. They do not have enough guards. It is the

[2] In the summer, lockdown was at 6 p.m.

[3] Adding another contrast to the prisoner experience in the two countries, Dutch prisoners were also (generally speaking) positively disposed towards mental health professionals who they trusted and valued. 21 out of the 29 participants had been in contact with a psychologist/psychiatrist. Sixteen were satisfied with the support and care they received. The five, who did not share this view, provided an account similar to that of the English lifers/CAT A prisoners, which was similarly shared by the other English participants. They argued that psychologists/psychiatrists behaved like robots, being more interested in recording information and reporting to the authorities than engaging with the prisoner and their needs. The effects of this was prisoners' inability and fear (in case restrictive safety measures were taken in respect of their treatment) to *turn the light on in the dark corners of their mind*, which worsened their mental health plight and made them paranoid. Like English prisoners, they argued that this did not enable them to actually deal with their problems and prepare for their release. The interrelated 'pains of psychological assessment and prisoners' self-government' are documented in other prison research (see, e.g. Crewe 2011). Crewe (2011: 513–520) highlights their intensification in the context of today's penality where risk

money, [it is] Hague. It is from high that they think about something; *we do this, that*. The officer has to do it and is also not happy about that. I think it is possible to get a lot of changes if the officers have the responsibility. But they only have the key.

Reintegration

As mentioned earlier, like the English when the Dutch talked about their reintegration, they differentiated between its micro- and macro levels. At micro-level, they would return to and join their families, and at macro level, society at large. In relation to the former, they too laid emphasis on the protection of their right to respect for private and family life, and identified the rights to work, fair remuneration, and to social assistance as necessary for their successful reintegration into society, placing like the English the onus of responsibility for their facilitation on the state.

---

identification and management are the dominant priorities. In his research, he documents the negative psychological impact of these two pains, which lead to increased prisoner anxiety and insecurity, and their distorting effects on their selfhood. As Crewe (2011: 522–525) notes, in the twenty-first century, the experience of imprisonment may be less physically oppressive but psychologically is 'tighter'. Prisoners are now called to actually actively participate in their control and management by engaging in a conscious modification of their behaviour.

In relation to prison (mental) healthcare in general, it is worth mentioning a personal observation during the course of the fieldwork in Dutch prisons. On my visit to a prison, on two separate occasions, I witnessed prison officers acting in the role of the chemist. At lockdown, they would give prisoners their medication, which was in sealed plastic bags. In my view, the practice put prisoners' (mental) health at risk since (a) if they had a cellmate, they could exchange medications, (b) or they could simply not take it, and (c) they could experience adverse reactions from the medication while locked up for 15 hours. I communicated my concerns informally to the prison officers and medical staff (a prison psychologist). The prison officers did not share my concerns. The answer was that the medication had already been prepared by the relevant staff, and the plastic bags had clear identifiers on them. The correct medication was delivered to the right people. The prison psychologist was more receptive to my concerns. They acknowledged the practical and ethical dilemmas involved but highlighted that since this was a custodial environment, as opposed to a civil mental health setting, adjustments had to be made. In a personal communication I had with a psychologist working in an acute civil mental health setting in England and Wales, my attention was drawn precisely to the need for a monitoring period after medication is given to patients in order to intervene promptly in case of side effects from medication and/or concealment of medication. The CoE Recommendation (98)7 on the ethical and organisational aspects of healthcare in prison reminds us that 'A medical prescription should remain the exclusive responsibility of the medical profession, and medicines should be distributed by authorised personnel only'. It is regrettable that the Recommendation does not define in more detail who this authorised personnel should be.

Return to Family

If we were to name the most fundamental human right in prison from both the English and the Dutch perspectives, it would be prisoners' contact with their families. Acknowledgement of its magnitude bore the same force in the two national settings and produced almost identical accounts.

Family contact was enormously significant for Dutch prisoners. Maintaining contact with their families and playing an active part in them re-affirmed their being *normal* and helped normalise to a degree the prison experience. In being able to perform their roles as parents and partners, they were able to escape their prisoner identity and develop a sense of real purpose and belonging. For these reasons, their families exerted an emancipatory influence on them that allowed them to visualise their reintegration. For the Dutch the reintegrative value of their family relations did not stem from their family's ability to positively shame them but from the trust their family placed in them. This is not the first time that we come across the importance that Dutch prisoners attributed to the aspects of familiarity and trust. They surfaced earlier in the peer support a cellmate could offer, and in the role of the prison officer as an interlocutor and mentor. Like in those instances, here too to trust and to be trusted were vital ingredients for prisoners' reintegration.

Like the English, the Dutch discussed the issue of family with reference to visits but, unlike their counterparts who were concerned both about their partners and children, they were predominantly preoccupied about their relationship with their children. They too called for changes in the provision of visits in terms of frequency and duration in want for more privacy, intimacy and quality time with their beloved ones. Despite their comparatively more favourable visiting arrangements, they wished visits of general nature had been more regular than once a week, longer than an hour and accommodating more than two people per session. Children's visits, which were normally once a month for two hours, with activities differing from one institution to another, were also seen as insufficient.

It is worth noting that they identified the change of visits from weekends to weekdays as problematic. After placements in or transfers to institutions far away from their hometowns, this new development was the second-greatest discouragement of visits that sabotaged in effect their family relationships. 'They considered it utterly thoughtless and heartless and listed a number of newly created complications that the former weekend arrangement demonstrated blatantly their tractability. Visits on weekdays were highly disruptive of visitors' lives' (Karamalidou 2012: 154). People who worked had to take leave and risked wage reductions if they wanted to visit every week. They were therefore disinclined to set off on a weekly prison journey, even more so if the prison was not close to their homes. Also, children would have to miss school, which made it even harder to visit.

Both men and women voiced concerns about their kids' emotional development in their absence, especially if it was long term. They remarked that the children of the imprisoned mothers and fathers were the *first victims* of their imprisonment. With implicit feelings of guilt, they belaboured the child's right to know why their parent was absent, observing that it was *wrong and unfair to let kids grow up thinking that they were not loved or that it was their own fault.* More frequently scheduled children's visits that took into account children's developmental needs based on their age were therefore indispensable. In this way, like other children, their own children could get to know their parents, spend time with and be emotionally supported by them. At the same time as parents they would be in a better position to explain matters early and to share some of the burden of their children's guardians.

Dutch female prisoners agreed with their English counterparts that having the choice to keep their babies with them was important. None of them thought that in reality they had much choice as they were unable to have their babies in a closed prison after they became 10 months old. They strongly believed that for both parties it was too soon to separate and argued fervently for an extension of the nine-month age limit. In acknowledgement of the security considerations, they called on the authorities to provide longer stay facilities in closed institutions for those assessed as dangerous to escape or to the public. In their opinion, women who did not pose such a risk and wanted to be with their child should have had the right to be transferred to Ter Peel.[4]

> It is ridiculous. One hour a week, and then from Monday to Friday when every normal person is working and kids go to school. They [visits] should be 2 hours and on weekends. It was not that way before. You had visits on Saturdays and Sundays; sometimes also during the week. They have to take a day off work. Kids have to skip school. If they want to come every week, they cannot ask for a day off every time. For how long can they do it? They will lose their job at some point. Some live far. They may need to take the next day off too. It also costs money, and you will be losing money if you cannot go to work. If they can visit on weekends, they can plan better and bring the kids. Kids need normality in their life and school.
>
> I believe we have a Father-Child day once a month, which is a visit in a more spacious room with toys and candies. It can be very important for a child 3–4 years old; not to be surprised when daddy comes home, thinking, *Who is this guy? Oh, yes, the guy from that building we used to go once a week.* You can focus all your attention on your child, really listening to them and them to you. I have a daughter, but I have never used it. It is painful.
>
> Prisoners' children seem to have no rights. It is not healthy for them not to be able to do normal things like any parent with their kids does. There are 4 officers present. You have no privacy. In X, it was much better than here. They were doing things to help the mothers. There were an inside and an outside house. In the outside house, there were space and activities. Your heart breaks when you cannot be with them, to tell them that you are also an individual, a woman except for being their mum; that things happen when you are an adult.

Return to Society

Like the English, the Dutch highlighted the instructional and instrumental value of work but comparatively, like the right to education the rights to work and a fair remuneration were a higher priority on the Dutch reintegration agenda.

---

[4]Ter Peel was at the time a semi-open prison and the only establishment in the country offering a similar provision to the English Mother and Baby Units. Imprisoned mothers could keep their babies there up to the age of four.

The Dutch complained about the menial nature of prison work, which they described as *boring*, *childish*, *for crazy people*, and *underpaid*. In their view, this showed that as a concept and aim, prisoner reintegration was not taken seriously. Prison work held no appeal to them except for as an opportunity for socialisation with other prisoners and interaction with staff. The absence of proper recreation time from the daily schedule meant that if they did not work, they would become socially alienated. Prisons were turned into business industries where commercial companies would bid for prison contracts, being attracted by cheap labour and high profits. It was a public relations exercise. The authorities employed such contracts as evidence of their commitment to contribute to the well-being of the communities that prisons served by instilling inter alia a work ethic in prisoners.

A genuine state commitment to their reintegration required the provision of meaningful and adequately paid work that they could engage inside the prison and gradually outside the prison walls. Here meaningfulness refers as much to the relevance of knowledge and skills for employability purposes as to their intrinsic worth. The implementation of hybrid employment schemes (part prison-based and part community-based) would ease their transition from prison to society as they would be able to test their social and job skills in real time and in a diverse environment.

In further support of the significance of meaningful prison work, participants pointed out that typically prisoners did not have a stable employment record either because they did not have adequate qualifications or as a result of their criminal lifestyles; and some were simply not interested in finding employment. So, they were not habituated to the idea of work. To appreciate the benefits of work and get into the habit of working, above all they had to be confident in their abilities. Work that required no mental input like existing prison work was 'demotivating and demoralising' (Karamalidou 2012: 154). It communicated to the person who was engaging in such work that this was the optimum that they were trusted to do.

The 12 euro wage contributed to prisoners' lack of motivation and interest in legal work. Prisoners described their pay as derisory, unethical and discriminatory, with a few calling it *slave pay*. It was unethical considering the strong campaigns in the Western world for fair trade practices and was discriminatory because their compatriots on the outside earned more while doing the same work. In this respect, it would be only fair and just, as well as conducive to building up their self-esteem and a work ethic, for the legal minimum wage to be extended to prisoners. Alluding to the importance of reintegration as a penological aim, the application of the minimum wage to prisoners had to be also accompanied by legislation placing a legal duty on employers to include in their workforce a certain number of released prisoners.

> They have these prison industries because they do not have to pay the same as outside. Everybody says, *you cannot buy this T-shirt or these shoes because they are made in Taiwan or China, and people make only $3 a day*. We do not even make $1 a day. Where is the money going? Paying you more shows respect for what you do and are. They show you that you worth it. How are you supposed to change your ways when your efforts are not valued?
>
> They should pay us the legally minimum wage that is outside. There should be a law that says that employers should employ X number of people coming out prison. I understand that they must check you first; like a paedophile should never work in a school, or a drug-addict in a place where there are drugs. But they can do this anyway.

Human Rights and Civic Identity

As already seen, the Dutch participants offered strong affirmations of their citizen status, manifested in their calls, for example for equality and equal treatment before the law, education and employment, highlighting the importance and contribution of the normalisation of prison life to their resocialisation and reintegration prospects. They also expressed strong civic and democratic sentiments, invoking principles and practices, such as democratic accountability in relation to the institutional treatment of prisoners' committees, and active and collective participation in common affairs through the prisoner committee mechanism and voting.

Like in the English case, Dutch prisoners' strong affirmations of their being still citizens behind bars, which ought to be reflected in their treatment and rights, did not translate into an appreciation of their own responsibilities. As mentioned in Chap. 5, this was an important finding that was even starker in the Dutch context, where prisoners' interpretations of human rights were heavily based on the social contract idea and the primacy of their social identity.

Prisoner Committees

Like their English counterparts, the Dutch referred to the aspects of accountability and transparency as important indicators of the authorities' recognition of and respect for their human rights. They too complained about the malleability of the prison rules that created confusion and led to tensions. To avert tensions and increase prisoners' sense of security, they argued for consistency in the application of the prison rules among similar institutions, or at least an easy access to them especially since prisoner transfers had become common.

Moreover, they called for changes in the operation and institutional treatment of prisoners' committees which they were proud of, citing them as an example of the embeddedness in the Dutch prison system of prisoners' right to complain.

In contrast to the English ad hoc operation of prisoner committees at wing level, prisoner committees have existed in Dutch prisons since the 1970s (Franke 1995: 265), being officially stipulated in the Dutch House (Prison) Rules. They bear some of the characteristics that the English proposed. Their members are prisoners elected by prisoners, with every wing having its own committee (Art 5, 1999 Dutch House Rules). The committees have though no executive powers. On every wing, prisoners can table proposals that are then put to the vote. Typically, proposals are concerned with issues arising out of prisoners' detention in the specific institution. The most popular ones are put forward for consideration by the prison management in the committee's meeting with the wing manager. It falls upon the governor to ensure that such meetings take place at regular intervals (ibid.)

In the prisoners' view, the purpose of these committees was to institute an additional monitoring mechanism in each establishment beside the Supervisory Committee in order to increase institutional levels of transparency and accountability. This did not materialise as there was no open and seamless dialogue between committee members and the prison management. Prisoners' proposals were often rejected without clear and prompt explanations given. Like in the English case, the timely dissemination of clear feedback was very important for the Dutch as it was the only way they could properly understand the institution's procedures, benefit from its services, and challenge its practices when these fell short of prescribed standards. Additionally, there was no set timetable for meeting with the management, and these meetings were not effectively monitored. Holding preferably monthly meetings attended by the governor, who had ultimately the power to initiate change, was seen as necessary for prisoner committees to be effective.

> We have here a new prisoner committee. They are trying to put things across to the management, but we never get a straight answer. This happens once every 6 weeks. You have to wait for the other units too. They should say that we-the prisoner committee, the unit manager, senior officers, the director, any other prisoners who want-will meet from now on once a month to discuss what the serious matters of the wing are. We have a democracy outside. There should be a dialogue like in a democracy. They should listen to the reasons…If you can see and talk to the director, you can let them know directly what is happening. Unless he comes down, sees it themselves and hears it from prisoners, things that need change will not change. He has the power to do this.
>
> They also have to explain why it is not possible. What message does this send out about the organisation of the country's services and institutions? What does it tell you about how we treat people?

Enfranchisement

One of the most notable differences between the English and Dutch prison systems regarding the legalisation of prisoners' human rights is their approach to prisoner voting. As of 2016 prisoners in England and Wales cannot vote whereas the Netherlands has enfranchised all prisoners (Hirst v. The United Kingdom 6 October 2005: para. 33). While the latter was largely unknown to the Dutch participants (out of the 29 interviewed only 8 knew that they could vote), in contrast to the English, nearly half of them (13 in number) raised the issue themselves, seeing in the right to vote one of their fundamental human rights qua prisoners qua citizens.

In the view of those 13, their criminal record did not take away their human ability to hold and express opinions as rational agents. There was nothing nonsensical about the argument that they rightfully had a say in how the society which they had lived in and would be returning to was governed. As an act and right, voting was important in two respects. It sensitised the individual that they were part of a common body so to speak, and therefore both shared a common present and future. If they were disillusioned with their present and aspired to a better future, they individually had to take action and also mobilise themselves as a body to effect change. Procrastination was futile and irresponsible because while they waited for someone to *rock the boat*, more and more people could be sinking under it, dragging them under it too.

> I think it is a basic right to have a vote. I am a human being, not a bin of garbage. There is also life here. If I do not agree with my government, I have also the right to comment on it. At some point we will be out again.
>
> I vote because this is how things here and out can change for the better. You get to talk about what you want. You cannot complain about the government and then not to vote.

Human Rights and Human Responsibilities

> A lot of people here do not read what the position in law is. So they do not know. They shout a lot of things. *Ok, read the book! You do not have to shout!* But, it is also from the other side. Sometimes, I ask the guards here, *have you ever read this?!* They say, *no*. Why not?! Because if you are interested in us and we have to be interested in the system, read it and you know.

One of the things that the above quote reminds us of is our fallibility and our resultant tendency sometimes to deflect (criticism) and disengage, and to reflect, in the best-case scenario, afterwards. Elements of this made a strong appearance near the end of the interviews when the subject changed from human rights to *human responsibilities*.

Like the English, the Dutch were asked whether they had human responsibilities in a similar fashion they argued for their human rights, and whether crime could be considered a human rights violation. Out of the 24, 18 held the view (some of them reluctantly) that on a closer examination each concept was implicit in the other for the purposes of promoting individual and general welfare. The general opinion was that their human responsibilities were (a) to follow the prison and society's rules; (b) to respect even those who were no respecter of persons; and (c) to desist from crime. One rejected the idea outright and four oscillated between the two positions, arguing that they could not envision how a notion of human responsibilities could be construed in a similar fashion.

Moreover, only five participants acknowledged the concept of crime as a human rights violation and the harm it caused to others. They referred to two kinds of victims and more than one type of harm involved. They identified as victims of crime the people directly affected by the offence and society at large. In their view, individual victims could suffer physically, psychologically and financially. They recognised that the psychological harm could sometimes be so grave that victims would go on living in a perpetual state of fear of falling again victims to crime. Irrational as this fear could become, it had a viral potency that was not to be underestimated. The reason was that fear of crime did not grow out of personal experiences alone. Distorted media representations of crime and populist political rhetoric were another two of its sources.

While the above contribution represented the minority view, the majority's response to the idea of crime as a human rights violation can be described as alarmingly detached and unsympathetic. The majority was of the view that the validity of this idea was conditional on either one of two factors. These were the direct infliction of physical harm upon another person and the absence of victim precipitation. The adjective *direct* denotes here that the harm had to be done by the perpetrator themselves. In this respect, two interviewees stressed that the aspect of direct physical harm was wrongly extended to drug dealing where responsibility laid on the users, not the dealers. It was, in their view, only the former who actually harmed themselves through their own substance abuse.

A representative sample of the two opposing views is found below:

> Some years back, I never used to think about the victim. It was as spontaneous thing. I needed money quickly to get drugs. As I grow older, and when I am alone in the cell, I sometimes think that the guy who I held the gun against in the armed robbery perhaps will never forget it. Maybe I have left him with a psychological trauma. Maybe, he now lives in fear.
>
> You are not only violating somebody's human rights. You are also violating society's rights. When someone robs a bank, time, appointments and many other things are lost because of his crime.
>
> Only if it is a killing because a person loses their life. Also, burglary because they may be violent if people are inside the house.
>
> It depends on the crime, for example kidnapping, yes; it damages somebody. They need more time to recover. In the case of murder, the person is dead. He does not know anything more. Ok, their family is hurt, but not their human rights.
>
> I am in jail for drugs. I sell them to people, but I do not force them to buy them. I have something they want. The judge called me a mass-murderer. I was so angry with him! It was not his job to give his personal opinion! His job was to give me my punishment based on what I did and what the law said.
>
> In my case, there are victims, but only with money. Someone's rights are violated just by the way they look, for example fat people. In a way, you can say yes. They have not asked for it.

Conclusion

Like the English, the Dutch argued for human rights recognition and protection, invoking their humanity and sociability. Human rights recognition and protection was a matter of principle and pragmatism for them. Human rights gave people *a fair chance to walk as a human [being] in life* and enabled them to become the *perfect human*. The *perfect human* was a being that lived their life in a society where they could develop themselves, progress and contribute in the company of others. The indispensability of human rights for a life worthy to be called human entailed that resocialisation and reintegration ought to be the fundamental aims of the prison, especially in a democracy governed by the rule of law. Disregard of these aims stripped the prison off its legitimacy.

In this context, drawing like the English on negative and positive rights and negative and positive state interference, the Dutch envisaged the prison primarily as a place for social and civic emancipation. In this respect, they identified the contribution of the prison officer as especially important. Reflecting historical differences between the English and the Dutch prison systems in the area of staff-prisoner relationships (see Chap. 2), the Dutch were (generally speaking) positively disposed towards officers who they essentially described as potential human rights ambassadors. Overall, these differences can be seen as a sign of the different cultural approaches to punishment between the two countries where remnants of the once strong commitment to resocialisation and reintegration *for all* are present in prisoners' views.

While the punitive direction of the preceding years seems not to have negatively affected prisoners' perceptions of officers, which implies an absence of antagonism and the existence of professionalism on the part of the staff, it affected the quality of their relationship and the prisoner experience. Double cells were a reality that led to prisoner insecurity and anxiety. Staff cuts and the harshening of the regimes saw the abolition of evening socialisation, which left prisoners with reduced opportunities for social interaction with fellow prisoners and staff where they could build and exercise all sorts of social skills. Also, the change in visiting arrangements from weekends to weekdays limited their contact with their family. All this shows that regressive, punitive developments are particularly aggressive, establishing themselves far more quickly than progressive developments that typically take time to flourish and deliver results.

7

Embedding Human Rights in Prison

Introduction

As a result of the legalisation of prisoners' human rights in Europe, we are at a stage now that European states and their prison administrations can no longer in principle ignore issues of human rights. In the risk-dominated wider socio-political context in which we live our lives and political decisions are made, it is perhaps no wonder that human rights themselves have become one more risk, which states and public bodies must factor in their decision and policymaking. In his assessment of the development of human rights into an organisational (legal) risk for the prison service in the UK, which can be equally applied to other European national prison systems, Whitty (2011) identifies a second type of risk, which he views as equally formidable in its effects. Whitty calls this 'legal risk+' and defines it as 'the capacity of human rights activism to propel an issue to centre stage, damaging an organisation's operations and reputation, irrespective of actual legal liability' (2011: 124).

Human rights as legal risk and 'legal risk+' are indeed a potent force of change in terms of their contribution to the development of a human rights-informed prison policy and prison management model. However,

A. Karamalidou, *Embedding Human Rights in Prison*,
DOI 10.1057/978-1-137-58502-8_7

as we have seen in Chaps. 1, 3 and 4, there is a parallel social and political reality that is hostile and/or not fully committed to the human rights idea in general and in prisons in particular. The hijacking of human rights by a risk discourse and penal populism and the unwavering popularity of imprisonment as punishment in Europe are potent counterforces to the potential of human rights as legal risk and 'legal risk+'.

While, unlike the *Rehabilitation Revolution* in English prisons, the 'human rights revolution' has reached such dimensions that Ignatieff (2001) wrote about *Human Rights as Politics and Idolatry*, it has its limitations. For example, in relation to the juridical aspect of the human rights revolution, judicial decisions are reactive by nature. In the majority of cases, findings of human rights violations cannot undo the harm done to the victims; they are already harmed. They do have an inbuilt preventative function, but this works at group level, not at individual level. 'Legal and policy changes as a result of positive findings of human rights violations strengthen the position of those who may or are likely to be in similar situation to that of the present victim in the future' (Karamalidou 2012: 150).

Moreover, as the human rights case law on life sentences and prisoner enfranchisement in England and Wales illustrates, judicial decisions produce incremental changes and can also be stalled or be strongly resisted for years. For example, *Newell* and *McLoughin* (2014) were heard in anticipation of the 2015 general elections and the pledged EU referendum against the background of aggressive media reporting on Europe and its conflation of the ECtHR with Brussels (McNulty et al. 2014). We cannot but wonder whether the political climate and the nature of the public debate on Europe exerted some kind of influence on the outcome of the case. After all, as Ignatieff (2001) wrote, human rights are a means of doing politics. The lack of any substantial progress in the area of prisoner enfranchisement is another example of the limitations of judicial decisions. Since *Hirst v UK* (2005), there have been a series of clone cases—*Greens and M.T. v UK* (2010), *Firth & Others v UK* (2014) and *McHugh & Others v UK* (2015)—all concluding that the blanket prisoner disenfranchisement violates Art 3 of Protocol 1 (European Court of Human Rights 2015). The government resists in making a decision on the issue for 11 years now. Last but not least, the changes to the ECtHR admissibility criteria and the renewed emphasis on the principles of subsidiarity and margin of appreciation (see Chap. 1) can arguably weaken human rights protection.

The Proactive Function of Human Rights in Prisons

English and Dutch prisoners' views point out the need to tap the proactive function of human rights, which is currently found in soft human rights law, such as CPT standards and EPRs, as the way to embed human rights in prison; and they shed light on how best to utilise this proactive function of human rights. Unlike its reactive function, the proactive function of human rights has a real-time and general application, benefitting all prisoners.

Based on prisoners' contributions, this proactive function has an educative, a psychotherapeutic, a humanising and an emancipatory potential. Taken together, prisoners see them as the vehicle for embedding human rights in prison and thus promoting prisoner rehabilitation and reintegration. Before we turn our attention to them, it is important to reiterate that participants did not privilege one category of human rights over another and applied the concepts of negative and positive state interference with regard to their protection to all human rights categories. Also, they did not treat human rights in an exclusive manner but in a complimentary one, applying sometimes the same human rights to the different types of the proactive human rights function.

Starting with the *educative* potential of human rights, it fosters prisoner awareness of human rights and an appreciation of their rights and responsibilities as members of society and citizens. Both English and Dutch prisoners said that they had received no information on their human rights as such by the authorities. It was only customary to be informed of their rights and duties under the prison rules. Human rights were not a topic of discussion among themselves or with staff. They were also uncertain about the legalisation aspect, whether they could bring a human rights claim before the courts, and what human rights were legally protected.

This was not the only gap in prisoners' awareness of their human rights. As we saw, in their majority, participants had a considerable difficulty in identifying what kind of *human responsibilities* they had and did not accept the idea of crime as a human rights violation, at least not explicitly. To remind ourselves, English participants chose not to comment while for the Dutch participants the idea was only valid in respect of violence that resulted directly in bodily harm or death.

There is no doubt that there is a need for raising prisoner awareness as much of their positively entrenched human rights as of the deeper layers of the meaning of the human rights idea along with what it means to be a citizen. Reflection needs intellectual stimulation and opportunities to use and apply critical thinking skills. In light of the above, the inclusion of human rights and citizenship education into the existing educational provision in prisons acquires urgency. Human rights and citizenship classes can provide prisoners with a platform where they can start critically exploring these concepts. In this respect, it is worth noting that in her 2016 review of education in English prisons, Dame Coates emphasised the need for a prison education that goes beyond 'simply addressing deficits in basic skills' (p. 29) and that it is not limited to the traditional classroom. Prison education needs to be diverse and innovative, and involve prison officers in its delivery so as to aspire and empower the prisoner, supporting them in their personal development as learners and human beings (2016: 20, 24–27, 29–30). In their work Warr (2016) and McMann (2016) make a strong case precisely for such a change in prison education, highlighting the transformative potential of both informal and more advanced learning opportunities for prisoners' personal and social development. The English prisoners' idea of prisoner committees and Dutch prisoners' strong endorsement of the civilising benefits of education re-affirm the need for a more creative and encompassing education in prisons. It is no coincidence that the Dame Coates review on education in the English prison system is entitled *Unlocking Potential*.

Moving to the *psychotherapeutic* potential of human rights, it promotes prisoners' self-awareness, enables them to come to terms with their circumstances, and empowers them to take positive action to change them. In this respect, prisoners identified as instrumental the rights to life, to privacy, to education, to adequate mental healthcare and to freedom of expression. With direct applicability to prison policy, they related the ability to choose to be alone in the cell to the rights to life and privacy. In the structurally controlled and relationally controlling prison environment, to be alone in the cell restored some normality in their daily lives and gave them space, in a literal and metaphorical sense, for (self) reflection. In particular the Dutch, who compared to the English, were relatively new to the practice of cell sharing, claimed to feel physically, emotionally and mentally threatened by the presence of a stranger in the same cell with them. They called for the practice to operate on a voluntary basis and to be informed of thorough regularly reviewed assessments of the two cellmates' compatibility with regard to their personality, offence history, individual needs, adjustment to the prison regime, and age. In general, participants credited the freedom to exercise volition in aspects, such as cell sharing (both national samples), vocational training and academic education (Dutch participants) with building their confidence and enabling them to become independent.

Echoing the CPT standard on the inclusion of a diversity of mental health professionals as part of prisoners' right to equivalence in healthcare (CPT 2015: para. 41), participants severely criticised the authorities' heavy reliance on prescription medication. What they were in need of and lacked was to have a safe space where they could release feelings and express thoughts that troubled them after an accumulation through the years of adverse experiences and ill-made decisions. Drugs alone could only manage their mental health troubles and risked introversion, increasing the likelihood of their becoming fixated on their problems. In order to prevent psychological regression, access to a more diverse mental healthcare was paramount.

Mental healthcare staff with a psychotherapeutic specialisation was not the only people that participants identified as being able to assist them in taking advantage of the cathartic and empowering effects of communication. According to the Dutch, prison officers could be especially helpful too. In their view, not only is the prison officer in a well-placed position to make such a contribution, but also it should be part of their role. A description of the prison officer's role from the prisoner perspective is drawn from the *humanising* potential of human rights.

The *humanising* potential of human rights facilitates meaningful interaction with others, which restores prisoners' self-respect, self-worth and dignity. The accent on the importance of meaningful interaction highlights the interdependence of our sense of selfhood and personhood. For the realisation of the *humanising* potential, participants identified as fundamentally important the human rights to respect for private and family life, freedom of expression, and to take part in cultural life. The prison officer is central to the *humanising* potential and also cuts across the *educative* and the *emancipatory* potential.

Both the English and the Dutch credited, albeit to a differing degree, the prison officer with the capacity to unlock the *humanising* potential. As we saw in Chaps. 5 and 6, the Dutch were more positively disposed towards officers whom they essentially portrayed as *human rights ambassadors*. In their view, not only is the prison officer well placed to perform such a role, but it should also be part of their job (role). While they acknowledged the ever-present divisions between officers and prisoners, in their view both parties had to demonstrate maturity and pragmatism. Re-affirming relevant research (see, e.g. Scott 2006; The Howard League for Penal Reform 2009; Liebling 2011), the prison officer has a strategic position in prison. They have daily and direct contact with prisoners that allows them to have first-hand knowledge of prisoners. This relational proximity between officers and prisoners poses too great an opportunity for prisoner rehabilitation and resocialisation to be wasted. The reality is that they depend on officers (see Liebling 2011: 485–486, 496), and their dependence goes beyond the opening of cell doors. They depend on officers to teach them how to exercise responsibility, work with others, negotiate disagreements and setbacks, and to be assertive; also to give them hope and purpose to survive the pains of imprisonment, which in certain circumstances, such as serving a life sentence, becomes increasingly difficult as the time passes. They also depend on officers' insights into their abilities and weaknesses, and on officers' guidance on how to develop and improve themselves. In the absence of family and friends, the officer embodies familiarity, stability and security. In this respect, the Dutch called for the re-introduction of evening socialisation, which in the past provided them with a dedicated space to interact with officers, and the English proposed the idea of prisoner committees where the interaction between prisoners and staff was credited with fostering awareness of the vicissitudes of life and the heterogeneity of its lifestyles.

In light of the impact an officer has on prisoner treatment and experience of detention, participants touched upon the issues of officer recruitment and training. Reflecting EPRs on *prison work as a public service and on the training of staff*, they argued that public and institutional perceptions of the prison officer had to recognise the complexity of the tasks, which the everyday reality of their job landed on their feet, as well as their contribution to society at large. As one Dutch participant put it succinctly, *someone has to do it*. Prison officers come into close contact with people of different backgrounds who have diverse life histories and acute vulnerabilities. Therefore, the challenges of their job are enormous. Their role and required competences should be re-designed to reflect their mentor, teacher and social worker function. Their training should also be versatile and continuous to enable them to cope with the diversity of the prisoner population and thus be able to adequately support prisoners.

For example, alluding to the high number of foreign nationals in Dutch prisons, one participant who was a foreign national himself remarked that a good command of the English language should be among the prerequisites for the job. Also, according to the lifers, there was a need for greater selectivity and specialisation in officer recruitment and training. Both aspects warranted careful consideration so as to ensure that the selected officers' personality and professional competences could accommodate, for example, the emotional, mental and psychological strain experienced by this specific prisoner group. Both remarks are especially current considering that foreign nationals represent just over 20% of the prison population (World Prison Brief Netherlands 2014) and there has been an increase in lifelong imprisonment.

Before we move to the *emancipatory* potential of human rights, we must add that the prison officer was not the only person with a valuable contribution to make to the prisoner experience. Prisoners' families also exerted a humanising influence. In the prisoners' view, the authorities' facilitation of meaningful family contact through the provision of longer, more frequent and private visits would encourage them to re-discover themselves and acquire a sense of purpose and belonging. These are essential ingredients for desistance from crime. In addition, concerns expressed among (some) English participants about a seeping confusion over their sexuality and gender identity re-affirms the humanising effect of conjugal visits that, as seen in Chap. 2, has been acknowledged by the Dutch since the 1960s.

Lastly, the *emancipatory* potential of human rights provides prisoners with the determination to return to society and equips them with skills for a successful reintegration. In this respect, participants identified as instrumental the human rights to respect for private and family life, to education, to vocational guidance and training, to work and a fair remuneration, and to social security.

Participants talked about their conflicting feelings of elation and fear about the time of their release. The closer the release date came, the more insecure they felt. Family and resettlement support were instrumental in enabling them to become independent and escape the passivity of institutionalisation. Family could soothe the pains of imprisonment and was empowering. It encouraged them to persist in their efforts to change their lives and assisted them, by example, in learning how to build and maintain human relations. Participants highlighted that preparation for release had to be a gradual process. Sentencing plans needed to set goals that reflected the different stages of their sentence, and resettlement support had to include opportunities to experience freedom in an incremental fashion. For instance, family visits and work in the community would help them re-adjust gradually to the pace and reality of the outside world. Such measures would also provide them with sufficient time to arrange important affairs, such as accommodation and social security assistance, which were typically the most pressing concerns in the immediate period following release.

Last but not least, prisoners highlighted the instructional and instrumental value of work. In their opinion, prison work failed miserably on both counts. As a result of prison overcrowding, English prisons had an insufficient number of work placements, which did not teach current employability skills and paid far too little for prisoners to gain a sense of independence. While Dutch shortages of work placements were minimised by splitting the working day into two shifts (4 hours in the morning and 4 hours in the afternoon) so that more people could work,

Dutch prisoners held similar views about the employability value of their prison work and their pay. Both English and Dutch participants stressed the importance of a decent prison wage, which was seen as empowering both psychologically and financially. In light of this, in the wider context of prisoners' right to equality and equal treatment, prisoners (in both national settings) called for the legal minimum wage to be applied to prison work too. In addition, the Dutch proposed a new legal duty on employers to include in their workforce a certain quota of newly released prisoners, as a way to give them *a fair chance* to overcome the stigmatisation of prison and its undermining of their reintegrative prospects.

Conclusion

The proactive function of human rights and what it needs for its realisation point out to one fundamental thing. Human rights as a strategy for penal reform can only be successful if we *commit* to a decarcerative penal policy. There is simply *no* alternative way. As the state of prisons in England and Wales plainly shows, overcrowded and at the same time understaffed prisons are not conducive to protecting prisoners' human rights, however well intended, dedicated and well trained the staff are. Such working conditions in such a challenging and unpredictable working environment are dangerous for both prisoners *and* staff, endangering the human rights of both groups.

As was just said, we must *commit* to a decarcerative penal policy. We cannot simply adopt 'a radical and realistic' approach that has the lifespan of a five-year Parliament, rushed through its early years. (*Rehabilitation*) *Revolutions* require strategic planning, and careful and joined-up assessments of the resources needed before they can take place. Otherwise, they are doomed to fail. Positive change needs time and resources for it to be embedded in everyday practice. The valuable lesson the Dutch experience teaches us is that regressive developments are particularly aggressive; they can quickly and permanently undo the progressive efforts and results of many years.

Taken together, the English and the Dutch prison systems provide other European penal systems a detailed roadmap of the pitfalls that must be avoided and the actions that must be taken if they aspire to develop and action a human rights-informed penal policy. But, most importantly of all, their prisoners highlight that this should not be just an aspiration. Instead, it should be a state (and society's) obligation based on the inextricable link between human rights recognition and protection in prison and the very legitimacy of prison as punishment. In light of the categorical importance of human rights for human life and a humane existence, a penal policy and a prison system that are not committed to the aims of rehabilitation, resocialisation and reintegration are morally bankrupt since they fail to deliver a punishment that the nature of the punished is worthy of.

Bibliography

Aas, K. F. (2011). 'Crimmigrant' Bodies and Bona Fide Travellers: Surveillance, Citizenship and Global Governance. *Theoretical Criminology, 15*(3), 331–346.

Aebi, M. F., & Delgrande, N. (2013). *Council of Europe Annual Penal Statistics SPACE I-Prison Populations Survey 2011*. Council of Europe & University of Lausanne. Retrieved February 15, 2016, from http://wp.unil.ch/space/files/2015/02/SPACE-I-2013-English.pdf

Aebi, M. F., & Delgrande, N. (2014). *Council of Europe Annual Penal Statistics SPACE I: Survey 2012*. Strasbourg: University of Lausanne and Council of Europe.

Aebi, M. F., Tiago, M. M., & Burkhardt, C. (2015). *Council of Europe Annual Penal Statistics SPACE I-Prison Populations Survey 2014*. Council of Europe & University of Lausanne. Retrieved February 15, 2016, from http://wp.unil.ch/space/files/2016/05/SPACE-I-2014-Report_final.1.pdf

Alston, P., & Weiler, J. H. H. (1999). An "Ever Closer Union" in Need of a Human Rights Policy: The European Union and Human Rights. In P. Alston with M. Bustelo & J. Heenan (Eds.), *The EU and Human Rights* (pp. 3–68). Oxford: Oxford University Press.

Andeweg, R. B., & Irwin, G. A. (2005). *Governance and Politics in the Netherlands* (2nd ed.). Basingstoke: Palgrave Macmillan.

A. Karamalidou, *Embedding Human Rights in Prison*,
DOI 10.1057/978-1-137-58502-8

Ashworth, A. (2007). Sentencing. In M. Maguire, R. Morgan, & R. Reiner (Eds.), *The Oxford Handbook of Criminology* (4th ed., pp. 990–1023). Oxford: Oxford University Press.

Ashworth, A., & Roberts, J. (2012). Sentencing: Theory, Principle, and Practice. In M. Maguire, R. Morgan, & R. Reiner (Eds.), *The Oxford Handbook of Criminology* (5th ed., pp. 866–894). Oxford: Oxford University Press.

Baker, E. (2013). The Emerging Role of the EU as a Penal Actor. In T. Daems, D. van Zyl Smit, & S. Snacken (Eds.), *European Penology?* (pp. 77–112). Oxford: Hart Publishing.

BBC News. (2006, November 2). 'Weekend Prison' Scheme Scrapped. Retrieved April 11, 2016, from http://news.bbc.co.uk/1/hi/uk/6109886.stm

Beck, U. (1992). *Risk Society. Towards a New Modernity*. London: Sage.

Beck, U. (2002 [2013]). The Terrorist Threat: World Risk Society Revisited. In E. McLaughlin & J. Muncie (Eds.), *Criminological Perspectives: Essential Readings* (3rd ed., pp. 630–645). London: Sage.

Becker, H. (1963 [2013]). Outsiders. In E. McLaughlin & J. Muncie (Eds.), *Criminological Perspectives* (3rd ed., pp. 256–266). London: Sage.

Bennett, J. (2007). Did Things Only Get Better? A Decade of Prisons Under Tony Blair and New Labour. *Prison Service Journal, 171*, 3–12.

Bingham, T. (2011). *The Rule of Law*. London: Penguin Books.

Blad, J. (2003). *Against Penal Instrumentalism*. Retrieved July 17, 2016, from http://www.iirp.edu/pdf/nl03_blad.pdf

Blakenburg, E., & Bruinsma, F. (1994). *Dutch Legal Culture* (2nd ed.). Deventer: Kluwer Law and Taxation Publishers.

Boin, A. (2001). Securing Safety in the Dutch Prison System: Pros and Cons of a Supermax. *Howard Journal of Criminal Justice, 40*(4), 335–346.

Boone, M. (2007). Selective Rehabilitation. In M. Boone & M. Moerings (Eds.), *Dutch Prisons* (pp. 231–248). The Hague: BJu Legal Publishers.

Boone, M., & Moerings, M. (2007). Growing Prison Rates. In M. Boone & M. Moerings (Eds.), *Dutch Prisons* (pp. 51–76). The Hague: Bju Legal Publishers.

Boone, M., & van Swaaningen, R. (2013). Regression to the Mean: Punishment in the Netherlands. In V. Ruggiero & M. Ryan (Eds.), *Punishment in Europe: A Critical Anatomy of Penal Systems* (pp. 9–32). Basingstoke: Palgrave Macmillan.

Boone, M. M. (2002). Imposed Versus Undergone Punishment in the Netherlands. *Journal of Comparative Law*, 6(4), 1–13. Retrieved September 10, 2015, from http://www.ejcl.org/64/art64-27.pdf

Bottoms, A. E. (1995). The Philosophy and Politics of Punishment and Sentencing. In C. Clarkson & R. Morgan (Eds.), *The Politics of Sentencing Reform* (pp. 17–49). Oxford: Clarendon Press.

Boutellier, H. (2004). *The Safety Utopia: Contemporary Discontent and Desire as to Crime and Punishment*. Dordrecht: Kluwer Academic Publishers.

Braithwaite, J. (1989). *Crime, Shame and Reintegration*. Cambridge: Cambridge University Press.

Broeders, D. (2010). Return to Sender? Administrative Detention of Irregular Migrants in Germany and the Netherlands. *Punishment & Society, 12*(2), 169–186.

Brugger, W. (1996). The Image of the Person in the Human Rights Concept. *Human Rights Quarterly, 18*(3), 594–611.

Buruma, I. (2006). *Murder in Amsterdam: The Death of Theo van Gogh and the Limits Tolerance*. London: Atlantic Books.

Casciani, D. (2006). *The Murder of Zahid Mubarek*. Retrieved September 10, 2015, from http://news.bbc.co.uk/1/hi/uk/3198264.stm

Cavadino, M., & Dignan, J. (2006a). Penal Policy and Political Economy. *Criminology & Criminal Justice, 6*(4), 435–456.

Cavadino, M., & Dignan, J. (2006b). *Penal Systems: A Comparative Approach*. London: Sage.

Cavadino, M., Dignan, J., & Mair, G. (2013). *The Penal System: An Introduction* (5th ed.). London: Sage.

Chalmers, D., Davies, G., & Monti, G. (2010). *European Union Law* (2nd ed.). Cambridge: Cambridge University Press.

Chaplin, R., Flatley, J., & Smith, K. (2011). *Crime in England & Wales 2010/11: Findings from the British Crime Survey and Police Recorded Crime* (2nd ed.). London: Home Office.

Charter of Fundamental Rights of the European Union. (2000). *Official Journal of the European Communities*. 364/01. Retrieved July 8, 2015, from http://www.europarl.europa.eu/charter/pdf/text_en.pdf

Chief Coroner. (2013). The Chief Coroner's Guide to the Coroners and Justice Act 2009. Retrieved June 23, 2016, from https://www.judiciary.gov.uk/wp-content/uploads/JCO/Documents/coroners/guidance/chief-coroners-guide-to-act-sept2013.pdf

Claessen, J. (2014). Life Imprisonment Means One's Entire Life! But Will this Last? Retrieved July 7, 2016, from http://law.maastrichtuniversity.nl/news-andviews/life-imprisonment-means-ones-entire-life-but-will-this-last/

Commissioner for Human Rights. (2008). Memorandum by Thomas Hammarberg Commissioner for Human Rights of the Council of Europe Following His Visits to the United Kingdom 5–8 February and 31 March–2 April 2008. CommDH (2008)27. Retrieved September 1, 2015, from https://rm.coe.int/CoERMPublicCommonSearchServices/DisplayDCTMContent?documentId=09000016806db836

Commission on Sex in Prison. (2014). Briefing Paper 2: Women in Prison: Coercive and Consensual Sex. The Howard League for Penal Reform. Retrieved February 22, 2016, from http://howardleague.org/wp-content/uploads/2016/03/Women_in_prison_sex_commission.pdf

Coroners Act. 1988. London: HMSO. Retrieved February 15, 2016, from http://www.legislation.gov.uk/ukpga/1988/13/pdfs/ukpga_19880013_en.pdf

Coroners and Justice Act. 2009. London: HMSO. Retrieved February 15, 2016, from http://www.legislation.gov.uk/ukpga/2009/25/pdfs/ukpga_20090025_en.pdf

Coroner's Rules. 1984. London: HMSO.

Council of Europe. (1998). Recommendation Rec (1998)7 on the Ethical and Organisational Aspects of Health Care in Prison. Retrieved August 20, 2015, from https://search.coe.int/cm/Pages/result_details.aspx?ObjectID=09000016804fb13c

Council of Europe. (2006). Recommendation Rec (2006)2 European Prison Rules. Retrieved March 16, 2016, from http://euromed-justice.eu/document/coe-2006-recommendation-rec20062-european-prison-rules-0

Council of Europe. (2010). *Protocol No. 14 to the Convention for the Protection of Human Rights and Fundamental Freedoms, Amending the Control System of the Convention.* Council of Europe Treaty Series- No. 194. Strasbourg: Council of Europe.

Council of Europe. (2012). Recommendation CM/Rec(2012)5 on the European Code of Ethics for Prison Staff. Retrieved August 20, 2015, from http://pjp-eu.coe.int/documents/3983922/6970334/CMRec+(2012)+5+on+the+European+Code+of+Ethics+for+Prison+Staff.pdf/5ba75585-6e2f-4e80-bcd7-090ef0a1b08e

Council of Europe. (2013a). Protocol No. 15 Amending the Convention for the Protection of Human Rights and Fundamental Freedoms. Strasbourg: Council of Europe.

Council of Europe. (2013b). Protocol No. 16 to the Convention for the Protection of Human Rights and Fundamental Freedoms. Strasbourg: Council of Europe.

Council of Europe. (2015). CPT Standards: CPT/Inf/E(2002)1-Rev. 2015. Retrieved January 23, 2016, from http://www.cpt.coe.int/en/documents/eng-standards.pdf

Council of Europe Parliamentary Assembly. (2006). European Prisons Charter. Retrieved August 28, 2016, from http://www.assembly.coe.int/nw/xml/XRef/Xref-XML2HTML-en.asp?fileid=17438&lang=en

CPT. (1993). Report to the Dutch Government on the Visit to the Netherlands Carried Out by the European Committee for the Prevention of Torture and Inhuman or Degrading Treatment or Punishment (CPT): CPT/Inf(93)15. Retrieved April 10, 2016, from http://www.cpt.coe.int/documents/nld/1993-15-inf-eng.pdf

CPT. (1996). Report to the United Kingdom Government on the Visit to the United Kingdom Carried Out by the European Committee for the Prevention of Torture and Inhuman or Degrading Treatment or Punishment (CPT) from 15 to 31 May 1994: CPT/Inf (96)11. Retrieved April 10, 2016, from http://www.cpt.coe.int/en/states/gbr.htm

CPT. (1998a). Report to the Netherlands Government on the Visit to the Netherlands Carried Out by the European Committee for the Prevention of Torture and Inhuman or Degrading Treatment or Punishment (CPT) from 17 to 27 November 1997: CPT/Inf(98)15. Retrieved April 10, 2016, from http://www.cpt.coe.int/en/states/nld.htm

CPT. (1998b). Report to the Government of the United Kingdom on the Visit to the United Kingdom Carried Out by the European Committee for the Prevention of Torture and Inhuman or Degrading Treatment or Punishment (CPT) from 8 to 17 September 1997: CPT/Inf.

CPT. (2000). Report to the Government of the United Kingdom on the Visit to the United Kingdom Carried Out by the European Committee for the Prevention of Torture and Inhuman or Degrading Treatment or Punishment (CPT) from 8 to 17 September 1997: CPT/Inf (2000)1. Retrieved April 10, 2016, from http://www.cpt.coe.int/en/states/gbr.htm

CPT. (2002a). Report to the Government of the United Kingdom on the Visit to the United Kingdom Carried Out by the European Committee for the Prevention of Torture and Inhuman or Degrading Treatment or Punishment (CPT) from 4 to 16 February 2001: CPT/Inf(2002)6. Retrieved April 10, 2016, from http://www.cpt.coe.int/en/states/gbr.htm

CPT. (2002b). Report to the Authorities of the Kingdom of the Netherlands on the Visits Carried Out to the Kingdom in Europe and to the Netherlands Antilles by the European Committee for the Prevention of Torture and

Inhuman or Degrading Treatment or Punishment (CPT) in February 2002: CPT/Inf(2002)30. Retrieved April 10, 2016, from http://www.cpt.coe.int/en/states/nld.htm

CPT. (2008). Report to the Authorities of the Kingdom of the Netherlands on the Visits Carried Out to the Kingdom in Europe, Aruba, and the Netherlands Antilles by the European Committee for the Prevention of Torture and Inhuman or Degrading Treatment or Punishment (CPT) in June 2007: CPT/Inf(2008)2. Retrieved April 10, 2016, from http://www.cpt.coe.int/en/states/nld.htm

Creighton, S., & King, V. (1996). *Prisoners and the Law*. London: Butterworths.

Crewe, B. (2006). Male Prisoners' Orientations Towards Female Officers in an English Prison. *Punishment & Society, 8*(4), 395–421.

Crewe, B. (2009). *The Prisoner Society: Power, Adaptation, and Social Life in an English Prison*. Oxford: Oxford University Press.

Crewe, B. (2011). Depth, Weight, Tightness: Revisiting the Pains of Imprisonment. *Punishment & Society, 13*(5), 509–529.

Criminal Justice Act. (2003). London: HMSO. Retrieved September 10, 2015, from http://www.legislation.gov.uk/ukpga/2003/44/pdfs/ukpga_20030044_en.pdf

Daems, T. (2013). Punishment and the Question of Europe. In T. Daems, D. van Zyl Smit, & S. Snacken (Eds.), *European Penology?* (pp. 27–52). Oxford: Hart Publishing.

Dame Coates, S. (2016). Unlocking Potential: A Review of Education in Prison. Ministry of Justice. Retrieved July 15, 2016, from https://www.gov.uk/government/uploads/system/uploads/attachment_data/file/524013/education-review-report.pdf

de Ruiter, C., & Trestman, R. L. (2007). Prevalence and Treatment of Personality Disorders in Dutch Forensic Mental Health Services. *American Journal of Psychiatry and Law, 35*(1), 92–97.

Department of Health. (2009). The Bradley Report: Lord Bradley's Review of People with Mental Health Problems or Learning Disabilities in the Criminal Justice System. Retrieved September 10, 2015, from http://www.rcpsych.ac.uk/pdf/Bradleyreport.pdf

DJI. (2000). *Penitentiary Programmes: Phase by Phase Return to Society*. The Hague: DJI.

DJI. (2007a). *(TBS) Placement Under a Hospital Order*. The Hague: DJI.

DJI. (2007b). *Annual Report 2007: Working Safely Towards Change*. The Hague: Ministry of Justice & National Agency of Correctional Institutions.

DJI. (2009). *Where Freedom Ends and may be Regained*. The Hague: DJI.

Downes, D. (1988). *Contrasts in Tolerance: Post War Penal Policy in the Netherlands and England and Wales.* Oxford: Clarendon.

Downes, D. (1998). The Buckling of the Shields: Dutch Penal Policy 1985–1995. In R. P. Weiss & N. South (Eds.), *Comparing Prison Systems: Toward a Comparative and International Penology* (pp. 143–174). Amsterdam: Gordon and Breach.

Downes, D., & Morgan, R. (1997). Dumping the 'Hostages to Fortune'? The Politics of Law and Order in Post-War Britain. In M. Maguire, R. Morgan, & R. Reiner (Eds.), *The Oxford Handbook of Criminology* (2nd ed., pp. 87–134). Oxford: Oxford University Press.

Downes, D., & Morgan, R. (2007). No Turning Back: The Politics of Law and Order into the Millennium. In M. Maguire, R. Morgan, & R. Reiner (Eds.), *The Oxford Handbook of Criminology* (4th ed., pp. 201–240). Oxford: Oxford University Press.

Downes, D., & van Swaaningen, R. (2007). The Road to Dystopia? Changes in the Penal Climate of the Netherlands. *Crime and Justice in The Netherlands, 35*(1), 31–71.

Downes, D., & Morgan, R. (2012). Overtaking on the Left? The Politics of Law and Order in the 'Big Society'. In M. Maguire, R. Morgan, & R. Reiner (Eds.), *The Oxford Handbook of Criminology* (5th ed., pp. 182–205). Oxford: Oxford University Press.

Drake, D. H. (2012). *Prisons, Punishment and the Pursuit of Security.* Basingstoke: Palgrave Macmillan.

Dumortier, E., Gutwirth, S., Snacken, S., & De Hert, P. (2012). The Rise of the Penal State: What can Human Rights Do About It? In S. Snacken & E. Dumortier (Eds.), *Resisting Punitiveness in Europe? Welfare, Human Rights and Democracy* (pp. 107–132). Abingdon, Oxon: Routledge.

Durcan, G., Saunders, A., Gadsby, B., & Hazard, A. (2014). *The Bradley Report Five Years on: An Independent Review of Progress to Date and Priorities for Further Development.* Centre for Mental Health. Retrieved September 15, 2015, from http://cdn.basw.co.uk/upload/basw_15825-2.pdf

Dutch Ministry of Security and Justice. (2015, September 2). Official Opening of Norgerhaven Prison to Norwegian Prisoners. Retrieved May 10, 2016, from https://www.government.nl/documents/speeches/2015/09/02/official-opening-ofnorgerhaven-prison-to-norwegian-prisoners-2-september-2015

Easton, S. (2011). *Prisoners' Rights: Principles and Practice.* Abingdon, Oxon: Routledge.

Ellison, G. (2013). Policing: Context and Practice. In A. Hucklesby & A. Wahidin (Eds.), *Criminal Justice* (2nd ed., pp. 57–82). Oxford: Oxford University Press.

Equality and Human Rights Commission. (2015). Preventing Deaths in Detention of Adults with Mental Health Conditions. Retrieved February 12, 2015, from https://www.equalityhumanrights.com/en/inquiries-and-investigations/preventing-deaths-detention-adults-mental-health-conditions-0

Equality and Human Rights Commission. (2016). Preventing Deaths in Detention of Adults with Mental Health Conditions: Progress Review. Retrieved June 16, 2016, from https://www.equalityhumanrights.com/en/inquiries-and-investigations/preventing-deaths-detention-adults-mental--health-conditions/preventing

European Commission. (2012a). The Values of Europeans: Standard Eurobarometer 77 Spring 2012. Retrieved January 12, 2016, from http://ec.europa.eu/public_opinion/archives/eb/eb77/eb77_value_en.pdf

European Commission. (2012b). Public Opinion in the European Union: Standard Eurobarometer 77 Spring 2012. Retrieved January 12, 2016, from http://ec.europa.eu/public_opinion/archives/eb/eb77/eb77_publ_en.pdf

European Commission. (2015a). Public Opinion in the European Union: Standard Eurobarometer 82 Autumn 2014. Retrieved January 12, 2016, from http://ec.europa.eu/public_opinion/archives/eb/eb82/eb82_first_en.pdf

European Commission. (2015b). Public Opinion in the European Union: Standard Eurobarometer Spring 2015. Retrieved January 12, 2016, from http://ec.europa.eu/public_opinion/archives/eb/eb83/eb83_first_en.pdf

European Commission. (2016). Public Opinion in the European Union. Standard Eurobarometer 85. Spring 2016. First Results. Retrieved August 15, 2016, from http://ec.europa.eu/COMMFrontOffice/publicopinion/index.cfm/Survey/get-SurveyDetail/instruments/STANDARD/surveyKy/2130

European Committee for the Prevention of Torture and Inhuman or Degrading Treatment or Punishment (CPT). (2015). CPT Standards: CPT/Inf/E(2002)1—Rev. 2015. Retrieved April 10, 2016, from http://www.cpt.coe.int/en/documents/engstandards.pdf

European Court of Human Rights. (2010). 50 Years of Activity: The European Court of Human Rights: Same Facts and Figures. Retrieved September 12, 2015, from http://www.echr.coe.int/Documents/Facts_Figures_1959_2009_ENG.pdf

European Court of Human Rights. (2015). Factsheet February 2015—Prisoners' Right to Vote (copy with the author).

European Court of Human Rights. (2016a). Factsheet April 2016—Detention and Mental Health. April (copy with the author).

European Court of Human Rights. (2016b). Factsheet April 2016—Detention Conditions and Treatment of Prisoners (copy with the author).

European Court of Human Rights. (2016c). Factsheet October 2016-Life Imprisonment. Retrieved October 1, 2016, from http://www.echr.coe.int/Documents/FS_Life_sentences_ENG.pdf

Faugeron, C. (1998). Prison: Between the Law and Social Action. In V. Ruggiero, N. South, & I. Taylor (Eds.), *The New European Criminology: Crime and Social Order in Europe* (pp. 104–118). London: Routledge.

Feeley, M. M., & Simon, J. (1992 [2013]). The New Penology. In E. McLaughlin & J. Muncie (Eds.), *Criminological Pespectives: Essential Readings* (3rd ed., pp. 510–523). London: Sage.

Feilzer, M. (2009). The Importance of Telling a Good Story: An Experiment in Public Criminology. *Howard Journal of Criminal Justice, 48*(5), 472–484.

Fowles, T. (2006). Counterblast: The Criminal Justice Act 2003. The End of an Era? *Howard Journal of Criminal Justice, 45*(1), 71–73.

Franke, H. (1990). Dutch Tolerance: Facts and Fables. *British Journal of Criminology, 30*(1), 81–93.

Franke, H. (1995). *The Emancipation of Prisoners: Two Centuries of Imprisonment in the Netherlands*. Oxford: Clarendon Press.

Garland, D. (2001). *The Culture of Control: Crime and Social Order in Contemporary Society*. Oxford: Oxford University Press.

Genders, E., & Player, E. (2014). Rehabilitation, Risk Management and Prisoners' Rights. *Criminology & Criminal Justice, 14*(4), 434–457.

Gewirth, A. (1983). The Epistemology of Human Rights. *Social Philosophy and Policy, 1*(2), 1–34.

Girling, E. (2006). European Identity, Penal Sensibilities, and Communities of Sentiment. In S. Armstrong & L. McAra (Eds.), *Perspectives on Punishment: The Contours of Control* (pp. 69–82). Oxford: Oxford University Press.

Goffman, E. (1961 [1991]). *Asylums: Essays on the Social Situation of Mental Patients and Other Inmates*. London: Penguin Books.

Government of the Netherlands. (1999a). 1999 Penitentiary Order. The Hague: Ministry of Justice (copy with the author).

Government of the Netherlands. (1999b). 1999 Penitentiary Principles Act. The Hague: Ministry of Justice (copy with the author).

Government of the Netherlands. (1999c). House Rules. The Hague: Ministry of Justice (copy with the author).

Green, D. A. (2008). *When Children Kill Children: Penal Populism and Political Culture*. Oxford: Oxford University Press.

Heringa, A. W., & Kiiver, P. (2007). *Constitutions Compared. An Introduction to Comparative Constitutional Law*. Antwerpen: Intersentia.

HM Chief Inspector of Prisons and HM Chief Inspector of Probation. (2008). The Indeterminate Sentence for Public Protection. A Thematic Review. Retrieved May 1, 2016, from http://www.justiceinspectorates.gov.uk/probation/wp-content/uploads/sites/5/2014/03/hmip_ipp_thematic-rps.pdf

HM Government. (2006). *Report of the Zahid Mubarek Inquiry*. London: The Stationery Office. Retrieved May 13, 2016, from https://www.gov.uk/government/uploads/system/uploads/attachment_data/file/231789/1082.pdf

HM Government. (2010). The Coalition: Our Programme for Government. Retrieved May 11, 2016, from https://www.gov.uk/government/uploads/system/uploads/attachment_data/file/78977/coalition_programme_for_government.pdf

HM Inspectorate of Prisons. (2015). Annual Report 2014–15. Retrieved March 15, 2016, from https://www.justiceinspectorates.gov.uk/hmiprisons/inspections/annual-report-2014-15/

HM Inspectorate of Prisons. (2016). Annual Report 2015–16. Retrieved July 30, 2016, from https://www.justiceinspectorates.gov.uk/hmiprisons/inspections/annual-report-2015-2016/

HM Prison Service. (2005a). Prison Service Instruction 11/2005. Criminal Justice Act 2003: New Sentences. London: HM Prison Service.

HM Prison Service. (2005b). Prison Service Instruction 18/2005. Introducing ACCT (Assessment, Care in Custody and Teamwork)-The Replacement for the F2052SH (Risk of Self-Harm). London: HM Prison Service.

HM Prison Service. (2008). Prison Service Instruction 27/2008. Criminal Justice & Immigration Act 2008 Sentencing Policy Changes. London: HM Prison Service.

Home Office. (2001). *The Halliday Report-Making Punishments Work: A Review of the Sentencing Framework for England and Wales*. London: Stationery Office. Retrieved September 10, 2015, from http://webarchive.nationalarchives.gov.uk/+/http://www.homeoffice.gov.uk/documents/halliday-report-sppu/

Hough, M., & Roberts, J. V. (2012). Public Opinion, Crime, and Criminal Justice. In M. Maguire, R. Morgan, & R. Reiner (Eds.), *The Oxford Handbook of Criminology* (5th ed., pp. 279–300). Oxford: Oxford University Press.

House of Commons Justice Committee. (2008). Towards Effective Sentencing. *Fifth Report of Session 2007–08*. Retrieved January 5, 2016, from http://www.publications.parliament.uk/pa/cm200708/cmselect/cmjust/184/184.pdf

Ignatieff, M. (2001). *Human Rights as Politics and Idolatry*. Princeton: Princeton University Press.

Indermaur, D., Roberts, L., Spiranovic, C., Mackenzie, G., & Gelb, K. (2012). A Matter of Judgment: The Effect of Information and Deliberation on Public Attitudes to Punishment. *Punishment & Society, 14*(2), 147–165.

Jewkes, Y. (2005). Loss, Liminality and the Life Sentence: Managing Identity Through a Disrupted Lifecourse. In A. Liebling & S. Maruna (Eds.), *The Effects of Imprisonment* (pp. 366–390). Cullompton: Willan Publishing.

Junger-Tas, J. (1998). Recent Trends in Sentencing Policies in the Netherlands. *European Journal on Criminal Policy and Research, 6*, 479–505.

Kalin, W. (2013). Late Modernity: Human Rights Under Pressure? *Punishment & Society, 15*(4), 397–411.

Karamalidou, A. (2010). *A Critical Assessment of Human Rights in English and Dutch Prisons.* PhD thesis, Middlesex University, London. Retrieved October 23, 2015, from https://eprints.mdx.ac.uk/7901/1/Karamalidou-phd.pdf

Karamalidou, A. (2012). The Educative and Emancipatory Potential of Human Rights in Prisons: Lessons from English & Dutch Prisons. In S. Georgoulas (Ed.), *The Politics of Criminology: Critical Studies on Deviance and Social Control* (pp. 145–172). Zurich: LIT Verlag.

Karamalidou, A. (2015). *The Return of the 'Difficult Patient'.* Retrieved September 10, 2015, from https://mdxminds.com/2015/03/10/the-return-of-the-difficult-patient/

Kaufmann, P. (1999). Prisoners. In K. Starmer (Ed.), *European Human Rights Law: The Human Rights Act 1998 and the European Convention on Human Rights* (pp. 453–492). London: Legal Action Group.

Kelk, C. (1983). The Humanity of the Dutch Prison System and the Prisoners' Consciousness of Their Legal Rights. *Contemporary Crises, 7*, 155–170.

Kelk, C. (2001). The Netherlands. In D. van Zyl Smit & F. Dunkel (Eds.), *Imprisonment Today and Tomorrow: International Perspectives on Prisoners' Rights and Prison Conditions* (2nd ed., pp. 479–507). The Hague: Kluwer.

King, R. D., & Resodihardjo, S. L. (2010). To Max or Not to Max: Dealing with High Risk Prisoners in the Netherlands and England and Wales. *Punishment & Society, 12*(1), 65–84.

Koenraadt, F., & Mooij, A. (2007). Mentally-Ill Offenders. In M. Boone & M. Moerings (Eds.), *Dutch Prisons* (pp. 167–186). The Hague: BJu Legal Publishers.

Kruttschnitt, C., & Dirkzwager, A. (2011). Are there Still Contrasts in Tolerance? Imprisonment in the Netherlands and England 20 Years Later. *Punishment & Society, 13*(3), 283–306.

Kunz, K. L. (2013). Is the Idea of a Sovereign Authority Based on Legal Rules and Human Rights Outdated? *Punishment & Society, 15*(4), 382–396.

Lacey, N. (2013). The Rule of Law and the Political Economy of Criminalisation: An Agenda for Research. *Punishment & Society, 15*(4), 349–366.

Lazarus, L. (2004). *Contrasting Prisoners' Rights: A Comparative Examination of England and Germany*. Oxford: Oxford University Press.

Legal Aid, Sentencing and Punishment of Offenders Act. (2012). London: HMSO.

Liebling, A. (2011). Distinctions and Distinctiveness in the Work of Prison Officers: Legitimacy and Authority Revisited. *European Journal of Criminology, 8*(6), 484–499.

Livingstone, S., & Owen, T. (1999). *Prison Law* (2nd ed.). Oxford: Oxford University Press.

Livingstone, S., Owen, T., & Macdonald, A. (2003). *Prison Law* (3rd ed.). Oxford: Oxford University Press.

Livingstone, S., Owen, T., & Macdonald, A. (2008). *Prison Law* (4th ed.). Oxford: Oxford University Press.

Mair, G. (1997). Community Penalties and the Probation Service. In M. Maguire, R. Morgan, & R. Reiner (Eds.), *The Oxford Handbook of Criminology* (2nd ed., pp. 1195–1232). Oxford: Oxford University Press.

McLoughlin and Newell [2014] EWCA Crim 188.

McMann, S. (2016). Rethinking Rehabilitation. *Prison Service Journal, 225*, 52–57.

McNulty, D., Watson, N., & Philo, G. (2014). Human Rights and Prisoners' Rights: The British Press and the Shaping of Public Debate. *Howard Journal of Criminal Justice, 53*(4), 360–376.

Melossi, D. (2013). The Processes of Criminalisation of Migrants and the Question of the European Union as a 'Land of Immigration'. In T. Daems, D. van Zyl Smit, & S. Snacken (Eds.), *European Penology?* (pp. 125–144). Oxford: Hart Publishing.

Midgley, M. (1978). *Beast and Man: The Roots of Human Nature*. Sussex: The Harvester Press.

Ministry of Justice. (2010). Breaking the Cycle: Effective Punishment, Rehabilitation and Sentencing of Offenders. Retrieved August 27, 2016, from https://www.gov.uk/government/uploads/system/uploads/attachment_data/file/185936/breaking-the-cycle.pdf

Ministry of Justice. (2011). News Release 2 January 2011: Deaths in Prison Custody 2010. Retrieved September 10, 2015, from https://www.gov.uk/government/news/deaths-in-prison-custody-2010

Ministry of Justice. (2013). Transforming Rehabilitation: A Strategy for Reform. Retrieved March 15, 2014, from https://consult.justice.gov.uk/digital-communications/transforming-rehabilitation/results/transforming-rehabilitation-response.pdf

Ministry of Justice. (2015a). Prison Population Projections 2015-2021 England and Wales. Retrieved January 10, 2016, from https://www.gov.uk/government/uploads/system/uploads/attachment_data/file/480031/prison-population-projections-2015-2021.pdf

Ministry of Justice. (2015b). The Harris Review: Changing Prisons, Saving Lives. Report of the Independent Review into Self-inflicted Deaths in Custody of 18–24 Year Olds. Retrieved September 14, 2015, from https://www.gov.uk/government/uploads/system/uploads/attachment_data/file/439859/moj-harris-review-web-accessible.pdf

Morgan, R. (1997). Imprisonment: Current Concerns and a Brief History Since 1945. In M. Maguire, R. Morgan, & R. Reiner (Eds.), *The Oxford Handbook of Criminology* (2nd ed., pp. 1137–1194). Oxford: Oxford University Press.

Morgan, R. (2008). Summary Justice: Fast-But Fair? Centre for Crime and Justice Studies. Retrieved May 11, 2016, from https://www.crimeandjustice.org.uk/publications/summary-justice-fast-fair.

Morgan, R., & Liebling, A. (2007). Imprisonment: An Expanding Scene. In M. Maguire, R. Morgan, & R. Reiner (Eds.), *The Oxford Handbook of Criminology* (4th ed., pp. 1100–1138). Oxford: Oxford University Press.

Morgan, R., & Newburn, T. (2007). Youth Justice. In M. Maguire, R. Morgan, & R. Reiner (Eds.), *The Oxford Handbook of Criminology* (4th ed., pp. 1024–1060). Oxford: Oxford University Press.

Morgan, R., & Newburn, T. (2012). Youth Crime and Youth Justice: Rediscovering Devolution, Discretion, and Diversion? In M. Maguire, R. Morgan, & R. Reiner (Eds.), *The Oxford Handbook of Criminology* (5th ed., pp. 490–530). Oxford: Oxford University Press.

National Audit Office. (2013). Managing the Prison Estate. Retrieved October 20, 2015, from https://www.nao.org.uk/wp-content/uploads/2013/12/10304-001-Full-Report.pdf

Noorduyn, C. (2008). Life is Life in the Netherlands. IBA Legal Practice Division Criminal Law Committee Newsletter (copy with the author).

Office for National Statistics (ONS) (2016). Statistical Bulletin: Crime in England & Wales: Year Ending June 2016. http://www.ons.gov.uk/peoplepopulationandcommunity/crimeandjustice/bulletins/crimeinenglandandwales/yearendingjune2016. Accessed 10 August 2016.

Office for the Commissioner for Human Rights. (2005). Report by Mr. AlVARO Gil-Robles, Commissioner for Human Rights on his Visit to the United Kingdom 4th–12th November 2004. CommDH(2005)6. Retrieved September 1, 2015, from https://wcd.coe.int/ViewDoc.jsp?p=&id=865235&direct=true

O'Malley, P. (2010). *Crime and Risk*. London: Sage.

Owen, B. (1998). *In the Mix: Struggle and Survival in a Women's Prison*. Albany: New York University Press.

Paine, T. (1791 [1996]). *Rights of Man*. Hertfordshire: Wordsworth Editions.

Pakes, F. (2004). The Politics of Discontent: The Emergence of a New Criminal Justice Discourse in the Netherlands. *Howard Journal of Criminal Justice, 43*(3), 284–298.

Pakes, F. (2005). Penalisation and Retreat: The Changing Face of Dutch Criminal Justice. *Howard Journal of Criminal Justice, 5*(2), 145–161.

Pakes, F. (2008). When the Gobal and the 'Glocal' Collide. *Prison Service Journal, 176*, 15–20.

Pakes, F., & Holt, K. (2015). The Transnational Prisoner: Exploring Themes and Trends Involving a Prison Deal with the Netherlands and Norway. *British Journal of Criminology, 57*(1), 79–93. doi:10.1093/bjc/azv104.

Penal Reform International. (2013). The Minimum Age of Criminal Responsibility. Retrieved August 20, 2016, from https://www.penalreform.org/wp-content/uploads/2013/05/justice-for-children-briefing-4-v6-web_0.pdf

Pratt, J. (2008). Scandinavian Exceptionalism in an Era of Penal Excess. Part I: The Nature and Origins of Scandinavian Exceptionalism. *British Journal of Criminology, 48*(2), 119–137.

Prison Reform Trust. (2010). Bromley Briefings Prison Factfile July 2010. Retrieved June 1, 2016, from http://www.prisonreformtrust.org.uk/uploads/documents/factfilejuly2010.pdf

Prison Reform Trust. (2011). Bromley Briefings Prison Factfile December 2011. Retrieved June 1, 2016, from http://www.prisonreformtrust.org.uk/Portals/0/Documents/Bromley%20Briefing%20December%202011.pdf

Prison Reform Trust. (2012). Bromley Briefings Prison Factfile November 2012. Retrieved June 1, 2016, from http://www.thebromleytrust.org.uk/Indexhibit/files/bbriefings2012.pdf

Prison Reform Trust. (2015). Bromley Briefings Prison Factfile Autumn 2015. Retrieved February 2, 2016, from http://www.prisonreformtrust.org.uk/Portals/0/Documents/Bromley%20Briefings/Factfile%20Autumn%202015.pdf

Prison Reform Trust. (2016). Bromley Briefings Summer 2016. Retrieved August 30, 2016, from http://www.prisonreformtrust.org.uk/Portals/0/Documents/Bromley%20Briefings/summer%202016%20briefing.pdf

Prisons and Probation Ombudsman. (2009). Disclosure Policy. Retrieved March 1, 2016, from http://www.ppo.gov.uk/investigations/investigating-fatal-incidents/disclosure-policy/

Prisons and Probation Ombudsman. (n.d.). Family Liaison. Retrieved March 1, 2016, from http://www.ppo.gov.uk/investigations/information-for-families/family-liaison/

Puddicombe, B., Corry, D., Fox, C., & Albertson, K. (2012). Payment by Results. *Criminal Justice Matters, 89*(1), 46–48.

R (Faulkner) v. Secretary of State for Justice and Another [2013] UKSC23.

R (Sturnham) v. Parole Board of England and Wales and Another [2013] UKSC23.

Resodihardjo, S. L. (2009). *Crisis and Change in the British and Dutch Prison Services: Understanding Crisis-Reform Processes.* Surrey: Ashgate.

Rousseau, J. (1762 [1999]). *The Social Contract.* Oxford: Oxford University Press.

Ryan, M. (2012). Delivering Pain in the Big Society. *Criminal Justice Matters, 89*(1), 22–23.

Sainsbury Centre for Mental Health. (2008a). *A Review of the Use of Offending Programmes for People with Mental Health Problems.* London: Sainsbury Centre for Mental Health.

Sainsbury Centre for Mental Health. (2008b). *In the Dark: The Mental Health Implications of Imprisonment for Public Protection.* London: Sainsbury Centre for Mental Health.

Sanders, A., Young, R., & Burton, M. (2010). *Criminal Justice* (4th ed.). Oxford: Oxford University Press.

Santegoeds, J. (2013). Torture and Ill-Treatment in Mental Health Care in the Netherlands. Submission on the Netherlands to the Committee Against Torture for the 50th Session of the CAT-Committee (6 May–31 May 2013). Stichting Mind Rights. Retrieved August 30, 2015, from http://tbinternet.ohchr.org/Treaties/CAT/Shared%20Documents/NLD/INT_CAT_NGO_NLD_12840_E.pdf

Scott, D. (2006). The Caretakers of Punishment: Prison Officer Personal Authority and the Rule of Law. *Prison Service Journal, 168*, 14–19.

Shine, J., & Morris, M. (2000). Addressing Criminogenic Needs in a Prison Therapeutic Community. *Therapeutic Communities, 21*(3), 197–219.

Shuker, R. (2010). Forensic Therapeutic Communities: A Critique of Treatment Model and Evidence Base. *The Howard Journal of Criminal Justice, 49*(5), 463–477.

Snacken, S., & van Zyl Smit, D. (2013). Distinctive Features of European Penology and Penal Policy-Making. In T. Daems, D. van Zyl Smit, & S. Snacken (Eds.), *European Penology?* (pp. 3–26). Oxford: Hart Publishing.

Struijk, S. (2015). Punishing Repeat Offenders in the Netherlands: Balancing Between Incapacitation and Treatment. *Behavioral Sciences and the Law, 33*, 148–166.

Sykes, G. (1958). *The Society of Captives: A Study of a Maximum-Security Prison*. Princeton: Princeton University Press.

Tak, P. J. P. (2003). *The Dutch Criminal Justice System* (2nd ed.). The Hague: Wetenschappelijk Onderzoek-en Documentatiecentrum.

Tak, P. J. P. (2008). *The Dutch Criminal Justice System* (3rd ed.). Nijmegen: Wolf Legal Publishers.

The Coroners (Investigations) Regulations. (2013). London: HMSO. Retrieved February 15, 2016, from http://www.legislation.gov.uk/uksi/2013/1629/pdfs/uksi_20131629_en.pdf

The Howard League for Penal Reform. (2009). *Turnkeys or Professionals? A Vision for the 21st Century Prison Officer*. Retrieved May 1, 2016, from http://howardleague.org/publications/turnkeys-or-professionals/

The Howard League for Penal Reform. (2014). Research Briefing: Breaking Point. Understaffing and Overcrowding in Prisons. Retrieved June 1, 2016, from http://howardleague.org/wp-content/uploads/2016/03/Breaking-point-10.07.2014.pdf

Treverton-Jones, G. D. (1989). *The Legal Status and Rights of Prisoners*. London: Sweet & Maxwell.

Tulkens, F. (2011). The Paradoxical Relationship Between Criminal Law and Human Rights. *Journal of International Criminal Justice, 9*, 577–595.

Tumim, S. (1996). The State of Prisons. In R. Matthews & P. Francis (Eds.), *Prisons 2000* (pp. 11–20). Basingstoke: Macmillan.

UN Committee on the Rights of the Child. (2016). Concluding Observations on the Fifth Periodic Report of the United Kingdom of Great Britain and Northern Ireland CRC/C/GBR/05. Retrieved September 1, 2016, from http://tbinternet.ohchr.org/_layouts/treatybodyexternal/Download.aspx?symbolno=CRC/C/GBR/CO/5&Lang=En

Vagg, J. (1994). *Prison Systems: A Comparative Study of Accountability in England, France, Germany, and the Netherlands*. Oxford: Clarendon Press.

van Dijk, J. J. M. (2010). Trends in Dutch Prisoners' Rates: Regression to the Mean or Enduring Exception? In H. Kury & E. Sjae (Eds.), *Punitivity; No. 1*. Bochum: Brockmeyer.

van Swaaningen, R. (2013). Reversing The Punitive Turn: The Case of the Netherlands. In T. Daems, D. Van Zyl Smit, & S. Snacken (Eds.), *European Penology?* (pp. 339–360). Oxford: Hart Publishing.

van Swaaningen, R., & de Jonge, G. (1995). The Dutch Prison System and Penal Policy in the 1990s: From Humanitarian Paternalism to Penal Business Management. In V. Ruggiero, M. Ryan, & J. Sim (Eds.), *Western European Penal Systems: A Critical Anatomy* (pp. 24–45). London: Sage.

van Zyl Smit, D., & Snacken, S. (2009). *Principles of European Prison Law and Policy: Penology and Human Rights*. Oxford: Oxford University Press.

Vinkers, D. J., Selten, J. P., Hoek, H. W., & Rinne, T. (2013). Psychotic Disorders Are More Common in Ethnic Minority than in Dutch Native Defendants. *Social Psychiatry and Psychiatric Epidemiology, 48*(9), 1399–1404.

Wacquant, L. (2012). The Punitive Regulation of Poverty in the Neoliberal Age. *Criminal Justice Matters, 89*(1), 38–40.

Wadham, J., & Mountfield, H. (2000). *Blackstone's Guide to Human Rights Act 1998* (2nd ed.). London: Blackstone Press.

Walmsley, R. (2015). *World Prison Population List* (11th ed.). Institute for Criminal Policy Research. Retrieved June 1, 2016, from http://www.prison-studies.org/sites/default/files/resources/downloads/world_prison_population_list_11th_edition.pdf

Warr, J. (2016). Transformative Dialogues: (Re)privileging the Informal in Prison Education. *Prison Service Journal, 225*, 18–25.

Westminster Legal Policy Forum. (2014). Keynote Seminar: Next Steps for Offender Management-Implementing the New Framework for Probation, Resettlement and Rehabilitation 28th January 2014 (copy with the author).

Whitty, N. (2011). Human Rights as Risk: UK Prisons and the Management of Risk and Rights. *Punishment & Society, 13*(2), 132–148.

Young, J. (1999). *The Exclusive Society*. London: Sage.

Table of ECtHR Cases

Baybasin v. The Netherlands, 6 October 2006 (13600/02)
Blackstock v. The United Kingdom, 21 June 2005 (59512/00)
Brand v. The Netherlands, 10 November 2004 (49902/99)
Curley v. The United Kingdom, 28 March 2000 (32340/96)
Downing v. The United Kingdom, 6 June 2000 (36525/97)

Edwards v. The United Kingdom, 14 March 2002 (46477/99)
Erkalo v. The Netherlands, 2 September 1998 (89/1997/873/1085)
Helling v. Germany, 9 July 2011 (20999/05)
Hill v. The United Kingdom, 27 July 2004 (19365/02)
Hirst v. The United Kingdom, 24 July 2001 (40787/98)
Hirst v. The United Kingdom, 6 October 2005 (74025/01)
Hutchinson v. The United Kingdom, 3 February 2015 (57592/08).
James, Wells and Lee v. The United Kingdom, 18 September 2012 (25119/09, 57715/09 and 57877/09)
Keenan v. The United Kingdom, 3 April 2001 (27229/95)
Lorse and Others v. The Netherlands, 4 May 2003 (52750/99)
McGlinchey and Others v. The United Kingdom, 29 July 2003 (50390/99)
Morsink v. The Netherlands, 10 November 2004 (48865/99)
Murray v. The Netherlands, 26 April 2016 (10511/10)
Nakach v. The Netherlands, 30 September 2005 (5379/02)
Oldham v. The United Kingdom, 26 September 2000 (36273/97)
Rutten v. The Netherlands, 24 October 2001 (32605/96)
Salah v. The Netherlands, 6 October 2006 (8196/02)
Schenkel v. The Netherlands, 27 January 2006 (62015/00)
Stafford v. The United Kingdom, 28 May 2002 (46295/99)
Sylla v. The Netherlands, 6 October 2016 (14683/03)
Van der Velden v. The Netherlands, 31 July 2012 (21203/10)
Van der Ven v. The Netherlands, 4 May 2003 (50901/99)
Vinter and Others v. The United Kingdom, 9 July 2013 (66069/09, 130/10 and 3896/10)
Von Bulow v. The United Kingdom, 7 January 2004 (75362/01)
Wynne v. The United Kingdom (no. 2), 16 January 2004 (67385/01)

Index

NUMBERS & SYMBOLS
1952 Prison Act, 33
1985 *Society & Crime*, 91
1990 Woolf Inquiry, 27, 28
1991 Criminal Justice Act, 40
1998 Crime and Disorder Act, 48
1998 EBI House Rules, 99
1998 HRA, 24, 31, 37, 41, 74, 117
1999 PPA, 32, 94, 99
2003 Criminal Justice Act, 42, 45
2007 Corporate Manslaughter and Corporate Homicide Act, 67
2009 Coroners and Justice Act, 46, 68
2012 LASPO, 81, 82, 86

A
abolition of doli incapax, 43
actuarialism, 42, 91, 98
anti-social behaviour, 41, 44, 45, 48, 92, 113, 143
anti-social behaviour order (ASBO), 44
Art 2, 31, 57, 59, 64, 66, 67, 94
  right to life, 3, 65, 122
Art 3, 57, 74, 75, 99, 103, 112, 190
  freedom from torture and inhuman or degrading treatment or punishment, 2, 12
  prohibition of torture and inhuman or degrading treatment or punishment, 2
Art 5
  right to liberty and security, 1, 14
Art 5(4), 74, 108
Assessment, Care in Custody and Teamwork (ACCT)
  suicide prevention, 60–2

A. Karamalidou, *Embedding Human Rights in Prison*,
DOI 10.1057/978-1-137-58502-8

autonomy, 16, 21, 118, 121, 125, 132, 136, 137, 141, 144, 149, 154, 155, 157, 159, 162

B

Baybasin v The Netherlands, 103
Bradley Report
 mental health, 52, 60–5
Breaking the Cycle, 51

C

Care Programme Approach(CPA), 60
Commission for Racial Equality (CRE), 58, 59
community of penal sentiment, 150
conjugal visits, 20, 24, 25, 133, 135, 196
Constitution of the Kingdom of the Netherlands, 30
Contrasts in Tolerance, 14, 17, 20, 23, 35, 89
coroners' inquest system, 56
Corston Review, 52
CPT inspection, 100
CPT Reports, 41
crime as a human rights violation, 148, 185, 192
culture of tolerance, 18, 21

D

Deaths in Prison
 Articles 2 and 3, 55
decarcerative penal policy, 14, 16, 113, 197
declaration of incompatibility, 31, 73
depersonalisation, 127, 132, 136, 139, 161
Diceyan, 29, 56, 149
differentiation, 95
dignified treatment, 154
doctrine of dualism, 30
doctrine of monism, 30
double cells
 cell-sharing, 162, 187
The Dutch concept of moral rights, 24
The Dutch legal right to complain, 25
Dutch rental prisons, 93
Dutch-style Garlandian crime and security complex, 92
duty of candour, 66

E

educative, 16, 139, 142, 148, 149, 174, 191, 194
Effective Detention, 91
EHRC Inquiry, 64
emancipatory, 16, 177, 191, 194–6
equality and equal treatment, 137, 155, 181, 197
European Court of Human Rights
 ECtHR, 1
external and internal differentiation, 95

F

family liaison, 67
freedom of expression, 69
freedom of thought, 118, 154

G

gender roles, 136

H

Halliday Report, 46, 47, 52
Harris Review, 64–8
Hirst v UK, 69, 190
humane and dignified treatment, 153
humanising, 16, 19, 191, 193–5
human responsibilities, 116, 142, 147–9, 185, 192
human rights ambassadors, 187, 194
human rights and civic identity, 142, 181
human rights and self-identity, 126
human rights and social identity, 136, 170
human rights awareness, 116
human rights potential, 12

I

infantilisation, 131, 132, 139, 144, 161
IPP prisoners, 49, 53, 70, 83–5
The ISD penal measure, 109

J

Justice for All, 45

L

Law in Motion, 91
legalisation of human rights, 14, 22
legalisation of prisoners' human rights, 16, 22, 37, 69, 183, 189
legal risk+, 189
legitimacy of imprisonment as punishment, 16
less eligibility, 15, 20
life and indeterminate sentences, 69
lifelong imprisonment, 73–4, 111, 112, 160, 162, 169, 195
life sentences, 15, 40, 47, 69, 70, 73, 74, 81, 83, 98, 110–12, 116, 190
Lorse & Others v The Netherlands, 99, 103

M

managerialist, 42, 43, 45, 82, 91, 113, 132
mandatory life sentence, 71–3, 110, 166
margin of appreciation, 14, 112, 191
mental health awareness training, 62, 64, 66, 150
Morsink and *Brand,* 107
Mubarek Inquiry, 59

N

negative and positive rights, 16, 141, 149, 187
Newell and *McLoughin,* 75, 190

O

offender responsibilisation, 172

offending behaviour programmes (OBPs), 53, 83–5, 150
one prisoner to a cell rule, 20, 34, 162

P
painism, 157
PbR
  payment by results, 51, 52
penal measure, 104
penitentiary programmes, 27, 95, 97, 98, 171, 172
personality disorder, 58, 61, 63
pillarisation, 18
politicisation of crime, 39, 44, 46
politicisation of human rights, 11
politics of accommodation, 18, 34
positive duty of care
  positive state interference, 29, 31
presumption of dangerousness, 83, 85
preventive detention, 15, 109, 110, 113
prisoner deaths, 15, 37, 55, 56, 59, 65, 66
prisoner disenfranchisement, 12, 70, 190
prisoner education, 142, 148
Prisons and Probation Ombudsman (PPO), 67
proactive function of human rights, 16, 191, 197
The Proactive Function of Human Rights in Prisons, 191
proportionality, 2, 29, 47, 71
Protocol 14, 13, 14
Protocol 15, 13
Protocol 16, 13
psychotherapeutic, 16, 191–3
public protection, 11, 15, 46, 47, 52, 62, 63, 69–71, 81–3, 91, 104, 113, 158, 159

R
recommendation (2003)22
  conditional release, 111
recommendation (2003)23
  life sentence and long term prisoners, 111
rehabilitation, 15–17, 19, 21, 23, 38, 46, 47, 51, 52, 54, 65, 70, 74, 84, 85, 87, 95, 98, 109, 111–13, 123, 124, 126, 127, 137, 142, 145, 149, 150, 154, 158, 159, 161, 163, 166, 170, 191, 194, 198
rehabilitation revolution, 22, 51, 53, 54, 87, 190
reintegration, 16, 74, 84, 94, 98, 111, 114, 123, 137, 139, 142, 144, 149, 170, 176, 177, 179–81, 187, 191, 196, 198
resocialisation, 15, 16, 111, 113, 158, 159, 162, 170–2, 174, 181, 187

S
selective incapacitation, 15, 110, 113
selective rehabilitation, 15, 95, 96, 98, 110
sentence planning, 84, 111, 140, 171
Sentencing Guidelines Council (SGC), 46

sexuality, 127, 132, 134, 136, 196
SOV, 109, 110, 172
subsidiarity, 14, 191
supermax facility, 99, 101

T

TBS combined sentences, 104, 106
TBS offenders, 105, 107
therapeutic community, 143
through a prison gate, 52
To A Safer Society, 92
Transforming Rehabilitation, 51, 52

V

Vinter & Others v UK, 70, 71, 73, 75, 112

W

Walker and James, 85
whole life tariff, 71, 75

The manufacturer's authorised representative in the EU is Springer Nature Customer Service Centre GmbH, Europaplatz 3, 69115 Heidelberg, Germany. If you have any concerns regarding our products, please contact ProductSafety@springernature.com

Printed and bound by CPI Group (UK) Ltd, Croydon, CR0 4YY
10/10/2026
02231221-0001